CAMBRIDGE LIBRARY COLLECTION

Books of enduring scholarly value

History

The books reissued in this series include accounts of historical events and movements by eye-witnesses and contemporaries, as well as landmark studies that assembled significant source materials or developed new historiographical methods. The series includes work in social, political and military history on a wide range of periods and regions, giving modern scholars ready access to influential publications of the past.

Sir Moses Montefiore

Originally published in 1884 as a centennial biography for Sir Moses Montefiore (1784–1885), this book draws on official records and informal writings to create a well-rounded account of Montefiore's life as, firstly, a financier and, later, a significant Jewish community leader. In an age of frequent pogroms and anti-Semitic prejudice in Europe, Montefiore immersed himself in philanthropic works after a religious awakening in 1824 in Palestine. By encouraging reforms, lobbying for the release of wrongfully imprisoned Jews and investing in Jewish projects all over Europe, he endeavoured to improve the lives and rights of Jews globally. Wolf (1857–1930) was himself a prominent political journalist and campaigner for Jewish rights. His book not only recounts Montefiore's life and achievements, but also incorporates the history of English Jews between 750 and 1837.

T0371584

Cambridge University Press has long been a pioneer in the reissuing of out-of-print titles from its own backlist, producing digital reprints of books that are still sought after by scholars and students but could not be reprinted economically using traditional technology. The Cambridge Library Collection extends this activity to a wider range of books which are still of importance to researchers and professionals, either for the source material they contain, or as landmarks in the history of their academic discipline.

Drawing from the world-renowned collections in the Cambridge University Library, and guided by the advice of experts in each subject area, Cambridge University Press is using state-of-the-art scanning machines in its own Printing House to capture the content of each book selected for inclusion. The files are processed to give a consistently clear, crisp image, and the books finished to the high quality standard for which the Press is recognised around the world. The latest print-on-demand technology ensures that the books will remain available indefinitely, and that orders for single or multiple copies can quickly be supplied.

The Cambridge Library Collection will bring back to life books of enduring scholarly value (including out-of-copyright works originally issued by other publishers) across a wide range of disciplines in the humanities and social sciences and in science and technology.

Sir Moses Montefiore

A Centennial Biography

Lucien Wolf

CAMBRIDGE
UNIVERSITY PRESS

CAMBRIDGE UNIVERSITY PRESS

Cambridge, New York, Melbourne, Madrid, Cape Town,
Singapore, São Paolo, Delhi, Tokyo, Mexico City

Published in the United States of America by Cambridge University Press, New York

www.cambridge.org
Information on this title: www.cambridge.org/9781108036689

© in this compilation Cambridge University Press 2011

This edition first published 1884
This digitally printed version 2011

ISBN 978-1-108-03668-9 Paperback

SIR MOSES MONTEFIORE.

A Centennial Biography.

(*From a Photograph taken by* J. E. MAYALL, F.C.S., F.R.M.S., 164, *New Bond Street.*)

SIR MOSES MONTEFIORE.

A Centennial Biography.

EXTRACTS FROM LETTERS AND JOURNALS.

By LUCIEN WOLF.

WITH PORTRAIT.

LONDON:
JOHN MURRAY, ALBEMARLE STREET.
1884.

LONDON :
BRADBURY, AGNEW, & CO., PRINTERS, WHITEFRIARS.

PREFACE.

THE following Biography has been compiled entirely from official records and other reliable data. I have to thank many kind friends for their assistance. Mr. E. H. LINDO, Secretary to the Spanish and Portuguese Synagogue, and Mr. LEWIS EMANUEL, Secretary to the Board of Deputies, opened to me the important archives committed to their care. Mr. J. B. MONTEFIORE, Mr. F. D. MOCATTA, Mr. H. GUEDALLA, Dr. L. LOEWE, Mr. EDWIN ARNOLD, and Signor CÉSAR OLIVETTI of Turin placed at my disposal a great deal of anecdotic and other information, and Mr. GUEDALLA most painstakingly revised the proof-sheets. Among the sources of information not acknowledged in the following pages, I must gratefully mention Mr. ISRAEL DAVIS' Biographical Sketch of Sir MOSES MONTEFIORE, reprinted from the *Times;* and the files of a large number of Jewish newspapers, particularly the *Jewish World* and *Jewish Chronicle* of London.

L. W.

CONTENTS.

CHAPTER I.

CHAPTER II.

CHAPTER VII.

THE DAMASCUS DRAMA.

CHAPTER VIII.

THE MISSION TO MEHEMET ALI.

CHAPTER XI.

RUSSIAN PERSECUTIONS : MISSION TO CZAR NICHOLAS.

CHAPTER XII.

A BUSY DECADE.

CHAPTER XIII.

THE MORTARA CASE, ETC.

CHAPTER XIV.

LADY MONTEFIORE.

CHAPTER XV.

THE JOURNEY TO MOROCCO.

CHAPTER XVI.

ANOTHER BUSY DECADE.

THE LIFE OF
SIR MOSES MONTEFIORE.

CHAPTER I.

FAMILY AND EARLY LIFE.

The Montefiore family—Origin of its name—Montefiores at Ancona—
Settlement of the family in Leghorn—Moses Vita Montefiore
comes to England—Commercial career—Jews in London in
1760—Descendants of the Jewish Hidalgos—Abraham Lumbrozo
de Mattos Mocatta—Benjamin D'Israeli—Moses Vita Montefiore's family—Adventures of Joshua Montefiore—Sir Moses'
father marries a daughter of Abraham Mocatta—Antiquity of
the Mocatta family—Mosé Mocato a literary contemporary of
Spinoza—Messrs. Mocatta and Goldsmid of London—Connection
with the Lamegos and Disraelis—Joseph Elias Montefiore—
His family—Birth of Moses Montefiore — Moses Montefiore's
education and apprenticeship.

ONE evening, in the early part of the year 1784,
a highly respectable Jewish merchant of the City of
London announced to his wife, in their cosy drawing-
room at Kennington, that he purposed paying a visit
to Italy at an early date, to buy some advantageous
parcels of straw bonnets, to which his correspondents
had drawn his attention. In those days, when not
merely the boring of the Mont Cenis, but railways
themselves, were undreamt of, such a journey was no
light matter. The wife, however, was young and

B

adventurous, and she gave her consent to the proposed
enterprise on one condition: that she was not left
behind. The husband prudently declined to contest
his partner's whim; the conjugal bargain was struck;
the company of the lady's brother was invited, and
the journey was undertaken. Not the least important
incident in this commercial expedition occurred at
Leghorn, on the evening of the 24th October, 1784.
The lady in question gave birth to a boy, whose name
was registered in the archives of the local synagogue
as Moses Haim Montefiore. The travellers were Mr.
and Mrs. Joseph Elias Montefiore, of London, and
Mrs. Montefiore's brother, Moses Mocatta, likewise
of London; the *nouveau-né* was the subject of this
book. In the Via Reale, opposite the new Leghorn
Synagogue, the house is still pointed out in which this
event took place, just one hundred years ago.

Little is known of the family history of the Montefiores beyond the four generations settled in this
country. It is generally assumed that they must have
come originally from the small town of the same
name in the Italian province of Ascoli Piceno. The
fact has, however, been overlooked that there are two
Montefiores in Italy, one in the neighbourhood of
Fermo, and the other near Forli. No certain evidence
exists to connect the family with either of these places,
although, from the frequent adoption by Jews of sur-
names from the names of the towns in which they
have resided, there is a strong probability that at
some period it was domiciled in one of the Montefiores.

At the same time the fact must not be lost sight of that names of flowers or connected with flowers have always been popular with Jews, and that the name Montefiore itself appears very frequently among Jews in the German equivalent Blumberg, together with many kindred names, such as Blumenbach, Blumenthal, Rosenberg, Rosenthal, Rosenfeld, Veilchenfeld, Lilienfeld, &c.

The earliest record which has been preserved of the Montefiore family is neither engraved on stone, nor inscribed on parchment. It exists appropriately enough in the shape of a silk ritual curtain, magnificently embroidered and fringed with gold, which, on festive occasions, is suspended before the Ark in the ancient Jewish Synagogue at Ancona. In the centre of this curtain is a Hebrew inscription recording its gift to the Synagogue in 1630 by Leone (Judah) Montefiore, whose wife Rachel, it states, had embroidered and inscribed it with her own hands. The Montefiores appear to have occupied a good position as merchants at Ancona, where, throughout the middle ages, their co-religionists enjoyed the reputation of a prosperous and industrious class. When Pius V. expelled the Jews from the States of the Church he expressly excepted those of Ancona, in order not to disturb the trade with the East, which was entirely in their hands. In the latter half of the seventeenth century, Amadio Montefiore and Ismael Montefiore appear, from entries in the Synagogue books, to have been prominent members of the Ancona Jewish Community.

At an early period some of the Ancona Montefiores
settled in Leghorn. The Jews of that city enjoyed
even greater prosperity than their brethren in the
Adriatic port. Their commercial genius was an important element in the development of commerce and
industry all over Italy, but in Leghorn the tolerance
of the Medicis secured them the freest scope for their
activity. Menasseh ben Israel, in his petition to
Cromwell for the re-admission of the Jews to England,
attributes the rise of Leghorn entirely to the industry
and "merchandising" of the Jews; and, indeed, their
commercial influence must have been very great, when
we find a writer relating, in the early part of the
eighteenth century, that the inhabitants generally, Jew
and Gentile, observed the Jewish Sabbath as a day of
rest from business. Early in the seventeenth century
there were Montefiores in Leghorn, who signed themselves "Montefiore d'Ancona," thus placing their
origin beyond all doubt. One of them, Isach Vita
Montefiore, was a merchant of standing about 1690.
He took into his business his nephew Judah, who had
come from Ancona to seek his fortune. Judah, in
process of time, married a daughter of the Medinas,
who presented him with four sons, the eldest of whom,
Moses Haim (or Vita*) Montefiore, was Sir Moses
Montefiore's grandfather.

Moses Vita Montefiore, the elder, was born December 28th, 1712, and married on March 29th, 1752,

* "Haim" is a common Hebrew name, signifying "Life," or, in
Italian, "Vita."

Ester Hannah, daughter of Massahod Racah, a Moorish merchant of Leghorn. The bride was only seventeen; and, according to a portrait of her, still extant, was of remarkable beauty. Moses Montefiore did not prosper at Leghorn; and six years after his marriage he resolved to emigrate to England, where several of his mother's relatives had made large fortunes, notably the wealthy Sir Solomon Medina, who financed Marlborough's campaigns, and was the Rothschild of the reign of Queen Anne. Accompanied by his youngest brother Joseph—who stayed, however, but a short time—Moses Montefiore landed in England in 1758, and immediately established himself as a merchant, trading with Italy. He lived and had his offices and warehouses at Nos. 13 and 15, Philpot Lane, in the city of London; and, according to his son Joshua, who has recorded the fact in his Bible, was "of high and respectable standing in society, and a merchant of eminence." After twenty years of successful trading, he took a house in Mutton Lane, Hackney, then a rural district, much affected by wealthy Jews. Here dwelt at their ease such notable Israelites as Ephraim Aguilar, the father of Grace Aguilar, and a scion of one of the most distinguished of the Portuguese Jewish families; his kinsman, the generous Abraham Lopez Pereira, who left a substantial sum to the churchwardens of Hackney to supply the local poor with coals in the winter season, in addition to noble legacies to the Synagogue; and David Alves Rebello, the gifted numis-

matist and writer on natural history. Close by, in
Bethnal Green, resided many more descendants of
the Jewish Hidalgos, among them Abraham Lumbroso
de Mattos Mocatta, an opulent Jewish broker, whose
daughter Rachel became the wife of Montefiore's son
Joseph, and mother of Sir Moses. Abraham Mocatta
was one of the patriotic band of London merchants,
who in March, 1774, when the rumours of a French
invasion in favour of the young Pretender were prevalent, waited on George II. with an address, expressing their " resentment and indignation at so rash an
attempt," and declaring their resolution "at this
critical conjuncture to exert our utmost endeavours
for the support of public credit; and at all times to
hazard our lives and fortunes in defence of your
Majesty's sacred person and government, and of the
security of the Protestant succession in your family."
Among the Italian merchants, with whom the elder
Montefiore competed in business, was one Benjamin
D'Israeli, of 5, Great St. Helen's, the father of Isaac
D'Israeli, author of " Curiosities of Literature," and
grandfather of the Earl of Beaconsfield, sometime
Prime Minister of England. Among the Hebrews he
must have frequently met in the ancient Spanish and
Portuguese Synagogue in Bevis Marks, were the
two Bernals, Abraham Ricardo, the father of the
economist; Ephraim, Baron d'Aguilar, ancestor of
General d'Aguilar, and father-in-law of Admiral Keith
Steward; Mordecai Rodrigues Lopez, grandfather of
the present Sir Massey Lopes; Naphtali Basevi, the

father-in-law of Isaac Disraeli; and the scions of many other ancient Hebrew families, such as the Abrabanels, Mendez da Costas, Villa-Reals, Alvarez, Lindos, Lousadas, Francos, Salvadors, Samudas, Nunes, Ozorios, Seixas, Fonsecas, Supinos, da Silvas, Garcias, de Castros, and Ximenes.

Moses Montefiore not only prospered; he completed the Mosaic blessing by multiplying as well. His wife bore him seventeen children, nine sons and eight daughters. Several of the daughters married well. Of the sons the first three were born at Leghorn, and the eldest, Judah, remained there in the care of his grandparents; the second, David, became a tobacco merchant, and carried on business in the Borough; the third, Samuel (grandfather of Mr. H. Guedalla), married Mr. Abraham Mocatta's daughter Grace, entered the export business, and settled in Mansell Street, Goodman's Fields; the fourth, Joseph Elias, was the father of Sir Moses; the fifth, Abraham, went abroad; the sixth, Joshua, became a lawyer and a soldier; the seventh and eighth, Eliezer (who married a grand-daughter of Simon Barrow, of Amsterdam), and Jacob, became partners, established themselves as general merchants in Camomile Street, City, and subsequently went to the West Indies; a ninth son, Lazarus, died in infancy.

The most remarkable of all Moses Montefiore's children was his sixth son, Joshua. Possessed of a well-stored mind and splendid abilities, he might have made an important name for himself had it not been for his roving disposition. At eighteen years of age he commenced to study law with James Cross, and, in the same year that his nephew, Sir Moses Montefiore, was born, he was admitted an attorney-at-law and solicitor in Chancery by Sir William Scott, Judge of the Admiralty Court, and Notary Public by the Court of Faculties of the Archbishop of Canterbury. While working at his profession he obtained considerable success as an author. His " Commercial and Notarial Precedents " quickly ran through three editions in London and two in the United States. His " Commercial Dictionary," which was dedicated by permission to Lord Ellenborough, was long regarded as the standard work of its kind. He also wrote the "Trader's Compendium," the "United States Trader's Compendium," an essay on the "Law of Copyright," and "Law and Treatise on Book-keeping." Joshua Montefiore was, however, not fitted for a stay-at-home life, and he seized the first opportunity of exchanging the pen for a sterner weapon. Towards the end of 1791 a colonising mania seized the citizens of London. Several merchants formed themselves into a society for the purpose of establishing settlements on or near the coast of Africa, and an expedition, consisting of 275 adventurers, was fitted out to take possession of the Island of Bulama. One of the directors was Moses Ximenes, afterwards Sir Maurice Ximenes, a prominent and wealthy Israelite, and among the adventurers was Joshua Montefiore, who gave up his legal practice to take part in an enterprise which accorded so well with his venturesome tastes.

The expedition turned out disastrously, and Joshua Montefiore was one of the few who survived its many trials and reverses. On his return home he wrote an account of his adventures. From this work it appears that having a taste for soldiering, the military arrangements of the expedition were from the outset confided to him. It was he who hoisted the British flag on landing at Bulama, and he, too, organised the whole offensive and defensive economy of the colony. Soon after the adventurers were settled, we find him in command of one of the vessels belonging to the expedition, keeping a look-out for suspicious craft and chasing and boarding Portuguese slavers. One day the colony was surprised by a war canoe full of armed " Indians," and it devolved upon him to pacify the chiefs by a diplomatic palaver. The "Indians" retired, and Joshua counselled his fellow-colonists, on the next appearance of the natives, to make overtures to them for the acquisition of the island by purchase, at the same time pointing out the injustice of holding by force land which did not rightly belong to them. His filibustering hearers stared amazed at this unexpected sermon, and flatly refused to follow his advice. The result was that when next the " Indians " landed a severe conflict took place, and the new colony was wrecked. Joshua Montefiore then travelled into the Papel country, met the Antula Indians, interviewed a native king, and dined with him on porcupine and squirrels. At Sierra Leone he visited another dusky potentate, the King of Nambana, whom he describes as " a very respectable old gentleman."

On his return home he was presented by Lord Boston to King George III., at his Majesty's special request, and was offered knighthood, which he declined. Finding it difficult to settle down to his old profession, he entered the army, and was the first Jew to hold a military commission in this country. He served in various parts of the world, and in 1809, as an officer in the York Light Infantry, was at the taking of Martinique and Guadaloupe. On his retirement he proceeded to the United States, where he practised as a lawyer, and published a weekly political journal, entitled " Men and Measures," which was subventioned by the British Government. In his seventy-third year he married a second time, and died in 1843, aged eighty-one, leaving issue by his second marriage, seven children, the youngest of whom was only six weeks old. Joshua Montefiore had cast his lot among strangers, but on his death-bed he called his eldest daughter to his side, and, asking her for pen, ink, and paper, wrote out from memory an English translation of the Hebrew burial service, which he enjoined her to read aloud at his funeral. He also desired to be buried in his garden at St. Albans, Vermont, and his wish was complied with. One of his sons, Mr. Joseph Montefiore, has achieved quite a reputation as a lawyer and journalist, and is now Editor of the Baldwin *Bulletin,* Wisconsin. Sir Moses Montefiore still retains a vivid recollection of his dashing "Uncle Josh," whose laced red coat and pigtail, and cocked hat and sword, together with his fund of tremendous anecdote, rendered him a huge favourite with his nephews.

On his mother's side Sir Moses Montefiore's lineage is of undoubted antiquity. "Mocatta" is an Arabic name which carries back the family bearing it to, at least, the period of the Moorish dominion in Spain. The Mocattas claim for themselves, however, a more remote antiquity, alleging that, as an Eastern Jewish family, they entered the Peninsula in the wake of the conquering armies of Tarik and Musa, in the eighth century. After the expulsions by Ferdinand and Isabella, part of the family settled in Venice, traded, flourished, became impoverished, and died out about a century ago, leaving their tombs on the Lido, the long island extending like a breakwater in front of the Venetian lagoon, where the Jewish cemetery was situated. The branch from which Sir Moses Montefiore is descended emigrated to Holland, and traded there. Some members presided from time to time over the Amsterdam Congregation. Others with literary tastes made graceful contributions to the poetical literature of the Hispano-Jewish exiles. A Mosé Mocato was a literary contemporary of Spinoza, and one of a band of twenty-one young Jewish poets who applauded in Hebrew, Spanish, and Latin verse the publication of Joseph Penso's Hebrew dramas. The literary traditions of the family have in recent years been worthily sustained by Mr. Frederic D. Mocatta, with an excellent sketch of the history of the Jews of Spain and Portugal.

When, in 1688, William of Orange entered England, a large number of Dutch Jews took up their abode in this country. Among them were the Mocattas, or Lumbroso de Mattos Mocattas, as they were called. In 1694, Mr. Isaac de Mocatta established in Mansell Street the firm which, about three-quarters of a century later, became Mocatta and Keyser, and in 1783, when Mr. Asher Goldsmid joined it, assumed the style which it still preserves of Mocatta and Goldsmid, bullion brokers to the Bank of England and the East India Company. Sir Moses Montefiore's maternal grandfather, Abraham Lumbroso de Mattos Mocatta, married about 1760 the heiress of the Lamegos, another ancient and distinguished family, one of the progenitors of which was Joseph Zapateiro de Lamego, a Jewish navigator of the fifteenth century, who first brought the intelligence to Europe that there was a South Cape of Africa, which could be doubled. Moses Mocatta, one of the sons of Mr. Abraham Mocatta—the names Lumbrozo de Mattos were dropped by Royal licence in 1780—was the author of several works, and translator of the celebrated controversial essay of Isaac Troki, *Chizuk Emunah.* He was a fellow traveller of his sister and brother-in-law in 1784, when his nephew Moses Montefiore was born at Leghorn. It may be mentioned that through the Mocattas a slight relationship is established between Sir Moses Montefiore and the late Earl of Beacons-

field. The mother of the Earl, *née* Sarah Basevi, was
sister-in-law to Sir Moses Montefiore's uncle, Moses
Mocatta, and also to Ephraim Lindo, whose brother
David Abarbanel Lindo was Sir Moses' uncle by mar-
riage with Abraham Mocatta's daughter Sarah. It was
David Abarbanel Lindo who performed on Lord
Beaconsfield the ceremony of initiation into the
Covenant of Abraham.

Joseph Elias Montefiore, the father of Sir Moses,
was born in London on the 15th October, 1759, soon
after his parents arrived in this country. He passed
his early years in his father's warehouses in Philpot
Lane, and eventually established himself on his own
account in Lime Street, Fenchurch Street. Here he
carried on a considerable business in Italian goods,
notably Leghorn straw bonnets and Carrara marbles.
On his marriage in 1783 he took a house at No. 3,
Kennington Place, Vauxhall, where, in addition to his
eldest son, seven children were born to him, two sons,
Abraham and Horatio, and five daughters, Sarah,
Esther, Abigail, Rebecca and Justina. All the sons did
well in life. Abraham, whose commercial career was
identified with that of his elder brother, was twice
married. By his first wife, a daughter of Mr. George
Hall, of the London Stock Exchange, he had one
daughter, Mary, who married Mr. Benjamin Mocatta,
and by his second wife, Henrietta Rothschild, he had
two sons (Joseph Meyer, of Worth Park, and Nathaniel
Meyer, of Coldeast), and two daughters, Charlotte
and Louisa, the latter of whom is the present Lady

Anthony de Rothschild. Horatio became a successful London merchant. He married Sarah, a daughter of David Mocatta, by whom he had a family of six sons and six daughters. His youngest son is Lieutenant-Colonel Emanuel Montefiore, late of Bombay. Of the daughters of Joseph Montefiore, the eldest, Sarah, married first, Mr. Solomon Sebag, of London, and secondly, Mr. Moses Asher Goldsmid, youngest brother of Sir Isaac Lyon Goldsmid. She was the mother of Mr. Joseph Sebag, and mother-in-law of Mr. H. Guedalla. The second, Esther, met her death by an accident in her fifteenth year; the third, Abigail, became the wife of Benjamin Gompertz, a well-known mathematician and actuary of the Alliance Insurance Company; the fourth, Rebecca, married Mr. Joseph Salomons, brother of the late Sir David Salomons, Bart.; and the youngest, Justina, found a husband in the same family whence her eldest brother took his wife. She married Mr. Benjamin Cohen, of Richmond, Surrey, who was for many years connected with the elder Rothschild. One of their sons is Mr. Arthur Cohen, Q.C., M.P.

All the sons of Mr. Joseph Montefiore received an elementary education at a local school, which they left early for the more serious business of life. Mr. Moses Mocatta, who lived in Kennington Place, a short distance from the Montefiores, superintended their studies in Hebrew and religion, and it was from him that Moses Montefiore derived that large-hearted interest in the traditions and fortunes of his race, which has enabled him to exert so potent an influence on their more recent history. On leaving school each of the sons was taught a trade. Abraham was apprenticed to Mr. Flower, the eminent silk merchant of Watling Street. It is a curious circumstance that Mr. Flower's grandson, Mr. Cyril Flower, afterwards became the husband of one of Abraham Montefiore's grand-daughters. Moses entered a provision house. One of his father's neighbours in Kennington Place was a Mr. Robert Johnson, head of the firm of Johnson, McCulloch, Sons, & Co., wholesale tea merchants and grocers, of 19, Eastcheap. An intimacy sprung up between the two families, and young Moses Montefiore became articled to the Eastcheap house. Here, in the closing years of the last century, he gained his first commercial experience.

CHAPTER II.

COMMERCIAL CAREER.

Moses Montefiore enters the Stock Exchange — Jewish brokers — Eminent Jews in the city—Abraham Montefiore joins his brother —Nathan Maier Rothschild establishes himself in London — Montefiore's marriage—Connection of the Montefiores with the Rothschilds—First news of Waterloo—Transactions of the New Court financiers—Death of Abraham Montefiore—Retirement of Moses Montefiore—The Alliance Insurance Company—Story of its establishment—The Imperial Continental Gas Association— The Slave loan—Park Lane sixty years ago.

Young Montefiore did not continue long in the trade for which his father had destined him. More rapid fortunes were to be made in the money business, in which at that period the house founded by his mother's family, Messrs. Mocatta and Goldsmid, " Brokers in Bullion, Specie, Diamonds and Pearls, Grigsby's Coffee House, near Bank," occupied a prominent position. Of a handsome presence, over six feet in height, engaging in his manners, and a Captain in the Surrey Militia, Montefiore was very much liked by his rich relatives, and was a frequent guest at the palatial residences of the Goldsmids at Morden and Roehampton. At Asher Goldsmid's house, on one occasion, he met Lord Nelson at dinner, and chanted the lengthy Grace after meals of the Hebrew

liturgy in his presence. His intimacy with Asher
Goldsmid's gifted son seems to have strongly influenced
his own character. Isaac Lyon Goldsmid was an
earnest philanthropist, as well as an astute financier.
The friend subsequently of Brougham, James Mill,
Mrs. Fry, and Robert Owen, a busy advocate of Negro
Emancipation, the restriction of capital punishment,
and the cause of popular education, he was eminently
fitted to be the companion of one who was destined
to rank conspicuously among the philanthropists of
the age.

Moses Montefiore having testified a desire to adopt
a Stock Exchange career, his uncles purchased for him
for £1200 the right to practise as one of the twelve
Jewish brokers licensed by the City. The fact that
the number of Jewish brokers was then limited is an
interesting indication of the restrictions under which
the Jews of England lived in Moses Montefiore's youth.
Sometimes even these restrictions were not considered
sufficiently narrow by enemies of the Jews. On one
occasion when a Jew applied to be admitted as broker
in the City of London, a petition was presented by
the Christian brokers, praying for its rejection. The
terms of the petition are extremely curious. It was
entitled : — "Reasons offered humbly to the Lord
Mayor and Court of Aldermen against a Jew (who is
a known enemy to the Christian religion), his being
admitted a broker." The reasons alleged were six in
number, and recited in substance that the Jews had
by statute no right to immunities and privileges of any

c

kind, and that every branch of trade would be injured
by admitting them as brokers.   The statement of fact
contained in these reasons cannot of course be disputed ; the prophecy, however, has happily failed to
be realised, even with the abolition of the restriction by which the number of Jewish brokers was
limited.*

On the Stock Exchange Moses Montefiore's amiable
disposition rendered him very popular.   His enterprise, industry, and steadiness, too, obtained for him
the confidence of many clients.   "Always remember
that it is better to earn a pound, than toss for two,"
said an old Scotch friend, to whom he applied for
advice when about to commence business on his own
account ; and this counsel would always occur to him
when he felt tempted to plunge into speculation.   His
enterprise is illustrated by his issuing a weekly price list
of securities at a time when such publications were
almost unknown.   At first his office was at Grigsby's
Coffee House, where he basked in the prestige of his
maternal uncle's patronage ; but later on he established
himself successively at No. 1, Birchin Lane, and 3,
Bartholomew Lane.   In course of time he was joined
by his brother, Abraham Montefiore, who had realised

* " The last recorded instance of a Jew purchasing the right to act
as broker took place in 1826, when Mr. J. B. Montefiore bought for
1500 guineas from Sir William Magnay, the then Lord Mayor, the
medal which formed the title deed of the privilege, and which had
lapsed by the death of the previous owner.   Two years after, the
absurd limitation was removed."—PICIOTTO, "Sketches of Anglo-
Jewish History," p. 386.

a small fortune in the silk trade, but was ambitious to turn over his money more rapidly than was possible in industrial undertakings. The firm of Montefiore Bros. carried on business in Shorter's Court, Throgmorton Street.

The year in which Moses Montefiore was admitted into the Stock Exchange also witnessed the entry into the same institution of David Ricardo, subsequently member of Parliament for Portarlington, and the ablest economist of his day. David Ricardo had seceded from Judaism, and left the parental roof as a mere youth ; and Christian strangers had helped him in his studies and his financial career. His father, to whom his apostasy was the source of an abiding sorrow, still carried on business as a merchant at Garraway's Coffee House. The Rothschilds of the time were Messrs. Benjamin and Abraham Goldsmid, of 6, Capel Court, whose town houses were in Finsbury Square and Spital Square, and who possessed princely estates at Morden and Roehampton. At this period Lord Beaconsfield's maternal and paternal grandfathers were still familiar figures in the City. Naphtali Basevi, or, as he was called in the Synagogue, Naphtali de Solomon Bathsheba, was a merchant in Wormwood Street, Broad Street; Benjamin D'Israeli had retired from the firm of D'Israeli and Parkins, of which he had been the head, and was living in Charles Street, Stoke Newington, but he still occasionally looked in to the City, and transacted business at Tom's Coffee House, Cornhill.

With all their industry and ability it is doubtful
whether the Montefiores would have been as successful
as they eventually were, had it not been for their connection with the boldest speculator and shrewdest
financier of the time, Nathan Maier Rothschild.   In
1812, when this connection commenced, Rothschild
was only thirty-five years old, but he had already
founded, on a secure basis, the English branch of the
world-famed house of which he was destined to become
the leading spirit.   In his twentieth year, such was his
father's confidence in him, that he had despatched him
to Manchester with £20,000 in his pocket to start in
business as a manufacturer of cotton goods, and within
five years he had increased this capital tenfold.   In
1802 his father's financial transactions with England
assumed such large proportions that he found it necessary to establish a branch of his banking business in
London.   He called upon Nathan to undertake its
organization and management.   The well-known pro-
bity of the elder Rothschild had made him the de-
positary of the fortunes of many of the French nobility,
who, fleeing from the terrors and conquering armies
of the Republic, knew not where to lodge their money
for safety.   Rothschild took it into his keeping, and in
due time transmitted it to his son in London, who
turned it to good account.   Unacquainted with the
sources of Nathan Rothschild's capital, the steady-
going city folk of those days looked askance at the
large transactions of the new financier; and when, in
1806, he asked the wealthy Levi Barent Cohen, of

Angel Court, Throgmorton Street, for his daughter, it was not unnaturally thought that the speculating stranger was more attracted by the young lady's dowry of £10,000 than by her personal charms. Mr. Cohen himself hesitated at first to give his consent to the marriage, whereupon, it is said, the future millionaire attempted to calm his intended father-in-law's fears by the characteristic remark: "If, instead of giving me one of your daughters, you could give me all, it would be the best stroke of business you had ever done."

The year in which the marriage took place (1806) was a fortunate one for the Rothschilds. It was the year which saw the power of Prussia broken on the field of Jena. Immediately after the battle, Napoleon, with his usual high-handedness, expelled the Elector William I. of Hesse-Cassel from his dominions, although he had previously recognised him as one of the neutral princes. Before his flight the Elector deposited large sums of money with Maier Rothschild, who had for some years acted as his Court agent, and these sums—said to have amounted to nearly £600,000 —the latter was successful in transmitting to his son in London. With this accession of capital Nathan Rothschild was enabled to enter upon a large extension of his financial operations. The times were propitious to so long-headed a capitalist. The coalition against Napoleon drew large sums of gold from England, and Rothschild became the paymaster of the allied forces. How sagaciously he utilised every opportunity for turning over his capital may be judged from the circumstance that he once bought bills of the Duke of Wellington at a discount, then sold to Government the gold wherewith to cash them, and finally undertook to convey the money to Portugal to pay the troops. It was he who organized the vast network of agencies all over Europe which gave the firm the earliest political information, and at the same time the means of turning it to the most comprehensive account. In the infancy of steam he had special steamboats to bring his news from Boulogne to Dover, and carrier pigeons to fly with it to London. The value of his Continental agencies was recognised in 1809 by the British Government, who, during that year, remitted through his house all the sums despatched to the Continent to keep up the struggle with Napoleon. When, in 1810, the money-market was left without an acknowledged head, owing to the death of Abraham Goldsmid, Rothschild became, by general consent, the arbiter of the Stock Exchange.

The connection of the Montefiores with this remarkable man was brought about in 1812, when Moses Montefiore married Judith Cohen, a daughter of Levi Barent Cohen, and sister-in-law of the future millionaire. Later on Abraham Montefiore espoused as his second wife Rothschild's sister Henrietta, and their daughter Louisa married in 1840 Rothschild's second son, Anthony.

Moses Montefiore took a house in New Court, St. Swithin's Lane, adjoining the one occupied by his brother-in-law. A warm friendship sprung up between the two men, and Montefiore became intimately associated with Rothschild in all his enterprises. His business career from this time is inseparable from that of his brother-in-law, for whom he acted as stockbroker. In 1813 the transactions of the firm in New Court entered on a phase of unparalleled magnitude. The allies arrayed an army of nearly a million of men against Napoleon, and Rothschild strained every nerve to keep Lord Castlereagh well supplied with funds. In that year he made his first public appearance as an English loan contractor, bringing out a loan for £12,000,000.

The time of the Napoleonic wars afforded a host of opportunities for the acquisition of wealth ; but what were chances to the majority of speculators were certainties to the financiers of New Court. Rothschild's agents kept him supplied with the latest intelligence, and in his counting-house more was known of the movements of armies and of the schemes of Continental statesmen than in Downing Street itself. Both the escape from Elba and the result of the battle of Waterloo were known to him before any other man in England. Sir Moses still relates to the few visitors he is allowed to receive how, at five o'clock one morning, he was roused by Mr. Rothschild with the intelligence that Napoleon had eluded the vigilance of the English cruisers and had landed at Cannes. Hastily dressing himself, he received instructions what sales to effect on the Exchange, and then Mr. Rothschild went to communicate his information to the Ministry. A French courier had brought the news, too precious to be entrusted to the usual pigeon-post, and when, in the evening, he was given a packet of despatches for the correspondents from whom he had come, Mr. Rothschild asked him, as he filled a stirrup-cup, if he knew what news he had brought. The man answered " No." " Napoleon has escaped from Elba and is now in France," announced Mr. Rothschild. For a moment the man looked incredulous. Then waving his glass, he shouted " Vive l'Empereur ! " and enthusiastically tossed off a bumper. As the courier took his leave Rothschild turned to his brother-in-law and said reflectively, " If that is the temper of the French I foresee we shall have some trouble yet."

Mr. Rothschild was not an ungenerous employer, and the little Frenchman, to whom he was indebted for many valuable services, he subsequently set up in business in Calais. When Sir Moses, in after-years, had occasion to visit the Continent, he frequently visited the ex-courier and indulged in a chat with him on the stirring times in which he had faithfully borne his part.

A change now took place in the transactions of New Court. The feverish anxieties of war time were over, and financial operations became founded on a firmer and more substantial basis. In other respects the character of the business carried on by Mr. Roth-schild and his colleagues was little altered. Instead of finding money to pay armies they now had to provide the means for re-organizing the unsettled European Governments. The French undertook to give compensation to the allies for every kind of damage caused by the armies of the Consulate and Empire, and to pay an indemnity of 700,000,000 francs. Altogether two milliards were required, and it devolved upon the Rothschilds to negotiate loans for the settlement of this huge claim.

In 1824 Abraham Montefiore died at Lyons, on his way home from Cannes, whither he had gone for the re-establishment of his health. He had been exceptionally fortunate on the Stock Exchange, and left behind him an immense fortune. Moses Montefiore had also accumulated considerable wealth, and now, past the midway of life, without children to work for or partner to assist him, he began to consider whether he might not free himself from the labours and anxieties of money-getting. As was his wont, he turned to his beloved wife for advice, and her counsel —" Thank God, and be content "—he followed. The year in which Sir Moses retired from business was the stormiest the City had known since the days of the South Sea Bubble, but, as in 1721 so in 1825, the Jewish financial houses stood as firm as a rock.

With a few companies, of which he was President or Director, Mr. Montefiore continued his connection. Among these were the Alliance Insurance Company, the Imperial Continental Gas Association, the Provincial Bank of Ireland, and the British, Irish, and

Colonial Silk Company. Of the two first he was a
founder. The establishment of the Alliance was
brought about by the unsuccessful candidature of Mr.
Benjamin Gompertz, a brother-in-law of Mr. Montefiore, for the post of actuary to the Guardian Office.
It was whispered at the time that Mr. Gompertz
owed his want of success to the fact of his being a
Jew, and much indignation was excited among his
co-religionists in consequence. Dissatisfaction also
prevailed in the Jewish community at the difficulties
which the existing companies interposed in the way of
granting fire policies to Jews, the impression appearing to prevail that arson had some peculiar charm for
the Hebrew. Mr. Montefiore consulted Mr. Rothschild on the subject, and suggested the formation of
a new insurance office. In this Mr. Rothschild con-
curred, although he was already a shareholder in the
Guardian, and very soon an influential directorate was
brought together. Curiously enough the strong Jewish
character of the new office became an important
element in its success. It had not then been ascertained that the Jews enjoyed a greater longevity than
other races, and their lives were consequently insured
at rates determined by the ordinary actuarial calcula-
tions. Some fifteen years later Hoffmann of Berlin,
and Bernouilli of Basle, commenced the elaborate
studies in vital statistics which have since proved that
Jewish lives are, on an average, nearly fifty per cent.
more valuable than those of any other known people.

The Gas Association was at first not so successful.

Its object was to extend the system of gas-lighting to the principal European cities. Only ten years before men of scientific eminence, among them Davy, Wollaston, and Watt, had declared that coal gas could never be safely applied to the purposes of street lighting, and an immense amount of prejudice still remained to be encountered. Progress was extremely slow, and for seventeen years Sir Moses took no director's fees. During his foreign tours he paid many anxious visits to the company's Continental establishments. He was frequently advised to terminate the operations of the company, but he declined. His courage and enterprise were ultimately rewarded. The company gradually turned the corner, and is now one of the most prosperous of the commercial societies in the City. Of both these companies Sir Moses still remains President, and it is his custom to give an annual dinner to all employed in their London offices. In 1836 the Royal Society recognised his exertions in the early introduction of gas by electing him a Fellow, as "a gentleman much attached to science and its practical use." His supporters on the occasion were Sir Richard Vyvyan, Dr. Babington, Dr. Pettigrew, Colonel Colby, and others.

Sir Moses was also one of the original directors of the Provincial Bank of Ireland, and so great was his interest in that undertaking that, when its offices were opened in Dublin, he made a special journey across St. George's Channel to issue its first note over the counter. Later in life he joined the board of the South

Eastern Railway Company on its formation ; and he
was also concerned in financing the loan of £20,000,000
by which the objects of the Slave Emancipation movement of 1833 were carried out.

On his retirement Mr. Montefiore sold his residence
in New Court, St. Swithin's Lane, to the Alliance
Insurance Company, and, as befitted a gentleman of
fortune and leisure, took a house in the fashionable
West.   This was in Green Street, Park Lane.   He
afterwards removed to his present address, 35, Park
Lane, then 10, Grosvenor Gate.   Mr. Rothschild
appears to have taken a house about the same time in
Piccadilly, and the brothers-in-law were, consequently,
still neighbours.   The district was then comparatively new, and as open and suburban as Kilburn and
Willesden at the present day.   The row of houses in
which Mr. Montefiore took up his abode was un-
finished, and where the Marble Arch now stands were
tea-houses and the booths of donkey and pony-keepers,
who hired out their cattle to children for a gallop down
the Bayswater Road.

CHAPTER III.

IT is May-day in the year 1827—a typical May-day.
Not a speck is visible in the gleaming sky, and the
trees of Hyde Park are clad in their full robes of
green. A concert of carolling and chirping songsters
comes from the leafy shadows, and the air is laden with
perfume from the flower gardens of the neighbourhood.
Eight o'clock has not yet struck, but notwithstanding
the earliness of the hour one of the houses in Park
Lane is already astir. A capacious travelling carriage
with four horses stands at the door, and servants are
busy packing away valises and trunks, and all the
requisites for a protracted journey.

Mr. and Mrs. Montefiore are about to undertake

their long-contemplated visit to the Holy Land, the cradle of their race, the theatre of the most remarkable episodes in its stupendous history. Many a time in the brief holidays snatched from the absorbing occupations of their City life, the worthy and pious couple had laid out plans for a visit in the following year to the hallowed soil in which so much of their historic sympathy centred, but when the time came something always occurred to prevent it—either political complications rendered travelling in the Mediterranean unsafe, or Mr. Montefiore could not be spared from the Stock Exchange—and so they were obliged to content themselves with another peep at Paris, or a short stay at Rome, or a visit to the birthplace of the Montefiores in the city of the Medicis, or sometimes only with a ramble along the South coast, amid scenes consecrated by the recollections of their honeymoon. Now, however, the City had ceased to have an imperative claim on Mr. Montefiore's time, and the cherished project was to be realised.

At six o'clock Mr. Montefiore had gone, as was his wont, to attend early morning service in the synagogue, and thither, as soon as the travelling carriage was ready, his wife proceeded, first stopping for a moment in Piccadilly to wave her adieux to young Hannah Rothschild,* who had risen thus early to bid her beloved aunt and uncle God speed. The carriage clattered

---

* Afterwards wife of the Right Hon. Henry Fitzroy, and mother of the present Lady Coutts Lindsay of Balcarres.

into the City, took up Mr. Montefiore in Bevis Marks,
and made its way towards the Dover Road. Breakfast
was taken at Dartford and dinner at Canterbury, and
at the end of twelve hours the travellers alighted at
Dover.

Very interesting is Mrs. Montefiore's diary* of the
journey which commenced so auspiciously on this
bright May morning; particularly as showing how
primitive still were the conditions of foreign travel
fifty years ago. It is not surprising to learn that, when
it took twelve hours to journey to Dover, three months
were required to reach Malta, and that only after seven
weeks more could Jerusalem be entered. Nor were
the circumstances of this voyage less striking and
romantic than one might expect from its primitive
character, albeit its date is so comparatively recent.

Mr. and Mrs. Montefiore embarked from Dover
under a salute of guns in honour of their fellow-
passenger, the Prussian Ambassador, who was about
to take leave of absence. The travelling carriage was
put on board, and served as a cabin during the passage.
Arrived at Calais, the Montefiores were joined by their
relatives, Mr. and Mrs. David Salomons, and together
they proceeded to post through France. Boulogne,
Montreuil, Abbeville, Grandvilliers, Beaumont, and
Charenton were reached in rapid succession, the out-
skirts of Paris were passed, a brisk run was enjoyed on
the Melun road, the Autun mountain was scaled, and

---

* Privately printed in 1836.

on the 11th May Lyons was reached. Here the happy party was saddened by the receipt of letters announcing the death of a relative, and their depression was not relieved when, in the course of the evening, Mr. Montefiore discovered that they were stopping in the hotel in which his brother Abraham had breathed his last three years before. So far, however, the journey had been a happy one. Every now and then we read of Mrs. Montefiore enjoying " a stage outside the coach with dear M——," " a little variety," adds the diarist, with almost girlish archness, " which made it pleasing to all parties." Little dreaming of the old age that one of their party was destined to attain, the travellers took an especial delight in relieving the wants of the aged poor on their route. At Chambery they assisted a poverty-stricken woman who was stated to be 114 years old ; at Lans-le-bourg one of the applicants for their bounty was 93 ; and at a village on the dreary mountain side of Radicofani, " which seems the asylum of poverty, Montefiore gave the curate a dollar for the oldest person in the place, who they said had only the heavens for his covering and the earth for his couch."

Having traversed the Mont Cenis without accident, and written a few grateful sentences in their prayer books for their " safe passage across the Alpine barrier," the travellers arrived at Florence in time to celebrate *Shebuoth* (the Feast of Weeks). The gentlemen went to the synagogue at seven in the morning, but the heat was so great that the ladies were obliged to conduct their devotions at their hotel. Naples, their last resting place on the European mainland, was reached during the rejoicings of the *festa* of *Corpus Domini,* and here the Montefiores bade farewell to their travelling companions.

Rumours now began to reach the voyagers of the dangers of travelling in the East. The Greek insurrection had attracted the official attention of Europe in consequence of the cruelties of Ibrahim Pacha in the Peloponnesus, and the relations between the Porte and the Powers were becoming strained. It was pointed out to Mr. Montefiore that, under these circumstances, a journey to Palestine was fraught with great peril. The Duke of Richelieu, on his way home from Egypt, happened, however, to stop at Naples, and he reassured the travellers. They determined to proceed. The *Portia,* a 176 ton brig, was engaged to take them to Messina, whence they were carried in a litter over the Sicilian mountains, and at Capo Passero embarked in a *speranara,* or two-masted open row-boat, for Malta. General Ponsonby, the Governor, received them most cordially, but did not allay their anxieties as to the safety of Eastern travel. So lawless had the high seas become in consequence of the disorganized state of Oriental politics, that it had been found necessary to despatch a large naval force against the pirates. Mr. Montefiore, high-spirited and sanguine, was with difficulty dissuaded from taking passage in an unescorted merchantman. On the 1st August news was received that an ultimatum had been

D

presented to the Porte by the British, French, and Russian Ministers, and again the travellers were warned that it would be "too enterprising" to proceed until a reply had been handed to the Powers by the Sultan. Still Mr. Montefiore "seems bent upon going at all events," and the *Leonidas*, a vessel of 380 tons burden, carrying twenty-two men, "which we trust will be amply sufficient to repel the attacks of pirates," was engaged for £550 to take him and his wife to Alexandria. Mrs. Montefiore now became indisposed —the anxieties of the journey had apparently told upon her—and it was not until the welcome intelligence was received that the *Leonidas* was to be convoyed to Alexandria by the *Gannet* sloop of war, that she was enabled to leave her chamber.

Having relieved the poor of the Malta congregation, and given a farewell breakfast to the chiefs of the Synagogue, the travellers again embarked. On the seventh day after their departure the *Gannet* gave chase to a supposed pirate, but "the valiant anticipations of making a capture were vain." Otherwise the voyage was quiet and dull. On the twelfth day they arrived at Alexandria, where they passed a couple of days examining the antiquities of the city. Then, in three days more, they partly sailed and were partly towed up the Nile in a cangia to Cairo. Here they explored the Great Pyramid under the guidance of a Bedouin, who told them he had acted in the same capacity to Napoleon, and on the 5th September they were presented to Mehemet Ali. The portrait of this re-

markable man, sketched by Mrs. Montefiore, is very
interesting :—

" The conversation was supported in a lively manner
by the Pacha for three-quarters of an hour. He smoked
and ordered coffee to be served. His pipe was richly
studded with diamonds and other precious stones. He
encourages every new invention and improvement, and
informed Montefiore of his having established silk and
other manufactories in his territories ; and that he
had planted numbers of olive and mulberry trees. His
extensive mercantile transactions were, however, a great
source of jealousy and dissatisfaction to his subjects,
who are thereby deprived of the advantages of competition and unfettered trade. He would not grant a
farmer a longer lease than a year, and fixed the price
of all the produce of the land himself. At the age of
forty-five he commenced learning to read and write,
which he persevered in to his satisfaction ; a singular
instance of strength of mind. All his vast transactions are managed by himself, and every written
document passes under his inspection. He told Montefiore that he never indulges in more than four hours
sleep during the night. He might prove a great
character in the world were he entirely unfettered."

This interview laid the foundation of a lasting
friendship. Mehemet Ali was so charmed with his
Jewish visitor that he proposed to him to act as his
agent in England. Although Mr. Montefiore's retire-

ment from business rendered his acceptance of this
offer impracticable, he has always maintained relations
of a friendly character with the Egyptian Court.
When, in after years, Said Pacha, a successor of
Mehemet, sent his son Toussoun to England to be
educated, his guardianship was confided to Sir Moses.

Another cangia took the travellers back to Alexandria, but there the chances of being able to reach
Jerusalem in safety became more than ever remote.
The Sultan—or "Grand Signor," as Mrs. Montefiore
calls him in old-fashioned phrase—had not deigned to
reply to the ultimatum of the Powers, and war seemed
imminent.   Mr. Montefiore was in despair; his good
wife, not so ardent to brave danger, philosophised on
the "futility and weakness of all human plans." Their
position was anything but enviable.   One person told
them that Abdallah, the Pacha of Damascus, was in-
imical to all Europeans, and "that a Frank by going
to Syria would run the risk of being massacred."   To
return was equally out of the question, for no convoy
was available, and the pirates had assembled in force.
"You will certainly be sold for slaves if you stir," said
Mr. Salt, the British Consul, and so they were obliged
to pass the Jewish New Year "pent up in a miserable
room, in a confined street, and suffocating from the
sands and hot blasts of the sirocco wind." Mrs.
Montefiore adds, complacently, that her husband "now
began to comprehend that travelling is not always
divested of disagreeables."

In this way they were detained several weeks in

Egypt; but eventually they resolved, in defiance of all danger, to set sail for Jaffa. Mrs. Montefiore donned the Turkish *bernische* and white muslin turban and veil, in order to pass for a Mussulman lady, in case of accidents. Several of the European gentlemen on board also assumed an Oriental garb; but Mr. Montefiore, gallant as ever, refused all solicitations to disguise himself. Fortunately Jaffa was reached in safety; and, after some parleying, the travellers were allowed by the Turkish authorities to land, and to proceed to Jerusalem.

By all classes of the population of the holy city they were received with overwhelming cordiality. So delighted were the Jews to welcome one of their own faith, who was affluent and honoured, that the Chacham, in his enthusiasm, likened Mr. Montefiore's visit to the coming of the Messiah. The Governor invited him to his house, offered him pipes and coffee, and ordered a scribe to add a handsome eulogium to his passport, to which he affixed his name and seal. The travellers had entered Jerusalem with the profoundest reverence; but this feeling was soon transformed into pity for its " fallen, desolate, and abject condition," as Mrs. Montefiore describes it. This is the account her diary gives of the state of the Holy Land :—

"Many were the solemn thoughts which rose in our minds on finding ourselves in this Holy Land: the country of our ancestors, of our religion, and of our former greatness, but now, alas! of persecution and oppression. We hear from every one of the extortions that are levied, and that there is no means of support, except such as is provided by the bounty of other countries, with the exception of the little help afforded by the few families who continue here from a principle of religious enthusiasm, and contribute all in their power to the support of the necessitous. There are four Synagogues adjoining each other, belonging to the Portuguese, who form the principal portion of the Jewish community. The Germans have only one place of worship, and the greater proportion of the population are from Poland. . . . There is no commerce; and shops are not suffered on terms which admit of their becoming profitable."

On the 21st October they left Jerusalem. During the whole of the preceding night seventeen Rabbis sat up praying for them in the Synagogue. The next morning the Portuguese high priest came at an early hour to give them his blessing; and then, amid the good wishes of a numerous multitude, who followed them to the gates, they set out on their return journey.

This visit to Jerusalem impressed the travellers deeply; it gave a deep-seated and serious purpose to their lives ; it cemented the foundations of that ardent interest in the fortunes of their oppressed race, and suffering humanity generally, which has written the name of "Montefiore" so large in the history of Judaism and philanthropy. How deeply this influence was felt, even at the early period of this first journey, may be seen in Mrs. Montefiore's eloquent words at the close of her chapter on Jerusalem :—

" ' Farewell, Holy City ! ' we exclaimed, in our hearts. ' Blessed be the Almighty, who has protected us while contemplating the sacred scenes which environ thee ! Thankful may we ever be for His manifold mercies ! May the fountain of our feelings evermore run in the current of praise and entire devotion to His will and His truth, till the time shall arrive when the ransomed of the Lord shall return, and come to Zion with songs and everlasting joy upon their heads.' "

The return journey was undertaken not a moment too soon; indeed, had it not been for the slowness with which news travelled in the year 1827, the departure of the Montefiores from Turkish territory might not have been altogether unmolested. The battle of Navarino had been fought the day before they left Jerusalem, and they arrived in Alexandria in time to hear the Arab women lamenting the disaster in the public streets. Nor had all danger from pirates passed away. Vessels preceding them had been attacked by the Greek buccaneers ; and at Alexandria they witnessed the arrival of one of these corsairs in the safe custody of a French cutter. The journey back to Malta was full of anxieties. Being without convoy, they asked the chief officer of the ship whether he would offer any resistance were he attacked. " Oh, certainly ! " was the encouraging reply. " Do you think I should tamely consent to have my ship pillaged, when I have the promise of Captain Montefiore's assistance, and four loaded guns to the vessel?" "Then we *have* a chance of having our throats cut!" blankly exclaimed Dr. Madden, who was of the party.

Their usual good fortune attended them, however; and, after a somewhat stormy voyage, Malta was safely reached. Here they met Admiral Sir William Codrington, to whom they had letters of introduction, and were entrusted by him with despatches, on the subject of Navarino, to the Duke of Clarence, afterwards William IV. Homeward then they travelled with all speed. H.M.S. *Mastiff* carried them in six days to Messina, and thence to Naples; and much the same route as the outward journey brought them in eight weeks to London.

The despatches, of which he was the bearer, Mr. Montefiore delivered at the house of the Duke of Clarence before going to his own home. Next morning His Royal Highness sent for him to Park Lane, to thank him personally for his complaisance. In the course of the conversation that ensued, His Royal Highness asked what people in the East were saying of Navarino? "That it could not be prevented," was the answer; "for, as the British commander himself said, ' when the British flag is insulted, an English admiral knows what is his duty!'" To which the Duke replied, musingly, "Inevitable! Inevitable!"

CHAPTER IV.

FOR nearly a quarter of a century previous to the
journey described in the last chapter, Mr. Montefiore
had been an earnest and active member of the Synagogue. From his earliest youth he had been a
punctual attendant at the services, and, from the time
he attained man's estate, a generous contributor to the
congregational funds. It was one of the rules of the
Portuguese Synagogue that no one should be eligible
for membership of the congregation before his twenty-
first year, and this rule was only waived under
exceptional circumstances, and on receipt of a petition
for admission from the youthful candidate. On the

4th November, 1804, an important meeting of the
Council of Elders was held under the presidency of
Mr. Jacob Samuda, the Warden President, for the
purpose of electing a new Chief Rabbi. After a long
deliberation the choice fell upon the learned Rabbi
Raphael Meldola, of Leghorn, and a hope was
expressed that this gentleman would succeed in
reviving the religious spirit of the congregation, which
since the death of the late Chacham Azevedo had
been very conspicuously waning. Towards the conclusion of the meeting the chairman announced that
he had received a petition from Mr. Moses Montefiore,
of Vauxhall, who, although only twenty years of age,
was desirous of being admitted a *Yahid*, or member of
the congregation. A few questions were asked, and
the prayer was unanimously granted. To no two
men is English Judaism more substantially indebted
than Chacham Meldola and Sir Moses Montefiore, and
it is an interesting coincidence that they were elected
members of the community, though in widely different
ranks, on the same day.

The Synagogue authorities had no reason to regret
their infraction of the law in admitting Mr. Montefiore.
A more regular attendant at the services had never
been seen within the Synagogue walls. Every
morning, at seven o'clock, he was in his place, piously
offering up his prayers to the God of his ancestors. As
his means improved, so year by year he increased his
contributions to the Synagogue exchequer; and, at the
meetings of the *Yehidim*, no one evinced a more earnest

interest in the affairs of the congregation. He soon
took rank in the community, and one by one served all
the various offices connected with the administration.
He was successively *Parnass* or Governor of the
Terra Santa and *Cautivos* funds, of the Hospital, the
Burial Society, and the Theological College. In 1814
he became *Gabay*, or Treasurer, and, in that capacity,
had doubtless much to do with the celebrated Synagogue account, which Isaac D'Israeli refused to pay in
that year, and which eventually led to the secession of
the D'Israelis from the Jewish community. Five
years later he reached the proud position of *Parnass*,
or Warden-President of the congregation. Six times
he has served this important post, the last occasion on
which his towering form was seen in the *Banca*
(warden's box) being in 1854. His assiduity in the
discharge of his duties may be seen by a reference to
the minute books of the congregation. He appears to
have been very rarely absent from the various meetings,
and hundreds of times his signature, in a neat Italian
hand, may be read at the foot of the records of the
proceedings. Previous to 1826 his autograph appears
in the Hebrew style, viz., "Moseh de Joseph Eliau
Montefiore;" subsequent to that date he adopted his
present signature, "Moses Montefiore," and, except
that it is somewhat firmer, it differs in no respect from
his signature at the present day.

In 1823 Mr. Montefiore presented the Synagogue
with an estate of thirteen houses in Cock Court, Jewry
Street, on the condition that the rents arising during

five years should be invested to form a repairing fund, and then the dwellings should be occupied by deserving poor. The "Montefiore Almshouses" are still an interesting feature in the Sephardic community.

Mr. Montefiore did not confine his attention to organisations immediately connected with the Synagogue. He co-operated in all the various societies which laboured for the communal welfare. His unostentatious but practical piety in this respect is illustrated by his connection with the *Lavadores*, an extra-Synagogual Society for washing the dead and preparing the bodies for burial. There is no more sacred duty incumbent on the Israelite than to perform the last offices for the dying and the dead. The importance of the duty in Jewish teaching has been beautifully expressed by Heinrich Heine :—

> "Drei Gebote sind die Höchsten :
> Gastrecht üben, Kranke pflegen
> Und zum Grabe hin den Todten
> Mit Gebeten zu geleiten."

As a matter of fact the teaching goes beyond mere prayer at burial. The duty is prescribed of washing and coffining the corpse, and so highly is this duty esteemed that the discharge of it is held to be a privilege to which only the most blameless Jews may be admitted. Hence in every community a voluntary society exists charged with this function, and the most jealous care is exercised over the admission of members. The wealthiest Jews are frequently found among them, and, in former years, member-

ship conveyed a higher distinction than wealth or
rank.   In foreign countries, when the Jews desire to
render particular honour to an eminent non-Jew, they
elect him an honorary member of their *Chevra Kadisha*,
as the society is called in the German communities.
One of these at Grosswardein recently elected M.
Tisza, the Hungarian Premier, a member, in acknowledgment of his defence of the Israelites against the
Anti-Semitic agitators.   The late Emperor Ferdinand
of Austria was a member of the *Chevra Kadisha* of
Prague, and whenever his name appeared on the rota
he never failed to appoint a Jewish substitute to
perform his duties.   The English Jews established
their society of *Lavadores* in 1723.   It consists of
twenty-five members, each of whom pays an entrance
fee and an annual contribution towards the expenses.
Mr. Montefiore was admitted a member in 1808.
Among the dead for whom he performed the last
offices was the very Chacham Meldola who entered the
Anglo-Jewish community on the same day that he was
elected a *Yáhid*.   On the seventieth anniversary of his
entrance into the society he was re-appointed its
Governor, although, of course, unable any longer to
undertake the work attached to the office.

Orthodox in his principles, and strictly observant of
the minute Jewish ceremonial, Moses Montefiore was
still a far-seeing and liberal man of the world.   His
superiority to ancient prejudices was illustrated by his
marriage.   There was a time when unions between
Spanish and German Jews were frowned upon by the

aristocratic denizens of Bevis Marks.   The pride of
the Sephardim, nurtured in the most brilliant age of
Spanish culture, of which they were at once the pro-
moters and the ornaments, had never been broken.
Even the colossal persecution under Ferdinand and
Isabella had not humbled them, and in their exile they
shrunk instinctively from fellowship with their German
and Polish brethren, upon whose sad history not one
ray of light had been shed, and who had been reduced
by ceaseless oppression to a lowly, pettifogging, almost
an ignoble race.   The barrier between the two
"nations," as they were called, although unsanctioned
by law or ritual, continued for a long time after the
German Jews in this country had vindicated their
native Hebrew energy and skill by commercial and
intellectual successes.   As late as 1744, when Jacob
Bernal, an ancestor of the present Duchess of St.
Albans, desired to wed a German Jewess, he had to
apply for leave to the *Mahamad* or Council of Elders
of the Synagogue, and then he only obtained permission under the most humiliating conditions.   This and
kindred prejudices had never found a supporter in
Moses Montefiore.   By his marriage in 1812 with a
" Tedesco "—for the Cohen family belonged to that
plebeian section of the community—he contributed to
break it down.   The folly and injustice of the division
between the two " nations " became apparent to him
as soon as he made the acquaintance of his wife's
accomplished family.   When he began to think over
the struggle the Jews would soon have to sustain in

order to win a legal and social equality with their
Christian fellow-citizens, his intelligence assured him
that any such division in the community was a source
of absolute danger to its interests. In almost every
city he has visited during his several missions to
foreign countries, he has preached the necessity of
communal union to his co-religionists. In Jerusalem
he spoke earnestly on the subject to the ecclesiastical
chiefs during his first visit. "Discord and differences
in the bosom of Judaism have been my greatest grief,"
he significantly said. in 1863, to a deputation which
waited upon him at Pesth, from the most orthodox and
unbending of the Jewish congregations in the city.

Deeply impressed with what he had seen of the
degraded condition of his co-religionists in the East,
during his tour in 1827, Mr. Montefiore resolved, soon
after his return to England, to take a still more active
part in the public life of the Anglo-Jewish community.
A survey of the condition of his brethren assured
him that it would be impossible for them to do anything of importance for the benefit of oppressed foreign
communities. It was obviously necessary that they
should win their own freedom first; and he was gratified to see, that for a struggle to this end both the
times and the condition of his co-religionists were
favourable. Mr. Montefiore's views on Jewish emancipation were not of an heroic kind, but they were
intelligent and practical. "I am an enemy of all
sudden transitions," he said in conversation some years
after. "The Jew must, in his claims and wishes, not

outstrip the age. Let him advance slowly but steadily;
let him gradually accustom his Christian fellow-citizens
to his gradual progress and success in public life, and
what may not be obtainable even by an arduous
struggle, will, after a certain time, fall into his lap like
ripe fruit." Mr. Montefiore thought he saw these
conditions fulfilled as he pondered on the subject
fifty-six years ago. There was union in the community; many of its members had won for themselves
distinguished positions in society, and the tendency
of national thought, as illustrated in Parliament by the
Catholic emancipation agitation, was distinctly liberal.

A representative body charged with the duty of
" watching " all chances of emancipation was already
in existence in the Anglo-Jewish community. The
Deputados, or " United Deputies of British Jews," was
formed in 1746, when the two houses of the Irish
Legislature were quarrelling over a Jewish Naturaliza-
tion Bill. The Irish House of Commons had twice
passed the Bill, and twice it had been rejected by the
House of Lords. The Bevis Marks Synagogue formed
a Committee of Diligence, to render assistance to the
party favourable to Jewish emancipation, but the Bill
was again and finally negatived by the Peers. Un-
daunted by their want of success, the Jews of London
set themselves to organise their forces. From the
" Committee of Diligence " was formed in 1760 the
" Deputies of the Portuguese nation," and towards the
end of the same year that body admitted to its deliberations representatives of the German congregations in

Duke's Place and Magpie Alley. For many years the
labours of the " Deputies " were not of any great
importance. The presentation of addresses to the
Crown, full of assurances of Jewish loyalty, on occasions of public rejoicing or public mourning, formed
the staple of their work. In 1795 their representations to Parliament procured the rejection of a clause
of doubtful bearing in the Sedition Bill, and in 1805
they prosecuted the *St. James's Chronicle* for the
publication of some offensive articles against the Jews,
and obtained an apology from the Editor.

This body, of which Mr. Moses Mocatta had become
President, was joined by Mr. Montefiore early in 1828.
An inspection of the minutes of the "United Deputies"
discloses from this date a sudden development in their
corporate activity, which it is impossible not to asso-
ciate with their new recruit. During the very month
of his election he became a member of a sub-committee
charged to draw up a petition in reference to the repeal
of the Test and Corporation Acts, and to present it to
the House of Lords. Indeed in this year the agitation
for the removal of Jewish disabilities in England was
for the first time placed on a firm basis. The *Deputados*
became the soul of the agitation, and Mr. Montefiore
the soul of the *Deputados*.

Two years later Mr. Montefiore solved one of the
Disability problems in his own person, by purchasing
the small East Cliff estate, near Ramsgate, notwithstanding that many eminent legal authorities still considered that the Jews could not lawfully possess real

E

estate in England.   It is true that in 1818 Sir Samuel
Romilly had held that Jews born in England were as
much entitled to own land as any other natives, at the
same time pointing out that no one had ever objected
to a title on the ground that the owner was a Jew;
nevertheless, down to the removal of all disabilities in
1853, this point was still doubted under the statutes or
ordinances of the 54th & 55th Henry III. (c.e. 1269),
which declared that no Jew should hold a freehold, and
it was never definitely settled.

East Cliff Lodge is a charming marine villa, in the
Strawberry Hill or modern Gothic style.   It consists
of a centre and two wings, with the summit embattled,
and each wing surmounted by an ornamental turret and
spire.   The dining-room, pronounced by local guide-
books " the most elegant specimen of Gothic domestic
architecture in England," is a noble apartment, having
a screen of columns at the lower end, and opening
from a vestibule by folding doors curiously wrought.
The grounds, which cover about thirteen acres, and
extend to the verge of the cliff, are laid out with great
taste and judgment.   Their principal attractions are
two subterranean caverns, reputed to be the work of
smugglers, which lead from the summit of the cliff by
a gradual descent, 500 yards long, to the beach below.
One cavern diverges in an easterly, the other in a
westerly direction.   Both are lighted by a series of
arched recesses, excavated out of the solid chalk, and
which, carpeted with turf and covered with shrubs and
flowers, present a very gay appearance during the

summer season. The house was built about 1795 by
Mr. Benjamin Bond Hopkins, who disposed of it to
Viscount Keith, better known as Lord Elphinstone.
It then became the property of the Marquis Wellesley,
brother of the Duke of Wellington. At one time it
was the favourite summer residence of Queen Caroline,
when Princess of Wales. Mr. Montefiore rented East
Cliff Lodge for some years before he purchased it.
One of the first uses to which he put the land when it
became his own was the building of a synagogue, which
he opened to all comers. The foundation stone was
laid in 1831, and the building was consecrated in 1833.
Soon after he had thus permanently taken up his
abode in Kent he was appointed a Deputy Lieutenant
for the county.

CHAPTER V.

AT what period the earliest Jewish settlement took
place in England is one of those difficult historical
questions of which nothing more certain is known than
that it is "involved in obscurity." A copyist's error in
the *Pesiktha Rabbathi,* by which " Mauritania " was
transformed into " Britannia," has suggested that the
Jews were already acquainted with Britain in the
Talmudic age. It has also been surmised that Hebrew
supercargoes accompanied the Phœnician mariners who
traded with the Cimbri and Damnonii of Cornwall
before the Roman invasion. The first mention of Jews
in any document connected with English history is in
the canons of Ecbright, Archbishop of York, which

contain an ordinance that "no Christian shall Judaize or presume to eat with a Jew." These canons were issued in the year 750.

After the Norman Conquest the Jews of England became numerous and wealthy. It is a mistake to imagine, with Professor Goldwin Smith, that they voluntarily "streamed" into the country as rapacious camp followers of the Conqueror. The truth is they were brought over here by William, with the deliberate design of their acting as engines of indirect taxation. "The Jews," says William of Newburgh, "are the Royal usurers," and it was in this capacity that they were domiciled in England. How they had become forced into this position is a melancholy story. Excluded from markets and trade guilds, prohibited from dealing in wines and cereals, forbidden to employ slaves at a time when all manufacturing industry was conducted by serf-labour, no means of earning their bread remained to them but usury. The Church smoothed their way to this occupation by prohibiting Christians (on the strength of the passage, Luke vi. 35) from taking interest of any kind on loans. Amid the universal want of ready money occasioned by the constant decrease in the stock of gold and silver, and the absence of any substitute for the precious metals, borrowing became a necessity with all classes, and the Jews, who had acquired considerable wealth by trading, were thus forced to lend. High interest increased their riches; and the English kings, whose taxing power was greatly crippled by the freedom of the Barons, consequently submitted them to crushing imposts. To enable them thus to make good the deficiencies in the revenue, they were specially taken into the Royal protection, and their rates of interest—once as high as 86¾ per cent.—were sanctioned by Royal decree.

It is not surprising that, under these circumstances, the Jews became hateful to the nation; but Mr. Freeman's picture of them, "stalking defiantly among the people of the land," is purely an effort of fancy. In their learning and their heroic fidelity to their religion, we have abundant evidence of their good sense. Jews taught geometry, logic, and philosophy in the University of Oxford, and Jewish schools or colleges were established in London, York, Lincoln, Oxford, Cambridge, and Warwick. Thither flocked Jew and Gentile to hear distinguished Rabbis expound the principles of arithmetic, Hebrew, Arabic, and medicine. The celebrated Ibn-Ezra visited England in 1159, and delivered lectures in London. During his stay he wrote his religio-philosophical work *Jesod Mora*. Among other learned Jews who lived in England before the expulsion were Rabbi Jacob, of Orleans, who taught in London, and Rabbi Benjamin, of Canterbury, both pupils of Rabbi Jacob Tam, the famous Tossafist, and grandson of Rashi. The fidelity of the Jews to their religion was illustrated by a thousand martyr deaths, but by nothing more gloriously than their beleaguerment in York Castle, when five hundred destroyed themselves rather than apostatise. It is impossible to read Isaac d'Israeli's

vivid sketch of this "scene of heroic exertion" without
feeling that to portray these men as the grasping and
arrogant bullies depicted to us in Mr. Freeman's pages
is little less than a calumny.

Massacres of Jews were, as a rule, sternly punished
by the English kings, who could ill afford to have
their "chattels" injured. When, however, exorbitant
taxes could no longer be squeezed from them, they
were ruthlessly abandoned to the fury of the populace.
The competition of the Caorsini, who disguised their
usury in commissions and expenses, first reduced their
value in the eyes of the King. The Government tried
to expel the new comers, but in vain; they were the
servants of the Pope, and no one dared touch them.
With the gradual relaxation of the Royal interest in
the Jews, the clergy grew bolder in denouncing them
as heretics. The public mind became inflamed; and
to gain popularity Edward I. passed the statute *De
Judaismo*, which, among other restrictions, prohibited
the Jews from practising the usury they had already
been compelled, to the King's great grief, to abandon.
Their expulsion from the country, amid horrible
cruelties, soon followed.

The Jews carried with them into exile the remembrance of many an outrage that marked their exodus
from Britain. Of one they preserved the tradition
through no less than five centuries. A number of
Jews were barbarously drowned in the Thames, close
by where London Bridge now stands. When the
old bridge was in existence the fall of the waters

at ebb tide caused a disturbance under one of the arches; and this, as late as eighty years ago, the Jewish gossips firmly believed was occasioned by the wrath of the Deity at the horrible crime committed there in the year 1290.

It is generally assumed that from this date until the Protectorate there were no Jews in England. Indeed, Mr. J. R. Green goes so far as to assert that " from the time of Edward to that of Cromwell no Jew touched English ground." Recent researches have proved, however, that in spite of proscription, Hebrews frequently visited these shores. The House of Converts, near Chancery Lane, received Jews continuously from the thirteenth to the eighteenth centuries; and the files of accounts preserved in the Record Office show that as many as seventy-two Jews resided within its walls during the early years of Edward III.'s reign. In the State papers relating to the marriage of Katherine of Aragon with Arthur, Prince of Wales, we are told that Henry VII. had a long interview with a Spanish envoy to discuss the presence of Jews in England. Roderigo Lopes, acknowledged to be a Jew, was Physician to Queen Elizabeth. The great legal luminaries, Littleton and Coke, both inveigh against the Jews with a vigour inexplicable, except on the hypothesis that members of the proscribed race were resident in England. It was not, however, until the time of Cromwell that Jews took up their abode in the land in any number. No actual revocation of the edict of expulsion seems to have taken place, but that some sort of permission to return was granted them it is impossible to doubt. In 1657 they considered their position sufficiently secure to justify them in purchasing a burial-ground ; and Cromwell's views on their readmission are put beyond all doubt, by the fact that he granted Menasseh ben Israel, the Jewish advocate, a pension of £100 a year.

Until the year 1829, when the Test and Corporation Acts were repealed, it was held by legal authorities that Jews in England had no civil rights ; and even as late as 1846 the Act *De Judaismo* was formally on the Statute Book. In 1673 the Jews were indicted for worshipping in public in their synagogues ; and in 1685 thirty-seven of their merchants were suddenly arrested in the Royal Exchange, under the statute 23 of Elizabeth, for not attending any church. Two years earlier it had been argued before the King's Bench by the Attorney-General, in the case of the East India Company *v.* Sand, that all Jews in England were under an implied licence, which the King might revoke, the effect of doing which would be that they would then become aliens. Even so great a judge as Lord Hardwicke held, in 1744, that a bequest for the maintenance of a Synagogue was void, because the Jewish religion was not tolerated in England, but only connived at by the Legislature. This decision was accepted as a precedent in 1786 by Lord Thurlow, and again in 1818 by Lord Eldon. In 1828, when Moses Montefiore set in motion the struggle for

Jewish emancipation, the English Jews, according to
Tomlins' "Law Dictionary," still laboured under serious
disabilities. "A Jew," we are told, "is prevented
from sitting in Parliament, holding any office, civil or
military, under the Crown, or any situation in corporate bodies. He may be excluded from practising
at the bar, or as an attorney, proctor, or notary, from
voting at elections, from enjoying any exhibition in
either university, or from holding some offices of
inferior importance."

When Mr. Montefiore joined the *Deputados* of Bevis
Marks, the question of Jewish Emancipation had
already a Parliamentary history. It had not, however,
been encouraging. Certainly in 1723 a slight concession had been made in respect to the oath of
abjuration, and in 1740 an impracticable Naturalisation
Act had been passed for the Colonies; but the
attempt of Mr. Pelham in 1753 to carry into effect a
wider scheme of Jewish Emancipation for the home
country had produced such an uproar that, for nearly
a century after, the bulk of the English Israelites
shrunk from publicly agitating for their rights. Mr.
Pelham's Act, historically known as "The Jew Bill,"
was at first passed by both Houses and received the
Royal assent, but it only lived for a few months. An
alarm for the Church and for religion spread through
the land. It was proclaimed from countless pulpits
that if the Jews were naturalised in Britain the country
became liable to the curses pronounced by prophecy
against Jerusalem and the Holy Land. Every dead

wall in the kingdom exhibited in varied orthography
the couplet,

> "No Jews,
> No wooden shoes."

Mr. Sydenham voted for the measure and lost his
seat for Exeter in consequence. A respectable clergyman named Tucker, who wrote a defence of the
Jews, was maltreated by the populace. The Bishop of
Norwich, who supported the Bill, was insulted on
his ensuing confirmation circuit. At Ipswich the boys
called upon his lordship "to come and circumcise
them," and a paper was affixed to one of the Church
doors to state that "next day, being Saturday, his
lordship would confirm the Jews, and on the day following the Christians." To such a pitch rose the popular
excitement that the Ministers beat a hasty and igno-
minious retreat. On the very first day of the next
session the Duke of Newcastle brought in a Bill to
repeal the previous measure, and it was rapidly carried
through both Houses. The incident elicited a
stinging commentary from Horace Walpole. "The
populace," he wrote, "grew suddenly so zealous for
the honour of the prophecies that foretold calamity
and eternal depression to the Jews, that they seemed
to fear lest the completion of them should be defeated
by Act of Parliament. The little curates preached
against the Bishops for deserting the interests of the
Gospel; and aldermen grew drunk at county clubs in
the cause of Jesus Christ, as they had used to do for
the sake of King James. A cabal of ministers, who

had insulted their master with impunity, who had
betrayed every ally and party with success, and who
had crammed down every Bill that was calculated for
their own favour, yielded to transitory noise and submitted to fight under the banners of prophecy in order
to carry a few more seats in another Parliament."

The remembrance of the intolerant spirit displayed
by the English people on this occasion, rendered the
Jews for many years exceedingly anxious to avoid anything that might direct public attention to them as a
body. The repeal of the Test and Corporation Acts
in 1828, however, aroused their hopes, and Mr. Montefiore, on behalf of the Board of Deputies, with the
assistance outside of Mr. N. M. Rothschild and Mr.,
afterwards Sir Isaac Lyon Goldsmid, endeavoured to
obtain a removal of the disqualifications pressing
upon Jews. Mr. Montefiore had several interviews on
the subject with the Duke of Sussex, whose sympathy
with the Jews had been already evinced in many substantial ways, and obtained from him a promise of his
interest and support. The Premier, however, was un-
favourable to any concession, on the ground that it was
inexpedient so soon after the passing of the Catholic
Relief Bill to excite the feelings of the country by
another measure of the same description. The movement consequently fell to the ground. Not for long,
however. In January, 1830, a petition to Parliament
was prepared, and a deputation from the Board of Deputies waited upon the Duke of Sussex, who again promised
his support. A host of petitions from Jews and non-

Jews all over the country poured into the House of
Commons, and on the 5th of April Mr. Robert Grant
moved for leave to bring in a Bill for the Repeal of the
Civil Disabilities of the Jews. Mr. Montefiore and
his brother Deputies were indefatigable in their efforts
to bring pressure to bear on Parliament to pass the
Bill. A committee of their body sat daily between
ten and four o'clock at the King's Head in the Poultry,
and incurred expenses amounting to little less than
£1000. Nevertheless, on the second reading of the
Bill, on the 23rd May, it was thrown out by 228 noes
against 165 ayes. Three years later another effort
was made and with better success. The Commons
passed Mr. Grant's Bill, but in the Lords it was thrown
out. Year by year, for four years more, the campaign
was prosecuted with unwearying zeal, Mr. Montefiore
in the meantime becoming the leader of the movement
by his election to the Presidency of the Board of
Deputies in succession to his uncle, Mr. Moses
Mocatta. Each year, however, the Lords proved
obdurate, and a pause in the struggle took place.

The agitation so far had not been altogether without
profit to the Jews. Mr. David Salomons had opened
the shrievalty to his co-religionists in 1835, and a Bill
to enable him to serve passed through Parliament
without opposition. Mr. Montefiore took advantage of
the Act to become a candidate for the same office in
1837, and was elected. Early in the year he headed
two deputations—one from the Board of Deputies, and
the other from the town of Ramsgate—to congratulate

the young Queen on her accession. When Her
Majesty subsequently entered the City of London on
Lord Mayor's day, the honour of knighthood was conferred on the new Sheriff as well as on the Lord
Mayor, the famous Mr. Alderman Wood, father of
Lord Hatherley. These were not the first occasions
on which Sir Moses had met Queen Victoria. In 1834,
when the Duchess of Kent and her daughter were residing at Townley House, Ramsgate, they frequently
rambled through the picturesque grounds of East Cliff
Lodge, and Mr. Montefiore courteously provided them
with a special key to his private gate. On his first visit
to Court he was graciously reminded of his hospitality.
"We always remember with pleasure the happy days
we spent at Ramsgate," cordially added the Duchess
of Kent, who was standing by the throne.

With another member of the royal family Sir Moses
had also established intimate relations; this was the
Duke of Sussex, uncle to the Queen. His Royal
Highness had taken a deep interest in the Jews. He
was a patron of their hospital, and presided at its
anniversary dinners. A diligent student of the
Hebrew language, and Jewish history and literature,
he also actively assisted in the movement for Jewish
emancipation. Sir Moses Montefiore was the first con-
forming Jew to receive the honour of knighthood, and
the Duke rightly interpreted the circumstance as
indicating the failure of anti-Jewish prejudice. He
took no pains to hide his satisfaction. When the
ceremony of investiture was performed he was present,

and at its conclusion he seized Sir Moses' hand, and heartily shaking it exclaimed, " This is one of the things I have worked for all my life ! "

The year of office Sir Moses served as Sheriff was distinguished by the large collections made for the City charities, and by the complete absence of capital punishment. The latter circumstance is a source of great pride to Sir Moses. There was certainly one criminal condemned to death, but with the assistance of a lady highly placed, a reprieve was obtained. Sir Moses, at that period, found few to sympathise with him in his humane dislike of the death punishment. His representations on the subject to Lord John Russell were coldly received, and when, while showing Marshal Soult over Newgate, he expressed his opinions on the subject to that inflexible disciplinarian, they evoked only an astonished stare.

During the same year he continued indefatigably to discharge his duties as President of the Board of Deputies. He began now, however, to turn his attention more towards the foreign Jews, whose oppressed condition had attracted his sympathies ten years before. The Emancipation struggle was safe in other hands, and he felt he could now leave it. His brother-in-law, David Salomons, his nephew, Lionel de Rothschild, his relatives, Isaac Lyon Goldsmid and Francis Goldsmid, were all prepared to invade the precincts of Parliament itself in the interests of Jewish emancipation ; but for so public a struggle Sir Moses Montefiore had no ambition.

CHAPTER VI.

AMID the engrossing labours of the Disability agitation, Sir Moses Montefiore had still found time to
communicate occasionally with foreign Jewish communities. Distress, however remote, never failed to
attract his attention, or to elicit from him sympathetic
and substantial assistance. The interest he evinced
in the welfare of his oppressed brethren spread his
fame far and wide among them. Dr. Wolff, the well-
known missionary, found, already in 1834, that his
name was known to the Jews of Bokhara, Samarcand,
Balkh, Khokand, and Herat.

Several circumstances now combined to determine
him to a more active and systematic treatment of the
various problems raised by the appeals addressed to
him from abroad. Not only was he enabled by the
lull in home affairs to give these problems more attention than formerly, but he had convinced himself that
it was of greater importance to the honour and fair
fame of Judaism that the Jewish character, as exempli-
fied by the great mass of his foreign brethren, should
be assisted to rehabilitate itself, than that every effort
should be concentrated on one or two agitations for
the repeal of local disabilities. Mr. Cobbett's taunt
that " the Israelite is never seen to take a spade in his
hand, but waits like the voracious slug to devour what
has been produced by labour in which he has no
share," had sunk deep in his heart, and he resolved to
seize an early opportunity of assisting the more down-
trodden communities of his co-religionists, to improve
their condition by agricultural and industrial labour.
He selected the Jews of Palestine for his first experi-
ment in this direction. His choice of these communities was determined partly by the fact, that the Holy
Land had a special attraction for him, and partly
because he had reason to hope that his influence with
Mehemet Ali, then lord of Syria, would enable him to
obtain a fair field for his operations.

Accompanied by his devoted spouse, he started
on his second voyage to the Holy Land on the
1st November, 1838. The journey was not a direct
one, as the travellers were desirous of enquiring into

F

the political and social condition of the Jewish communities of the Continent.   To this task they devoted
close upon seven months.

In Lady Montefiore's private journal* many interesting particulars are preserved concerning the
Continental Jews at this period.   Their condition
was not altogether unsatisfactory, although the sun of
civil and religious liberty had not yet dawned.   At
Brussels the travellers found a community of about
eighty families, possessing a neat little synagogue, in
which sermons in German were delivered weekly.   At
Aix-la-Chapelle the community, though very poor,
were erecting a new synagogue, towards the expense of
which the travellers contributed.   At Strasbourg ritual
reforms had already been introduced ; but at Avignon,
once the home of so many learned Rabbis, there were
no regular religious services, and no means of obtaining *Kosher* food.   Marseilles had some excellent communal schools, in which Hebrew, French, and Latin
were efficiently taught ; but in Nice, then a town of
the kingdom of Sardinia, the Jews were so oppressed,
that the Chacham told Sir Moses it was with the
greatest difficulty he retained his position in the
community.   Notwithstanding the disabilities to which
they were subjected, the Jews had, with touching loyalty,
erected a handsome monument, with a Hebrew inscription, commemorating the visit of the King Charles
Felix to the town.

* Privately printed in 1844.

Skirting the shores of the Mediterranean in their travelling coach and six, the Montefiores arrived on the 3rd of January at Genoa, where they attended the ancient Synagogue, and relieved the poor, principally immigrants from Northern Africa. The community they found in a very impoverished state. Proceeding to Florence, where there was a Jewish population of 3000, they met with the first indications in Italy of a liberal policy towards the Jews. The Tuscan Government, although maintaining many of the old restrictions, had recently given its Hebrew subjects considerable freedom in commercial matters. They were allowed, *inter alia,* to farm the tobacco revenues ; and many of them were extremely well off. In the Papal States, on the other hand, the old mediæval regulations were maintained. " How painful ! " exclaims Lady Montefiore, in her diary, " it is to find our people under so many disadvantages here (Rome). Three thousand five hundred souls are obliged to maintain themselves by shops, and in a confined part of the city. Arts, sciences, mechanism are prohibited. Four times in the year two hundred are obliged to attend a sermon for their conversion. It is said that no proselytes are made, except occasionally from among the most destitute. Leo XII. deprived them of the privilege granted by Pius VII. of keeping shops out of the Ghetto." Lady Montefiore did not confine the expression of her feelings on this subject to the privacy of her diary. While entertaining a Papal Monsignore, she tells us, "I did not

conceal from him the indignation with which I should
be animated at finding myself denied all opportunity
of acquiring distinction by the free and honourable
exertion of such ability as might be conferred upon
me by the Author of my being."

It was during this visit to Rome that Sir Moses
Montefiore first encountered Dr. Louis Loewe, a Jewish
scholar, who for close upon half a century has acted
as the benevolent Hebrew's lieutenant in all his
philanthropic enterprises. An accomplished linguist
and earnest Israelite, Dr. Loewe was well fitted for
duties, the adequate discharge of which required a
wide acquaintance with foreign languages almost as
much as a good Jewish heart. Dr. Loewe had already
obtained considerable reputation as a linguist, and
while in England had enjoyed the patronage of the
Duke of Sussex. He had travelled extensively in
Ethiopia, Syria, Palestine, Turkey, Asia Minor, and
Greece. Arabic literature he had read with Sheik
Mohammad Ayád Ettantavy; Persian he had studied
under Sheik Refá; and Coptic he had learnt of a
Coptic priest. His career had been an adventurous
one, and now, on his return from an Eastern tour, he
was prosecuting literary researches in the Vatican
library, under the auspices of the Cardinals Mezzo-
fanti, Angelo Mai, and Lambruschini. Dr. Loewe
spent Passover with the Montefiores at Rome, and
read and expounded to them the Passover service.
He subsequently accepted an invitation to accompany
them to the Holy Land.

The Mediterranean was no longer infested with the
pirates who, on the previous journey, had been so
serious a source of anxiety; but the eternal Eastern
Question, in another of its protean shapes, still rendered the dominions of the Padishah unsafe for European travellers. Shortly before leaving Rome a private
message was conveyed to Lady Montefiore from the
Baroness James de Rothschild at Naples, informing her
that there was good reason to believe that the Sultan
was about to make an effort to recover Syria from
Mehemet Ali, by force of arms, and advising her to
persuade her husband not to pursue his projected tour.
Sir Moses was deeply concerned at this intelligence,
calculated as it was to defeat his cherished plans; but
he buoyed himself up with the hope that he might
effect the object of his mission before the actual outbreak of hostilities, and he adhered to his determination to proceed. No sooner had he arrived at Malta,
however, than he was met by other and more serious
objections. The plague had broken out in the Holy
Land, and the gates of Jerusalem were closed; the
country was stated to be infested with brigands; and
the heat of 'a Syrian summer, he was warned, would
severely try a European constitution. Sir Moses was
still not to be dissuaded from his enterprise, but he
began to feel considerable anxiety on his wife's score.
He suggested to her that he should proceed alone.
"This I peremptorily resisted," writes Lady Montefiore, " and the expression of Ruth furnished my heart
at the moment with the language it most desired to

use : ' Entreat me not to leave thee, or to return from
following after thee ; for whither thou goest I will go,
and where thou lodgest I will lodge.' " Two days
later the attached couple embarked in the English
steamer *Megara,* and within a week they cast anchor
in the Bay of Beyrout.

The journey through the Holy Land resembled
almost a royal progress. As the friend of Mehemet
Ali, Sir Moses was received by the authorities with
distinction ; as a benevolent and wealthy Israelite,
desirous of seeing Palestine prosper, he was welcomed
by the poverty-stricken inhabitants with enthusiasm.
Immediately on his arrival at Beyrout, the Governor
waited upon him, and begged him to take up his
quarters in his own house. The following day a
numerous congregation assembled in the Synagogue
and offered up special prayers for the safe accomplishment of his undertaking. At Safed, where he passed
the Pentecost holidays, the rejoicings were of the
wildest description. Deputations met him on the road
and presented addresses. Crowds of people—young
and old, rich and poor—danced around him, shouted,
clapped their hands, sounded their Darrabukas, and
chanted songs of praise. As he entered the city guns
were fired, and the streets and the tops of the houses
were thronged with men, women, and children. The
Governor, Abd-el-Khalim, attended by the Cadi and
other influential Mussulmen, paid him a ceremonious
visit, and expressed a hope that, " as Queen Esther
had delivered her people from destruction, so might

the Hebrews, suffering in Palestine under such accumulated distresses, be relieved by his (Sir Moses') efforts." Not less cordial was the reception at Tiberias. Deputations from all the congregations awaited Sir Moses outside the walls, and the Governor, mounted on a beautiful Arab steed, and attended by a numerous suite, presented him with an address of welcome. Then, with music and dancing, and amid deafening cries of "Live the protector!" he entered the town. On the 7th June he arrived outside Jerusalem, but in consequence of the plague raging in the town, encamped on the Mount of Olives. The Governor, Mohamed Djisdor, paid a visit to his encampment and pressed him to enter the city; eventually he consented. The conversation at this interview, which was interpreted by Dr. Loewe, and has been preserved by Lady Montefiore, is worth quoting :—

The Governor : "May your day be bright and blessed!"

Sir Moses : "And yours full of blessings and comforts!"

The Governor.—"May the Almighty prolong your life!"

Sir Moses.—"And yours continue in happiness."

The Governor.—"The air is delightful here."

Sir Moses.—"Most beautiful. I should think the breezes of this mountain would convey health and every other blessing to the Holy City."

The Governor.—"Doubtless all blessings arise from

this mountain; particularly as you have pitched your tent upon it."

Sir Moses.—"Blessed be he who bestows so much honour upon me by his kind and flattering expressions!"

The Governor.—"I say what my heart feels, and that which the whole world witnesses with me!"

Sir Moses.—"I wish it were in my power to show my friendly feelings towards you, as well as to others who think so kindly of me."

The Governor.—"I wish to impress on your mind, that not only the Jews, but the Mussulmans, Christians, and every other class of the inhabitants are most anxious for your entrance into the Holy City."

Sir Moses.—"I am perfectly convinced of the worthy and distinguished character of its inhabitants, and that such it should be is not astonishing, subjected as it is to the careful observation of such a Governor as yourself; and had it not been on account of Lady M., I should have entered the town the very day of my arrival."

The Governor.—"God shall prolong your life. Only under the watchful eye of our lord, Ibrahim Pacha, and yourself, can happiness be increased. At the time when our lord came to Jerusalem I went to meet him. He said to me, 'Achmet!' I replied, 'Effendina!' 'You know the age when it was said, This is a Christian and that a Jew, and there is a Mussulman! but now, Achmet, these times are past. Never ask what he is: let him be of whatsoever religion he may do him justice, as the Lord of the world desired of us.' "

Sir Moses.—" These are my sentiments. Make no distinction. Be like the sun which shines over the whole world—all are blessed by its light, all strengthened and refreshed by its warmth, whether they be Jews, Christians, or Mussulmans."

The Governor.—" Long live Effendina! His sword is very long! Look at the spot on which your tents are pitched. Ten years ago five hundred men would have been needed to make your abode here secure. At present you may walk with a bag of gold in your hand. Not a soul would molest you."

Sir Moses.—" You are perfectly right. I can myself bear witness to the change that has taken place in this country. Twelve years ago, when I visited this town, I often heard the complaints of travellers. Even at that time I personally experienced no inconvenience. But now that Mehemet Ali governs, we not only travel in security, but are furnished by his Highness with letters of introduction to the various authorities of the country."

The Governor.—" Mehemet Ali knows how to appreciate distinguished persons like yourself; and I assure you I am longing to show you every proof of my respect. But while you are sitting here in quarantine our means are limited, and it is impossible for us to manifest the delight which would otherwise be evidenced. Follow my advice. Enter the city, and I will come and accompany you with the whole of my suite. The day

of your appearing among us shall be a festival to all
the people. I will send you a beautiful Arabian horse ;
in short, whatever you like, whether soldiers, horses,
or servants. Depend upon it, by my head, by my
eyes, by my beard, all shall be ready in a moment ! "

Sir Moses.—" I feel highly obliged to you, and am
fully assured of your goodwill. I promise you that I
will enter, be it the will of God, on Wednesday morning, when I shall be happy to avail myself of the kind
offer of your company."

The Governor.—" You have poured torrents of
blessings on my head ; and I shall not fail to be here,
at whatever hour you desire, with the Khakham
Morénu, whether before or after sunrise. We are
all your servants."

The Governor was as good as his word, and a
princely reception was accorded to Sir Moses Montefiore. We cannot do better than quote the description
from Lady Montefiore's bright narrative :—

" At a quarter past three we were called, in order to
commence early preparations for entering the city.
The Governor arrived at six o'clock, attended by his
officers and suite. Coffee, cibouks, and a plate of
cake were served, his excellency giving a piece of the
latter to each of his suite. After some conversation,
we rose to depart. M—— expressed his wish to ride
his own horse, thinking that sent for him too spirited,
but the Governor replied that two young men were
appointed to walk by his side. All the party being
mounted, the Governor led the way, attended by his

officers. The chief of the cavalry arranged the order of march, and two soldiers with long muskets were appointed immediately to precede me. The scene produced by this descent of the Mount of Olives, passing as we were through the most romantic defiles, and with long lines of Turkish soldiers, mounted on noble Arab horses and dressed in the most costly costume, cannot be easily described. More honour, they said, could not have been paid even to a king. We entered the city through the Gate of the Tribes. The streets were narrow, and almost filled up with loose stones and the ruins of houses which had fallen to decay. Our guards on each side were busily engaged in keeping off the people, a precaution rendered necessary to lessen the danger of contagion. Having passed through the bazaar, we entered the Jewish quarter of the town, and which appeared the cleanest of any we had traversed. The streets, every lattice, and all the tops of the houses were thronged with children and veiled females. Bands of music, and choirs of singers welcomed our arrival with melodies composed for the occasion, while every now and then the loud, quick clapping of hands gave signal that the whole vast crowd of spectators was striving to give expression to popular delight. Having reached the Synagogue, the Governor entered with us, and then said, addressing M——, he would leave us to our devotions, and that his officer should attend us, when we pleased to return to our encampment. M—— was called to the Sepher, and offered prayer for all our

friends in England, as well as for those present. I
was allowed the honour of lighting four lamps in front
of the altar, and putting the bells on the Sepher.
Blessings were then given for M—— and me, and for
the party. We then went successively to three other
Portuguese, and two German Synagogues. Blessings
at each place of devotion were offered up for us, and
no sight can I imagine more impressive or delightful
than that which was thus exhibited."

In each of the Holy Cities Sir Moses made elaborate
enquiries into the state of the Jewish population. He
endeavoured to acquaint himself so thoroughly with
the condition of every individual, that, in the schemes
he was contemplating, no one Jew should be neglected.
Besides visiting the Jewish quarters and personally
noting all he saw, he instructed Dr. Loewe to take a
kind of census of the Hebrew population. For this
purpose statistical forms were prepared and distributed,
and when filled up, they gave copious particulars
respecting the communities and their institutions. A
collection was also made of such suggestions for
effecting improvements, as any thoughtful persons in
each locality might care to commit to writing. The
Jewish population seemed to regard Sir Moses'
schemes with much favour. Elaborate reports were
supplied by the Rabbis, in which many excellent and
practical suggestions were made. Lady Montefiore
sums them up in the words:—" Energy and talent
exist. Nothing is needed but protection and
encouragement."

But Sir Moses did more than make these statistical enquiries ; he munificently relieved the pressing wants of the poor in each of the Holy Cities, and without distinction of creed. Anticipating that he should find the people in a very sorry state, through the devastations of earthquake and plague, and the marauding forays of the Druses, he provided himself before leaving Alexandria with a large sum of money in specie, for distribution in the Holy Land. The safety of this money was no small source of anxiety during the journey from Beyrout to Safed. The country was alive with brigands, and Sir Moses and his companions were compelled to arm themselves to the teeth ; even Lady Montefiore carried pistols in her holsters. One night, when the escort whose duty it was to look after the tents lost their way, Sir Moses and Lady Montefiore had to sleep in their rugs, while Dr. Loewe and the courier kept watch with loaded fire-arms. With their usual good fortune the travellers escaped molestation, and the money was successfully distributed at Safed and Tiberias. Careful enquiries were first made in order to avoid imposture, and then the poor were admitted to Sir Moses' presence in batches of thirty, and each man and woman was presented with a Spanish dollar, and with half that sum for every child under thirteen years of age. Orphans and children over thirteen received a full dollar. With rare consideration, Sir Moses arranged to receive separately in the evenings, those who shrunk from exposing their poverty to the public gaze. At Jerusalem he was unable to perform this interesting ceremony, as his stock of money had become exhausted, and there was no banker in the city to honour his credits; he was compelled therefore to give the authorities drafts on Beyrout. One of the happy results of this importation of ready money was, that in Safed and Tiberias the price of a measure of corn fell immediately from five piastres to two.

His enquiries completed, Sir Moses made all haste to lay his plans before Mehemet Ali. He reached Alexandria on July 13th, and was cordially received by the Pacha, who listened attentively while he unfolded his schemes. Mehemet Ali promised every assistance, and expressed himself anxious to improve the condition of his Hebrew subjects. " You shall have any portion of land open for sale in Syria," he said, " and any other land which by application to the Sultan might be procured for you. You may have anyone you would like me to appoint as Governor in any of the rural districts of the Holy Land, and I will do everything that lies in my power to support your praiseworthy endeavours." He further gave instructions to his Minister of Finance, Burghos Bey, to confirm these assurances in writing.

A new era seemed dawning for the Jews of the Holy Land. Sir Moses returned to England with a light heart, and prepared to put his plans into execution. But—

> " The best laid schemes o' mice an' men,
>   Gang aft a-gley."

He was still conning over the voluminous data he had
collected, and was constructing in his mind the foundation of a new commonwealth for Palestine, when
he was suddenly called upon to proceed again to the
East—this time, not as a peaceful reformer, but as the
champion of his people, charged to vindicate their
honour in the face of a foul conspiracy. He cheerfully
laid aside his agricultural schemes, and girded up his
loins for the new enterprise. When he returned home
in the following spring, crowned with laurels, and
hailed on all sides as the deliverer of Israel, his
triumph was clouded by one sad thought—the projects
to which he had devoted the whole of the previous year
were no longer possible. Mehemet Ali had ceased to
be lord of Syria, and his improving rule had been
replaced by the asphyxiating authority of the
Stamboul Effendis, under whom questions of social
well-being could expect little furtherance.

CHAPTER VII.

THE DAMASCUS DRAMA.

The " Red Spectre" of Judaism—Its history and origin—Revival of the Blood Accusation at Damascus in consequence of the disappearance of Father Thomas—The fanaticism of the monks and the designs of the French Consul—M. de Ratti Menton sets himself to manufacture a case against the Jews—Secures the co-operation of the Governor of the city—Arrest, torture, and confession of a Jewish barber—A Jewish youth flogged to death —Further arrests—The prisoners submitted to terrible tortures— Wholesale seizure of Jewish children—Ratti Menton's *mouchards* —Another confession—The bottle of human blood—Two of the prisoners die under torture—Protests of the Austrian Consul—A mass over mutton bones—Attempt to excite the Mussulman populace—The prisoners condemned to death—The "Red Spectre" at Rhodes—Anti-Jewish risings.

SOME eighteen centuries and a half ago the city of Alexandria was distracted by an agitation against the Jews, which, in many of its features, was a perfect type of the anti-Semitic movements we have witnessed during the present century. The charges against the Hebrew people were then the same as now. One writer discovered that they were an unsociable tribe; another affirmed that their religion was a danger to the State. The Rohling of the day was an Egyptian named Apion, who declared that the Jews were required by "a secret tradition" to make use of human blood in

their Passover ceremonies, and that, consequently, they
were obliged to sacrifice annually a certain number of
Gentiles. The public mind became inflamed, and
Flaccus Aquilius, the Roman Prefect, desirous, like
many a modern functionary, of ingratiating himself
with the people, took no measures to prevent the riots
and massacres that eventually occurred.

No circumstance of this ancient anti-Jewish agitation
has been more frequently repeated than the charge of
the ritual use of human blood. This " Red Spectre "
of Judaism has haunted the whole history of the
Hebrew dispersion, and has written the larger portion
of its martyrology. It clung even to the skirts of
Christianity in the early days of its temporal impo-
tence, when its Hebrew origin was still fresh in men's
minds. Athenagoras found himself compelled to appeal
to Marcus Aurelius for protection against the calumny;
and Origen, in his reply to Celsus, was obliged to cite
from the Old Testament the many prohibitions of the
use of blood as evidence of the impossibility of the
alleged practice. In course of time, however, Christians themselves adopted the fable, together with many
other of the superstitions of paganism, and, by a
triumph of prejudice, fastened it on the very people
whose traditions they had relied on to rebut it when it
was related of themselves. Notwithstanding that the
post-Biblical legal codes of the Jews worked out into
elaborate detail the Scriptural laws on this subject, the
Church obstinately persisted in repeating the charge.
No Christian ever disappeared about Easter time but

G

the cry immediately arose that he had been murdered
by the Jews. The calendar bristles with saints who
are supposed in the flesh to have been victims of this
"damnable practice of Judaism." Miracles were
wrought by their bodies and their reliques ; and their
shrines have been visited by thousands of pilgrims.
To this day the accusation is persisted in, and there
are still people in Europe who believe that ritual
murder is a practice of orthodox Judaism.

The origin of this extraordinary delusion has per-
plexed many historical scholars. The most probable
theory seems to be that it was only a natural corollary
of the vague impression of the Pagan world that
Judaism was a form of sorcery. In the supernatural
medicine chest blood has always occupied an important place. Even in Biblical times its magical virtue
was the burden of a vulgar superstition ; for we read
of harlots washing themselves in Ahab's blood, no
doubt under the impression that some peculiar
beautifying property attached to the blood of a king.
Homer, Horace, and Pliny speak of the magical use of
blood. Gower in his *De Confessione Amantis* states it
to have been prescribed to Constantine for the cure of
his leprosy ; but that he refused to try it, and for his
piety was miraculously healed :

> "The would him bathe in childes bloode,
> Within seven winters' age ;
> For as thei sayen, that shulde assuage
> The lepre."

It is very likely that the superior healthiness of the

Jews, and their immunity from many epidemic diseases, helped to fix more firmly in the popular mind the idea that they occasionally fortified themselves with doses of human blood. The specific association of the accusation with the Passover has been attributed to the red wine drunk on the first evening of the festival. *Red* wine is chosen because, according to an old Jewish legend, when Pharaoh was once seriously ill he caused his body to be bathed daily in a bath of the blood of Jewish children in order to regain his health. The fate of these children and other Jews, stated to have been murdered in Egypt, is commemorated on the Passover by drinking *red* wine; and it is conjectured that supporters of the Blood Accusation imagine this wine to be blood.

In the spring of 1840 the Jews of Europe were startled by a revival of the blood calumny in a peculiarly virulent form. Paragraphs appeared in the *Times*, the *Leipziger Allgemeine Zeitung*, the *Semaphore de Marseilles*, and other influential journals, announcing that a charge of ritual murder had actually been brought home to the Israelitish community of Damascus. Sir Moses Montefiore immediately caused enquiries to be made into the truth of the allegation, but it was with great difficulty that any reliable information could be obtained. Ultimately, however, the true story leaked out, and, as its harrowing details assumed tangible form, it caused a thrill of horror to run through the whole of Western Europe.

Early in the year a Capuchin friar, named Thomas

G 2

de Calangiano, had, together with his servant, unaccountably disappeared. The reverend gentleman was well known all over Damascus, where he exercised the profession of physician, visiting in that capacity all classes of the population, Mussulmans, Catholics, Armenians, and Jews. A rumour at first pervaded the town that a quarrel had taken place between him and a Turk, and that the latter had been heard to swear that the "Christian dog" should die by his hand. It was even said that a fight had taken place. Very mysteriously, however, the story died away; and one fine morning a mob of Christians crowded into the Jewish quarter, shouting that the Jews had murdered Father Thomas, to employ his blood in their superstitious rites. Whether this demonstration was promoted by the Catholic clergy or not, it is impossible to say; but the barbarous surmise by which it was actuated does not seem to have been at all repugnant to the feelings of these holy men. On the contrary, it appears to have suited their interests to give it all the support in their power, in order, apparently, to avoid a conflict between themselves and the dominant Mussulman population, which would have certainly taken place had an investigation been made of the clue afforded by the rumoured quarrel. Besides, as Graetz has shrewdly remarked, a monk killed by the Jews would have given them another saint, and furnished them with an additional claim on the purses of the faithful.

The expediency of the course adopted by the

monks recommended itself with peculiar force to the
tortuous mind of the French Consul, the Count de
Ratti-Menton, an unscrupulous schemer, whose moral
character may be inferred from the fact that he had
already been dismissed from offices of trust in Sicily
and Tiflis. He acquiesced in the accusation against
the Jews with alacrity, not merely on the score of the
personal interests of the local Christians, but, as he
diplomatically thought, to serve the political ends of
France in the East by currying favour with the
Mussulman population. He immediately set himself
to manufacture a case against the Jews; and for this
purpose took into his confidence a trio of the most
notorious rascals in Damascus, Hanna Bachari Bey,
a well-known Jew-hater; Mohammed El-Telli, an
adventurer, who had already extorted money from the
Jews on a trumped-up charge of ritual murder; and
Shibli Ajub, a Christian Arab, who was actually under-
going at the time a term of imprisonment for forgery,
of which he had been convicted mainly on the evidence
of a Jew.

The Governor of Damascus, Sheriff Pasha, needed
no pressing to consent to the proceedings of the
French Consul. Gallic influence was then paramount
in the councils of Mehemet Ali, who was relying
on the specious promises of Louis Philippe to enable
him to defy the European Allies of the Sultan. It
was consequently more than a provincial official's head
was worth to offend a diplomatic agent of the French
Government. Besides, Sheriff Pasha was not in-

sensible to the prospect of plunder held out by a
well-devised Blood Accusation.

The stage thus cleared, the curtain rose on the
first act of the drama.   Bachari Bey, after a long and
mysterious enquiry, discovered a person who was
willing to swear that, on the day of the Padre's disappearance, he had seen him and his servant enter a
house in the Jewish quarter of the city.   The tenant
of the house in question, a poor barber, was waited
upon by the satellites of the French Consul, and
sternly interrogated.   He showed so much trepidation
and confusion, that it was resolved to arrest him, and
he was handed over by Ratti-Menton to Sheriff Pasha
for further examination.   This took the form of 500
lashes, but it failed to extort a confession.   More
exquisite torture was resorted to, but still the poor
barber steadfastly denied all knowledge of the crime.
He was then thrown into a pestiferous dungeon to
regain strength for further torture.   During his in-
carceration Shibli Ajub made his acquaintance as a
fellow prisoner, and, acting upon instructions from
without, endeavoured to gain his confidence, with a
view to eliciting from him the fate of Father Thomas.
But still he protested that he knew nothing about it;
and all the machinations of his wily interlocutor were
powerless to induce him to incriminate either himself
or any of his brethren.   At last, growing impatient,
Shibli declared himself in his true character.   Adopting
an imperious tone, he called upon the half-distracted
barber to confess his guilt at once; he told him that

he was an agent of the Pasha, and if the truth were not immediately avowed, the torture would there and then be resumed. In an agony of terror the miserable creature threw himself at Shibli's feet, and frantically implored his mercy. Shibli coldly repeated his interrogatories, when the barber, yielding to his fears, gasped out that he was guilty. So, at least, Shibli reported to his superiors, at the same time stating that the barber had mentioned as his accomplices several Jewish merchants of Damascus, who all, curiously enough, turned out to be very wealthy men.

In the meantime Sheriff Pasha had sent for the Jewish ecclesiastical chiefs, and had commanded them to discover the criminals within three days. The whole community were in consequence summoned to the Synagogue by the Rabbis, and a proclamation was read, calling upon any Jew who knew aught that might lead to the detection of the murderers, to instantly make it known under pain of excommunication. The community were likewise enjoined to institute a diligent search for the criminals. In consequence of this proclamation, a young man, a Jew, who kept a tobacconist's shop in the Moslem quarter, close by one of the city gates, came forward, and stated that the missing priest and his servant had passed by his door at six o'clock on the evening of the day on which he was last seen; that he had solicited them to purchase *tumbeki*, but that they had passed on to the house of a Turkish merchant, which they had entered.

The young man was taken before the Pasha, to whom he repeated his story; but the latter, instead of inquiring into its truth, angrily accused him of being an accomplice, and ordered him to be mercilessly flogged. The youth perished under the bastinado. He was the first martyr in this terrible tragedy.

Ratti-Menton lost no time in communicating to Sheriff Pasha the nature of the barber's alleged confession; and seven of the most influential Jews in the town—David Arari, his son and two brothers, Moses Abulafia, Moses Saloniki, and Joseph Laniado, the latter a man over eighty years of age—were forthwith arrested. Examined by the Governor, they one and all asserted their innocence. At the suggestion of Ratti-Menton the bastinado was called into requisition; but still they denied all knowledge of the missing monk. Then they were submitted to the most excruciating tortures. They were soaked with their clothes for hours at a stretch in large tanks of cold water; their eyes were punctured; they were made to stand upright without support for nearly two days; and when their wearied bodies fell down, they were aroused by the prick of soldiers' bayonets; they were dragged by the ear, until their blood gushed; thorns were driven between the nails and flesh of their fingers and toes; fire was set to their beards till their faces were singed; and candles were held under their noses, so that the flames burnt their nostrils. But still no admission of guilt passed their lips. Sheriff Pasha then bethought himself of another and still more fiendish plan. He

ordered sixty Jewish children, ranging in age from
three to ten years, to be forcibly torn from their
mothers, and locked up in a room without food, in
the hope that the bereaved parents would frantically
denounce the murderers. This infernal expedient
also failed. Then maddened by their want of success,
Sheriff Pasha and Ratti-Menton invaded the Jewish
quarter with a troop of soldiers, and demolished several
houses ostensibly to find evidence. Nothing was discovered; and the enraged Governor before taking his
leave swore a tremendous oath, that if the body
of Father Thomas were not soon produced, many
hundred Jewish heads should pay the penalty.

All this time Ratti-Menton's *mouchards* had not been
idle. They had managed to obtain for themselves the
entrée to the houses of the imprisoned Jews, and day
after day they had spent in cajoling the servants.
Mohammed El-Telli had specially attached himself to
one of Arari's servants, Mourad El-Fallat, and eventually he prevailed upon him to admit that he had killed
Father Thomas at his master's orders, and in presence
of the other prisoners. This was held by Ratti-
Menton to be a confirmation of the barber's narrative,
notwithstanding the discrepancy that both the self-
accusers claimed to have alone committed the deed.
A search for the remains of the murdered man was at
once instituted, and resulted in the finding of a piece
of bone and a rag in a drain near Arari's house. The
bone was declared by Ratti-Menton to be a portion of
the priest's skull, and the rag a part of his cap. The

guilt of the accused was now considered established, and all that remained to be discovered was the blood, for the sake of which the Padre was alleged to have been murdered. The seven prisoners were again dragged before the Pasha and examined, but to no purpose. Torture was then once more tried. The aged Laniado died under the bastinado. Worn out with pain, one of the prisoners whispered to a gaoler that he had given the blood to Moses Abulafia. The latter, after receiving another thousand blows, and hardly knowing what he was saying, stammered out that he had hidden the bottle in a certain closet. Abulafia was carried on the backs of four men to the closet indicated by him, where, of course, no traces of blood were found. The tortures were then resumed, but without any other result, than that David Arari shared the fate of Joseph Laniado, and Abulafia purchased immunity from further molestation by turning Mussulman.

Towards the beginning of March suspicion fell upon six more Jews, among them one Isaac Levi Picciotto, an Austrian subject. He appealed to his Consul, M. Merlato, for protection, and the latter, who had watched the proceedings of Ratti-Menton with undisguised abhorrence, refused to deliver him up. All kinds of so-called evidence of his guilt were offered, and threats were even used towards his protector, but M. Merlato proved immovable. About the same time more bones were discovered, and although they were pronounced by physicians to be sheep's bones, Ratti-Menton declared them to be the skeleton of the missing

priest. He even went to the extent of ordering the
monks to celebrate a mass over the remains, and then
sent another insolent message to the Austrian Consul,
demanding of him the Jew Picciotto.

M. Merlato now thoroughly lost his patience. The
horror with which he had silently watched the French
Consul's proceedings became intolerable, and he felt
compelled to remonstrate with him publicly. This he
did in no measured terms, at the same time threatening
to communicate with his Government. The gravity of
his position seems to have now dawned upon Ratti-
Menton for the first time, and he hastily devoted himself to the task of transferring the responsibility for
the outrages from himself to the Mussulman population, who, strange to say, had taken but a very languid
interest in the whole affair. In order to excite their
fanaticism, he caused to be translated into Arabic a
lying anti-Jewish work, the *Pompta Bibliotheca*, of
Lucio Ferrajo, in which the ritual use of human blood
by Jews is sought to be demonstrated by forged
extracts from the Talmud. The riots he anticipated
would follow from this publication did not, however,
take place. Then he resolved to put a bold face on
the whole matter. He held a mock judicial enquiry,
at which he admitted the *Pompta Bibliotheca* as
evidence, and his own creatures as witnesses, and
ultimately decided (1) that the Jews used human blood
in their Passover services, and (2) that the imprisoned
Jews had murdered the priest Thomas de Calangiano
for the purposes of their Passover. As a result of this

finding, he formally demanded of the Governor the
execution of the prisoners ; and Sheriff Pasha, with an
equally ostentatious respect for legal procedure, promised to apply immediately to Cairo for a confirmation
of the death sentences.

While this tragedy was being enacted at Damascus,
a no less unhappy revival of the Blood Accusation
occurred in Rhodes. In that island, a Greek boy, ten
years of age, had disappeared, and a rumour at once
spread that the Jews had killed him. The Consuls of the
European Powers, in their zeal for Christian interests,
called upon the Mussulman Governor, Jussuf Pasha,
to adopt severe measures against the Jews. Among
the bitterest accusers of the persecuted Hebrews were
the British Consul, Mr. Wilkinson, and his son. The
Austrian Consul alone protested against the disgrace-
ful return to mediæval superstition. On the representations of two Greek women that the missing boy
had been last seen in the company of a certain Jew,
this unhappy individual was seized and thrown into
prison. Then, to the lasting shame of Christian
civilisation, the Consuls attempted to extort a confession by torture. They flogged their prisoner, they
burnt his flesh with red-hot irons, and dislocated his
bones on the rack. The result was, of course, the
same as at Damascus—the wretched Hebrew, delirious
with pain, aimlessly moaned out the names of several
of his co-religionists. These were in their turn seized
and charged, not only with the murder, but also with
having extracted the blood from the body of the

Rhodes.

missing boy, and transmitted it to the Chief Rabbi at
Constantinople. No confession being forthcoming, they
were also tortured and imprisoned. Then the gates
of the Ghetto were ordered to be closed, and no food
was allowed to enter for three days. Still no discovery
was made; and it was finally attempted to manufacture
a case by smuggling a dead body into the Jewish
quarter at night. The vigilance of the Jews defeated
this infamous plan.

The news soon spread that another Jewish ritual
sacrifice had been detected, and popular risings against
the Israelites took place in several towns of Syria.
What Ratti-Menton had been powerless to effect by his
transparent intrigues, was brought about by the consternation caused by the new discovery at Rhodes. At
Djabar, near Damascus, the mob rose and sacked the
synagogue. At Beyrout and Smyrna serious riots
broke out. For a moment it seemed as if the whole of
Eastern Judaism was about to be engulfed in a wave
of fanaticism.

This was the terrible story that startled the Jews
of Western Europe about the middle of April, 1840.

CHAPTER VIII.

THE MISSION TO MEHEMET ALI.

To the Jews of England the new Blood Accusation
was a source of the deepest anxiety. Under any circumstances the revival of so sinister an appeal to
vulgar fears and prejudices would have been of serious
moment, but occurring in the midst of a critical
struggle for their emancipation, and in connection
with political complication, which rendered an adverse
decision by no means improbable, its aspect in 1840

was of an exceedingly grave character. The Roman Catholic Church had irrevocably committed itself to the guilt of the Damascus Israelites, and France, masking her designs on Syria by a Pharisaical championship of the Eastern Christians, had bound herself to a similar conclusion. In the diplomatic conflict between Louis Philippe and the Quadruple Alliance, a French success meant certain conviction of the imprisoned Jews at Damascus ; and, in presence of M. Thiers' warlike attitude, such a success was by no means unlikely. To the Powers it was probably a small matter, in the aggregate of interests at stake in Egypt, whether a few Jews were or were not found guilty of murder; but, to the Jews as a body, and particularly those of England, no more serious question had occurred for many years. The alleged murder was, it must be remembered, a ritual murder, and for a civilised European Power like France to give its countenance, however incidentally, to the theory of the possibility of such a murder, was to arm the enemies of the Jews—and they were by no means few—with the most powerful weapon they had possessed for ages. Far-seeing Jews in England felt this. They saw, too, its practical bearing on their own struggle for freedom, and their action was consequently prompt.

On the 21st April Sir Moses Montefiore convened a meeting at his residence in Park Lane to consider the news from the East. Many Jews eminent in the community attended, in addition to the members of the Board of Deputies; Mr. Isaac Lyon Goldsmid, Mr.

David Salomons, Mr. A. A. Goldsmid, Dr. Loewe, and Dr. Barnard Van Oven were among those present. M. Crémieux, then Vice-President of the Consistoire Central, and a busy advocate at the French bar, attended on behalf of the Jews of France. The story of the sufferings of the Eastern Israelites was placed before the meeting in the shape of letters from Damascus, Beyrout, Alexandria, and Constantinople, and a communication was also read from the Rev. S. Hirschel, the then Chief Rabbi of Great Britain, solemnly repudiating the charge of shedding human blood for ritual purposes. After a spirited discussion, a series of resolutions was adopted, expressing the concern, disgust, and horror of the meeting at such unfounded and cruel accusations against their Eastern brethren, and at the barbarous tortures inflicted upon them ; entreating the Governments of England, France, and Austria to take up the cause of the unhappy Jews, and appointing a deputation to wait on Lord Palmerston (who was at the time Her Majesty's Secretary for Foreign Affairs), with Sir Moses Montefiore at its head.

The reception accorded to Sir Moses and his colleagues at Downing Street was extremely gratifying. Lord Palmerston expressed abhorrence of the persecution at Damascus ; assured the deputation that the influence of the British Government should be exerted on behalf of the Jews, and promised that instructions should immediately be sent to Colonel Hodges, at Alexandria, and Lord Ponsonby, at Constantinople, directing them to use every effort to prevent a continuance of the outrages. On the same day M. Crémieux had an audience of the French King, but with not quite so satisfactory a result. "I know nothing of all you have told me," coldly replied Louis Philippe, "but if, in any part of the world, there are Jews who appeal to my protection, and it is in the power of my Government to afford that protection, you may depend upon it that it will be granted." In Austria, on the other hand, very efficient action was taken. Prince Metternich, pleased to find that his diplomatic agents in the East had already declared themselves on what he was shrewd enough to perceive would prove the side of justice and right, addressed a personal remonstrance to Mehemet Ali, and instructed the Austrian Consul Laurier to insist upon the fullest reparation to the Damascus Israelites.

The result of these vigorous movements on the part of the Western Jews was to cause great uneasiness in the mind of the Egyptian Viceroy. M. Cochelet, the French Consul at Alexandria, did his best to laugh away Mehemet's anxieties, and for a time the latter yielded himself up entirely to the Frenchman's advice and consolations; but at last a joint representation by the foreign Consuls convinced him that the Powers were in earnest, and he hurriedly sent orders to Sheriff Pasha to stop the outrages, and directed that an armed force should proceed to Damascus to quell disturbances and maintain order. He also appointed a Commission of Enquiry, consisting of the English, Austrian,

H

Russian, and Prussian Consuls, with permission to take evidence at Damascus, and to conduct their proceedings according to European rule.

Nothing could have been more satisfactory to the Jews. Unfortunately the political atmosphere was too heavily charged with intrigue for so straightforward a course to be pursued to the end. The warlike policy of the French Ministry had brought about serious differences between M. Thiers and his Royal master, and the former was desirous, at all hazards, to obtain for himself the support of a majority in the Chambers. Just at that moment the Clerical party were equally anxious that no enquiry should be held in respect to the Damascus outrages, and, to conciliate them, M. Thiers instructed M. Cochelet to protest in the strongest possible manner against the appointment of the Consular commission. Mehemet Ali, apprehensive amid his increasing difficulties of alienating his only friend among the Powers, allowed himself to be intimidated, and forthwith cancelled the appointment.

It now became necessary for the Jews of Europe to renew their agitation. Conferences and meetings were held at Sir Moses Montefiore's house, and communications were opened with foreign and colonial communities. Eventually, on the 15th June, it was resolved to send a mission to Mehemet Ali, and the zealous President of the Board of Deputies was asked to undertake its leadership. With his usual devotion to the interests of his brethren he accepted the onerous appointment, and a subscription to defray the expenses was imme-

diately set on foot. The Sephardi congregation in
Bevis Marks handsomely gave £500 from their
Cautivos fund ; other Synagogues offered according to
their means. Meetings in support of the action of the
London Israelites were held, and contributions were
raised at Hamburg, Leghorn, New York, Philadelphia,
St. Thomas, and Jamaica. M. Crémieux was deputed
by the Jews of France to accompany Sir Moses Monte-
fiore, but he failed to obtain from the French
Government the slightest support ; even recommenda-
tions to French officials in the East were denied him.
M. Thiers had been irritated by a debate on the
Damascus affair that had taken place in the French
Chamber at the instance of M. Achille Fould, and this
was doubtless his revenge. It had a very desponding
effect upon M. Crémieux, who, on his arrival in
London, bitterly declared, " La France est contre
nous ! "

Before the departure of the Mission two significant
demonstrations in its favour took place in London, the
first in the House of Commons, the second at the
Mansion House. The debate in Parliament was
initiated by Sir Robert Peel, who, " in the interests of
general humanity," called upon the Ministry to insist
upon an investigation of the Damascus mystery.
" Thus," said the speaker, " they will be enabled to
rescue that great portion of society, the Jews, who, in
every other country in which they live have, by their
conduct in private life, conciliated the general estimation and goodwill of their fellow-subjects, from a

charge which is founded on prejudice, and must subject them to the most grievous injustice." Lord Palmerston's reply was all that could be desired. Full reports had not yet been received from the East, but strong representations had been made to Mehemet Ali. "Upon hearing of the circumstance," said the Minister, "I immediately instructed Colonel Hodges at Alexandria to bring the subject under the serious attention of the Pasha of Egypt, to point out to him the effect which such atrocities as these must produce on the public mind of Europe, and to urge him, for his own sake, to institute such enquiries as would enable him to punish the guilty parties, if guilty parties there are, and to make such an atonement as is in his power to the unfortunate sufferers." The demonstration at the Mansion House was still more gratifying. It was convened by the Lord Mayor, Sir Chapman Marshall, in response to a memorial signed by 210 members of Parliament, merchants, bankers, &c., and was influentially attended. The speakers included Mr. J. A. Smith, M.P., Dr. Bowring, Lord Howden, and Daniel O'Connell, and among the company were Sir Denham Norreys, M.P., Mr. James Morrison, M.P., Mr. W. Attwood, M.P., Mr. Martin Smith, M.P., Mr. S. Gurney, the Hon. and Rev. Baptist Noel, Sir C. Forbes, Mr. John Dillon, and Thomas Campbell, the poet. Several effective speeches were delivered, and, amid much enthusiasm, resolutions were passed setting forth the commiseration felt by all true Christians for the persecuted Jews of Damascus and Rhodes, declaring their abhorrence at the use of torture and their disbelief in the confessions obtained thereby, and expressing their deep regret that, in this enlightened age, a persecution should have arisen against the Jews, originating in ignorance and inflamed by bigotry. The Lord Mayor was empowered by the meeting to present copies of these resolutions to all the foreign ambassadors as well as to the British Government. Thus encouraged, Sir Moses Montefiore left London on the 7th July, accompanied by Lady Montefiore, M. Crémieux, M. Munk, Mr. Alderman Wire, Dr. Loewe, and Dr. Madden. Before his departure he was graciously received by Her Majesty the Queen, and was furnished by the Foreign Office with recommendations to the diplomatic agents of Great Britain in the East. He was also provided by the Jewish ecclesiastical authorities with important documents formally repudiating the charge of ritual murder.

Notwithstanding the hostile attitude of the French Government, the Mission were well received at their various halting-places in France, especially at Avignon, Nîmes, Carpentras, and Marseilles. At the latter town good news reached them from Rhodes. A special tribunal, under the presidency of Rifaat Bey, had, after a short but exhaustive enquiry, come to the conclusion that the accusation against the Jews was unfounded. The prisoners had been restored to their homes, and Jussuf Pasha, the Governor, dismissed from his post by the Sultan. At Leghorn, on the other hand, discouraging intelligence was received from Syria.

That province was in open rebellion against the rule of
Mehemet Ali ; Suleiman Pasha, one of the Viceroy's
generals, had been attacked and taken prisoner, and
Beyrout was blockaded. The dangers of the expedition were pointed out to Sir Moses Montefiore, but he
declined to desert the cause he had undertaken,
whatever the risks to which he might be exposed. On
the 27th July the Mission arrived at Malta, where
they learnt that the insurrection in Syria was on the
point of being quelled. Continuing their voyage, they
reached Alexandria on the 4th August.

Sir Moses Montefiore at once delivered his creden-
tials and despatches to Colonel Hodges, and requested
that he would procure for him an immediate audience
with the Pasha. At the same time all the foreign
Consuls, with the exception of M. Cochelet, tendered
their support to the Jewish representative. On the
6th August Sir Moses was courteously received by
Mehemet Ali, to whom he presented a petition asking
for permission to proceed to Damascus for the purpose
of obtaining evidence on behalf of the imprisoned Jews,
and to see and interrogate the prisoners. He further
prayed that safety should be guaranteed to the members
of the Mission and all persons giving evidence.
Mehemet Ali promised to consider the petition. Two
more interviews took place, but no decision was arrived
at. On one pretence or another Sir Moses was then
put off from day to day, and it soon became evident
that intrigues were being carried on against him, the
nature of which he could only suspect from M. Cochelet's

frequent interviews with the Viceroy and his open unfriendliness to the Mission. M. Cochelet had daringly shown his animosity by declining, contrary to all etiquette, to present M. Crémieux to the Viceroy.

Sir Moses proved equal to the difficulties of the situation. The embarrassment of Mehemet Ali in respect to Syria was becoming daily more critical, and it was obvious that, while there was still a hope of peace, he would not care to strain his relations with the Powers by a conflict with the entire consular body. Sir Moses accordingly arranged that another petition should be drawn up, but this time by the Consuls, who should present it in person to the Pasha. This move had its desired effect. The day before the petition was to be presented an English merchant of Alexandria, Mr. Briggs, called upon Sir Moses and informed him that the Pasha was willing to release the prisoners provided the whole matter was allowed to fall into oblivion. The Jewish Mission had not desired merely the release of the Jews, but a new trial to enable them to clear their character. Considering, however, the perturbed political state of the country, Sir Moses agreed to waive his demands for a trial, provided Mehemet Ali discharged the prisoners at once. Mr. Briggs repeated the observation to Mehemet Ali, whereupon His Highness, still under the influence of M. Cochelet, made out the Firman in the shape of a pardon. This was, of course, not acceptable to Sir Moses, who returned it, with the remark that the discharge must be granted as an act of justice, or he should not be able to accept it at all. Ultimately the firmness of the Jewish champion prevailed, and the Firman was amended as he wished. Subsequently an order of general protection to the Jews was also given, together with permission to the members of the Jewish Mission to proceed to Damascus. At a concluding interview Mehemet Ali personally assured the Hebrew embassy of his complete disbelief of the Blood Accusation.

Sir Moses Montefiore and his colleagues had intended to carry the Firman themselves to Damascus, but their design had to be abandoned, partly in consequence of the dangers of the journey, and partly because it was feared that an outbreak of fanaticism on the part of the Christians might follow such a visit. An authenticated copy of the order of release was forwarded to Sheriff Pasha by other channels, and the British Consul was requested to see that it was carried out. The Firman arrived on the 6th September. M. de Ratti-Menton endeavoured for a time to oppose its execution, but unavailingly. The nine prisoners—seven of whom had become crippled for life by the tortures to which they had been subjected—were released, and it was publicly made known that the Jews who had fled might return to their families. To a large proportion of the Mohammedan population the Firman gave great satisfaction, but the Christians did not disguise their disappointment. With solemn pomp they erected in the Church of the Capuchins, over the mutton bones discovered by Ratti-Menton, a memorial tablet, setting forth that beneath were interred the remains of Father Thomas, "who had been murdered by the Jews."

The members of the Jewish Mission, before returning home, attempted to sow the seeds of some permanent improvement in the condition of the Eastern Israelites. Sir Moses Montefiore made a careful study of their political arbitration ; M. Crémieux preached to them of the advantages of secular education. The latter then left for Europe, and received a perfect ovation on his homeward journey.

Sir Moses was preparing to follow his colleague's example, when a change in the political situation necessitated an alteration in his plans. An open rupture had, at last, taken place between Mehemet Ali and the Quadruple Alliance, and at Kaleb-Medina the Egyptian forces had been totally defeated. Alexandria itself was blockaded by Admiral Napier, and at Damascus the monks, taking advantage of the new complications, were fiercely preaching a crusade against the Jews. Sir Moses Montefiore rightly judged that, to accomplish the mission with which he had been entrusted, it was now necessary to obtain from the new master of Syria the same assurances that he had received from the old. He accordingly sailed for Constantinople, and on the 28th October was received in audience by the Sultan, Abdul-Medjid. He has himself described his interview with the Commander of the Faithful. In a letter to the Board of Deputies he wrote as follows:—

"At the appointed time, accompanied by George

Samuel, Esq., D. W. Wire, Esq., and Dr. Loewe, with Frederick Pisani, Esq., first Dragoman to the British Embassy, I proceeded to the palace. We went in state. On our arrival, we were saluted by a guard of honour and a military band, and ushered into an elegant apartment, where H.E. Reschid Pasha and Riza Pasha awaited our arrival. Pipes and coffee were handed round. In a few minutes an officer announced that his Imperial Majesty was ready to receive us. Preceded and followed by a great many officers, we walked across a garden, and were introduced into the State apartments, where we found His Majesty seated. We advanced to the right, when the great officers of State took their places on the left of His Majesty. I read an address, which was translated into Turkish by Mr. Pisani. His Majesty made a most gracious reply, which was afterwards reduced into writing, and sent to me by H.E. Reschid Pasha. As soon as His Majesty had finished his reply, he requested me to come nearer to him, when I was presented by H.E. Reschid Pasha, and His Majesty then desired I would present the gentlemen accompanying me, which I did, severally, by name. Immediately we retired from the presence we were conducted to a room below, where sherbet was served round, and we received the congratulations of the Ministers present; after which we left the palace and returned home, in the same state with which we went. Thus ended an audience most gratifying to my feelings, because I was assured the honour conferred upon us reflected back upon those who sent us, as well as upon all our co-religionists. This is my apology for being so minute in detailing circumstances which might otherwise appear unimportant. I have not yet got the Firman, but I have no reason to doubt that I shall receive it in sufficient time to enable me to leave here by the next packet for Malta. So important, however, do I consider it, that I shall not hesitate to make a further sacrifice of my comforts, and winter here rather than leave the city without its being in my possession."

On the 11th November he received the Firman from Reschid Pasha. In this document not only is the groundlessness of the Blood Accusation demonstrated, but the equality of the Jews with the other subjects of the Padishah is declared, and any molestation of them in their religious or temporal concerns prohibited. Sir Moses does not over-rate the importance of this Firman in the following extract from one of his letters to a friend in England :—

" There can be no doubt but that the Firman will be productive of lasting benefit to our people. It has been received with joy I cannot describe by those to whom I had the pleasure of reading it, and by those to whom its contents were made known during the course of our voyage. . . . . . In the East it is as much appreciated as were the Acts for the Repeal of the Catholic Disabilities and the Test and Corporation Acts at home, by those who were interested in such

repeal. It is, indeed, the ' Magna Charta' for the
Jews in the Turkish dominions. How can I express
my gratitude to Him in whose hands are all our affairs,
that He has been pleased to prosper our labours, and
enabled us to vindicate the innocence of our brethren !
Thus the clouds that hung over them, and which for a
time threatened to obscure the brightness and glory of
our religion, have, by the merciful goodness of God, been
driven away ; I trust for ever.   And I pray that peace
may now be upon all Israel !   I cannot but congratulate you, and all our friends in England, upon the
triumphant success which has attended our labours.
Sustained by God—upheld by your prayers and
sympathies—we have surmounted many difficulties,
endured much privation and anxiety, and at last have
been rewarded for all, by the assurance that we have
not left our country in vain."

Before quitting Constantinople Sir Moses Montefiore
devoted considerable attention to the educational wants
of his brethren in the Turkish capital.   At a meeting
of the principal men in the community he rebuked
them for their unwisdom in concentrating all their
energies on the study of Hebrew, without giving due
attention to the vernacular of the land in which they
lived.   He then requested Dr. Loewe to draw up a
kind of proclamation to the Jews of the Ottoman
Empire, pointing out the importance of studying the
Turkish language.   Copies of this proclamation were
distributed broadcast, and posted on the portals of

every Synagogue. Sagacious statesmen in Turkey cordially approved of this action of Sir Moses. Reschid Pasha is reported to have said to him : " If you had done nothing more than this in Constantinople, you should consider yourself amply compensated for the trouble and fatigue you have undergone. In advising your brethren to acquire a knowledge of the Turkish language you have been instrumental in enabling them to raise themselves to some of the highest offices in the Empire." Events have justified this remark of Abdul-Medjid's shrewd Vizier. To-day many posts of dignity and usefulness at the Sublime Porte are occupied by Jews.

On his way home Sir Moses Montefiore, with characteristic thoroughness, gave two more finishing-touches to the great work he had so happily completed. At Rome he saw Cardinal Rivarola, the head of the Capuchin Order, and obtained from him a promise that instructions should be sent to Damascus, commanding the removal of the memorial tablet to Father Thomas, which described the Padre as having been murdered by Jews. The order was sent, but the Damascus monks disregarded it, and for twenty years the stone with its lying inscription was allowed to remain. At Paris Sir Moses was presented to the French King by the British Ambassador, and handed to His Majesty a copy of the Sultan's Firman declaring the innocence of the Damascus Jews. Louis Philippe congratulated the Jewish champion on the success he had achieved, although he could not but have felt some degree of humiliation in doing so. It was not only that the Firman marked the defeat of French ambitions in the East, but the circumstances of the interview itself seemed full of sly mockery at the mistakes of France. That a Jew should read a lesson on toleration to a French monarch was in itself bad enough, but that he should read this lesson on the authority of a Turkish Sultan, who had just got the better of France in a political struggle, must have been extremely awkward.

In England Sir Moses Montefiore was received with great rejoicings. A Day of Thanksgiving was appointed for the 8th March, 1841, and special services were held in the Synagogues. A testimonial monument in silver designed by Sir G. Hayter, and measuring three and a half feet in height, was presented to him by the Jews, and the Queen showed a graceful appreciation of his labours by granting him permission to add supporters to his arms, a privilege usually only accorded to peers and knights of orders. All over Europe and America, and even in the far East, the Jews celebrated with enthusiasm the success of their champion. In Germany it was proposed to institute a new Purim in his honour, and Isaac Erter, the most elegant of modern Hebrew stylists, wrote a considerable portion of a work in Biblical verse to be read in the Synagogue on each anniversary, as the Book of Esther is read on the day which commemorates the defeat of the conspiracy of Haman.

The Jews did not overestimate the significance of Sir

Moses' triumph. It has had far-reaching consequences in Hebrew history, the beneficial effects of which are still unexhausted. "Damascus" became the watchword of a new struggle for freedom, which reached from the shores of the Persian Gulf to the banks of the Thames—a struggle to throw off not only political shackles but the demoralizing effects of centuries of persecution. It taught the Jews the necessity of a common effort to raise themselves to the level of modern culture, so that not only might they win a political equality with their fellow-men, but that their traditions might be worthily sustained. It founded Jewish solidarity on a new and intelligent basis, and to-day the *Alliance Israelite Universelle*, with its brilliant record of political successes and its network of schools covering the East from Bagdad to Salonica, is its practical outcome.

The Jewish triumph derived no small amount of its lustre from the straightforwardness and honesty with which it had been obtained. Amid the dark intrigues of the Eastern embroglio of 1840 the conduct of Sir Moses Montefiore and his colleagues is one of the few circumstances on which the mind can dwell with pleasure. More than one offer of venal assistance was made to them, but they were scornfully rejected. The rich and vivacious table talk of Sir Moses Montefiore comprises no more striking anecdote than that in which he is wont to relate how he subsequently repelled the charge that the Firman of the 12th Ramazan had been bought. In the course of his negotiations with Cardinal Antonelli on the Mortara affair he had occasion to refer to the Firman, whereupon the Cardinal slyly asked how much of Rothschild's gold he had paid for it ? " Not so much," warmly answered Sir Moses, " as I gave your lackey for hanging up my coat in your hall."

CHAPTER IX.

FIVE YEARS OF HOME WORK.

Synagogal labours—Sir Moses' popularity—Visits to the Congrega-
tional Schools—He helps to promote education in the Jewish
Community—Jews' College, the Jews' Hospital, and the Free
School—The Board of Deputies—Its constitution and functions—
Sir Moses corresponds with Sir James Graham and Sir Robert
Peel in respect to various Bills before Parliament—Foreign
Affairs—The Holy Land—Sir Moses Montefiore establishes a
Loan Fund, a Printing Establishment, and a Linen Factory at
Jerusalem—Assists agricultural schemes, and founds a Free
Dispensary—He raises a Relief Fund for the Jews of Smyrna—
Promotes the building of a Khan at Beyrout—The Blood Accu-
sation at Marmora—Sir Moses Montefiore and Sir Stratford
Canning—The Jews of Morocco—Correspondence with Bokhara
—The "Reform" Movement in the Anglo-Jewish Community.

MISCELLANEOUS work in the community at home
occupied the next five years of Sir Moses Montefiore's
life. This was the work nearest his heart, and he
devoted to it all his energies. To labour for the
ancient Synagogue round which so many solemn traditions gathered, to assist in administering the affairs
of its dependent institutions — monuments to the
benevolence and intelligence of his own kith and kin
—were almost passions with him. He attended the
meetings of every institution to which he belonged
with old-world punctuality. In the President's chair

at the Board of Deputies he represented the political interests of his brethren with dignity and zeal. The Synagogue knew no more familiar figure than his. On Sabbath mornings, when in town, he would religiously walk from Park Lane to Bevis Marks, accompanied by his affectionate wife, the Law prohibiting riding on the Day of Rest. In the afternoons he generally attended *Mincha* service at the Western Synagogue of the German Jews in St. Alban's Place, St. James'. At the time of which we are writing he had already been four times *Parnass*, or Warden President, of the Spanish and Portuguese congregation, viz., in 1819, 1826, 1832, and 1840.

His co-religionists recognised his piety, and repaid his devotion to their interests with affectionate homage. In the small community which centred at Bevis Marks he was regarded almost as another "Prince of the Captivity," and he acknowledged this high estimation of himself by a generous discharge of the responsibilities of his implied seigniory. One of the sights of the London Jewry forty years ago was his annual visit to the Spanish and Portuguese Congregational Schools. This always occurred at Purim time, on the occasion of the distribution of prizes. It was the great gala day of the institution. The classes would assemble in their full strength to receive him, as, beaming with smiles, and bowing right and left, he made a kind of Royal progress of the establishment, the boys and girls meanwhile singing a hymn of welcome in their lustiest tones. Lady Montefiore and Dr. Loewe usually accompanied him on these pleasant pilgrimages, and behind him marched the Beadle of the Synagogue, Mr. Genese, carrying a heavy bag of newly-minted silver coin, the chink of which sent a thrill through the school. When the formal business of the day had been disposed of, and the prizes distributed, Sir Moses would deliver a brief address, and then each of the pupils, over three hundred in number, would be called up to receive a present—ranging from a florin to a crown piece—from the "lucky bag" carried by the Beadle. With each present came a hearty shake of the hand and a cordial "I wish you a merry Purim." The less bashful scholars would answer, "Thank you, Sir Moses, I wish you the same;" whereupon the philanthropist would say, "Thanks; I hope we shall *all* be happy," with grave emphasis on the "all." Lady Montefiore was passionately fond of children, and she would pet and caress the younger pupils as they toddled up to the platform to receive their present; sometimes she would take them in her lap and kiss them. No one was forgotten on these happy Purim visits. When the "lucky bag" was emptied, there were equally lucky slips of paper for the teachers, and a golden guinea or so for the door-keeper. To this day the ceremony is continued by a representative of the venerable baronet.

Sir Moses Montefiore's activity in the promotion of education was not confined to these schools, or even to the Sephardi "nation." He had been, in earlier years, a governor of the "Beth Hamedrash," or Talmudic

I 2

College, founded in 1734 by the pious Benjamin Mendes da Costa, and he continued to take a deep interest in the work of that institution. The theological literature resulting from the studies pursued within its walls found in him a generous patron. He particularly encouraged the Rev. D. A. de Sola in his literary enterprises, and the subject and plan of that gentleman's useful work on " The Blessings " originated with him.

Of Jews' College, a theological seminary established some years later by leading members of the German community, he was one of the founders. The scheme originated in 1838, but it was only after the return from Damascus, in 1841, that any measures were taken for its realisation. Mr. Jacob Franklin, the editor of the *Voice of Jacob,* was its most active promoter, and it was his wish that it should be established as a memorial of the success of the Jewish Mission to Mehemet Ali. Sir Moses Montefiore wrote to Mr. Franklin from Constantinople approving the plan, and when, on his return to England, he paid over to the treasurers of the Damascus Fund a personal contribution of £2,200 towards the expenses of his Mission, Mr. Franklin very reasonably suggested that this sum should be utilised for the purposes of the proposed College. The growing differences in the community at the time prevented the realisation of the project, and Sir Moses' £2,200 were distributed among the contributors to the Damascus Fund as representing a surplus in the accounts. It was not until 1845, when Dr. Adler was appointed Chief Rabbi, that the scheme was revived, and then still eleven years elapsed before it was carried into effect. When, ultimately, the College was started in 1856, Dr. Adler and Sir Moses Montefiore, to whose exertions its establishment was in a great measure due, became respectively its President and Vice-President.

In the Jews' Free School and the Jews' Hospital, two more educational establishments of the German Jews, Sir Moses also took considerable interest. At the time of which we are writing he had passed the President's chair of both institutions. Of the latter, a creation of the Goldsmids, he was elected President in 1837, succeeding his relative, Mr. Sheriff, afterwards Sir David, Salomons. In 1843, when the Duke of Sussex died, he was instrumental in persuading the late Duke of Cambridge to succeed his brother as a patron of the institution. Also, in the provinces, Sir Moses was an active worker in the cause of education. The same year that he interviewed the Duke of Cambridge in the interests of the Jews' Hospital, he laid the foundation stone of the Hebrew National Schools, at Birmingham, and in the following year he presided at their formal opening.

During his temporary absence in the East in 1840 his place as President of the Board of Deputies had been filled by Mr. Hananel de Castro; but immediately on his return to England he was re-elected by acclamation. The *Deputados* had special reasons for holding Sir Moses in high esteem, independent of the consideration that his mission to Damascus had

earned for him a fame which reflected upon the body
over which he presided.   It was due to his intelligent
administration that the Board had become the most
important representative body in the Anglo-Jewish
community.   No sooner had he been elected its President in 1835, than he set himself to remodel its
constitution in such a way as to make it the accredited
mouth-piece of the Jews of England.   At his instance
a scheme was elaborated for admitting to the Board
delegates from every Jewish congregation that might
desire the privilege of being represented; and this
not only enhanced the importance of the Board, but
it had the larger effect of promoting and consolidating
the union of the community for political purposes.
A mass of miscellaneous business of a highly important kind now occupied the Board.   Under the Marriage Acts it became the duty of its President to
certify Synagogue secretaries as registrars for marriage
purposes; and this imparted to it a certain official
standing, which no other Jewish institution enjoyed.
Under the provisions of the constitution of the old
Committee of Diligence, of which it was the heir, it
had to watch the progress of legislation at home, in
order to safeguard Jewish interests; while in consequence of the exhaustion of the *Cautivos* Fund of
the Spanish and Portuguese Congregation, the duty
devolved upon it of receiving and considering such
appeals as were formerly addressed to that body by
oppressed foreign Jewish communities.

Upon the multifarious duties arising from these

functions Sir Moses entered immediately on his re-election to the Presidency. In addition to taking part in the various measures promoted by the Board for sustaining the Civil and Religious Liberty agitation, he was indefatigable in pressing upon Government Jewish grievances and claims in respect to minor legislative matters. Thus, in 1842, we find him corresponding with, and interviewing Sir James Graham on the operation of the Poor Laws, by which pauper Jews were excluded from out-door relief. During the same year he induced Sir Robert Peel to introduce a clause into the Income Tax Bill, placing Jewish Synagogues on an equal footing with other places of worship in respect to imposts on property and income. In the following year again he was in correspondence with Sir James Graham on the subject of a Burials Bill and a Factory Bill. In almost every instance he succeeded in obtaining valuable concessions for his co-religionists.

The foreign business of the Board had a more especial attraction for him; for he alone of all its members knew how real were the hardships of Jewish life in the Ghettos of the Continent and the East. It so happened, that, as the Deputies had no funds of their own—their annual expenses were assessed on the Synagogues they represented—and could not therefore act with the requisite promptitude in emergencies when immediate relief was required, the larger portion of the foreign business fell to Sir Moses' personal administration, which was unhampered by circumlocutory statutes and standing orders.   His name, too, was so much better known abroad than that of the Board, that in the majority of cases the appeals were addressed direct to him in his private capacity, and only brought under the notice of the Board when public action became necessary.   This was especially the case with the business connected with the Holy Land.

The changes in the suzerainty of Syria having defeated for a time the agricultural schemes he had elaborated in 1837, Sir Moses endeavoured by other means to effect an amelioration in the lot of the Palestinian Hebrews.   In 1842, Colonel Churchill, whose acquaintance he had made in the East, addressed to him some very interesting letters, proposing that efforts should be made by the Jews of Europe to promote a re-establishment of the Kingdom of Judah in Palestine.   Sir Moses, who is a devout believer in the literal restoration, answered Colonel Churchill sympathetically, but expressed his opinion that the time was hardly ripe for a practical consideration of the project.   At the same time, as Colonel Churchill was about returning to the East for a stay of several years, he asked him to take charge of a fund he was desirous of providing, for the promotion of thrift among the Jews of the Holy Land, by advancing loans to the industrious poor in amounts varying between 500 and 1,000 piastres.   During the same year he laboured assiduously to introduce useful industries among the Jews of Palestine.   He sent a

printing press to Jerusalem, which gave employment
to several persons, and produced many useful works,
and he also established a linen manufactory on a considerable scale, with a girls' school attached to it. To
ensure the factory being conducted on the best modern
principles, he sent out a technical instructor to take
charge of it, and had three native Jews brought to
England, and taught the art of weaving at Preston.
The needle-women and laundresses of the Holy City
he also assisted to carry on their trades efficiently;
and, with a view to attaching the Jews of Safed,
Tiberias, Hebron, and Jaffa, more firmly to husbandry,
he supplied them with oxen and all the necessary
appliances of agriculture. The charitable requirements
of the communities were also not neglected. Among
many other matters, Sir Moses took a deep interest in
a scheme put forth in 1842 by Dr. Philippson, of
Magdeburg, for the establishment of a Jewish hospital
at Jerusalem. Appeals for subscriptions were issued,
and Sir Moses had the necessary architectural plans
prepared. The realisation of the project, however,
lagged, and, as there was at the time much sickness in
the Holy City, Sir Moses, at his own cost, despatched
thither a medical man, Dr. Fränkel, and established a
dispensary, which he has ever since maintained. The
large amount of good achieved by this prompt action
is sufficiently illustrated by the fact, that the very first
day the dispensary was opened sixty patients were
treated, and the number increased daily.

But it was not only the Jews of the Holy Land for

whom Sir Moses Montefiore laboured. A few months after his return from Constantinople, a disastrous fire destroyed the Jewish quarter of Smyrna. Urgent appeals were addressed to the Western communities, and Sir Moses raised a considerable Relief Fund. Two years later he interested himself in a project for building a Khan for Jewish travellers at Beyrout, which was successfully carried out. In 1844 the Blood Accusation was revived in the island of Marmora. Sir Moses placed the facts of the case before Sir Stratford Canning, who had succeeded Lord Ponsonby as British Ambassador to the Porte, and he procured a public trial at Constantinople, which resulted in the acquittal of the accused. Sir Moses took the opportunity afforded by his correspondence with "the great Eltchi" to induce him to give some attention to the condition of the Hebrews in the Ottoman Empire. Sir Stratford received his representations very cordially, and a month or two later was enabled to report that he had prevailed upon the Turkish Government to make a grant of land to the poor of Constantinople for a new burial ground, of which they stood in need. The Jews of Morocco, Tripoli, Tunis, and Persia, appealed in turn to Sir Moses at this period, and were all more or less assisted. In 1845 he memorialised the Emperor of Morocco to grant his Jewish subjects the same rights as had been guaranteed to the Jews of Turkey, under the Firman of the 12th Ramazan, and received a satisfactory reply—satisfactory, that is, as far as

promises were concerned. So extensive had his influence in the East become at this time, that when
Colonel Stoddart and Captain Conolly were thrown
into prison by the Emir Nazrullah, of Bokhara, the
British Government made strenuous efforts to convey
a letter from him to the Jews of the Khanate, asking
them to interest themselves in the fate of the English
emissaries. Unfortunately the letter only arrived
after they had been put to death, but in one sense it
had the desired effect. The warm terms in which it
was couched led the Bokhara Jews to imagine that the
English officers were fellow Israelites, and they
" interested themselves in their fate " to the extent of
mourning their loss in the synagogues.

In work of this description Sir Moses Montefiore
not only gratified his philanthropic tastes, but found
relief from the cares and anxieties which at this time,
more than at any other period of his career, beset his
position in the Anglo-Jewish community. Towards
the middle of 1841, a schism had taken place among the
English Jews, and a congregation in the west end of
London had been started on lines differing somewhat
from those which had guided the foundation of the
City synagogues two hundred years before. Sir Moses
Montefiore, whose orthodoxy has ever been of the
most rigid type, strongly opposed the new movement,
and the community became a prey to the bitterest
dissensions. In comparing to-day the so-called
" Reform " synagogue with the orthodox Jewish congregations, it is difficult to understand how such a

movement could have caused the commotion it did at
the time of its inception.   Sir Moses Montefiore himself was not uncompromisingly wedded to the old
order of things, notwithstanding that he led the
orthodox party on this occasion.   We have seen, for
example, how he disapproved of the ancient differences
between the Spanish and German congregations, and
he gave a further and emphatic illustration of his
opinion on this subject in 1845, by proceeding to
Dover to receive, on behalf of the Jews of England,
the new German Chief Rabbi, Dr. N. M. Adler, on
his arrival in this country.   One of the grounds, too,
on which the new synagogue was opposed, was, that
it violated an ancient statute of the Bevis Marks
congregation, prohibiting the establishment of district
synagogues ; and yet, in 1844, Sir Moses himself promoted the establishment of a Western branch of the
Spanish and Portuguese Synagogue, by offering £5,000
towards the expense of its erection.   The fact seems
to have been, that the orthodox party was actuated
rather by vague fears of what might take place if a dis-
satisfied section of the community were to establish a
synagogue independent of the constituted authorities,
than of disapproval of what was actually contemplated
by the seceders—fears that have been amply justified
by the dangerous course since pursued by Jewish
Reform in America and elsewhere.   The " Reform "
movement in England, however, turned out to be little
more than a premature anticipation of the natural
progress of forty years.   How mild it was is evidenced

by the fact, that when Dr. Fränkel, the reforming
Chief Rabbi, of Dresden, was asked to place himself
at its head, he declined on the score that it did not
contemplate changes of a sufficiently radical character;
and, a few years ago, Professor Marks, the Chief
Minister of the West London congregation of British
Jews—as the new synagogue called itself—publicly
declared, in the presence of the Rev. Dr. Hermann
Adler, the Delegate Chief Rabbi, that there would
have been no secession in 1841 had the orthodox
synagogue then been as it is now. At the present
time, there is little appreciable difference between the
various synagogues of Great Britain. The Jews of
England, as a body, are the most orthodox and united
of Occidental Jewish communities; and it is in no
complimentary spirit, but as indicative of an important
and undeniable fact, that all classes among them
concur to-day in paying homage to Sir Moses Montefiore. They recognise in him the most representative
of English Jews—a thorough embodiment of their
views and aspirations.

CHAPTER X.

THE sessions of the Board of Deputies (1841—46),
referred to in our last chapter, were particularly notable
for their connection with the Jewish Question in Russia
—the most serious question of modern Jewish history.
Through a correspondence opened with Sir Moses
Montefiore in 1842, the Western Hebrews were for the
first time made aware of the terrible condition of their
Russian co-religionists; and, in the subsequent action
of the Board of Deputies, the foundations were laid of

the movement for their relief which has ever since
been gallantly carried on in the happier countries of
Europe. The Russo-Jewish Question is something
more than a Jewish or even a Russian Question. It is
one of the most extraordinary problems presented by
the complex phenomena of modern society; and it
appeals loudly to the humanitarian sense of civilised
Europe for a speedy and equitable solution.

The ostensible reason for the oppression and
persecution of the Jews of Russia is that they constitute a pernicious element in the Empire; as a
matter of fact, they are the victims of religious hatred.
The struggle between Judaism and Christianity has
been more serious in Russia than in any other country;
and, consequently, the hatred of the Jew has become
more deeply rooted in the national sentiment. How
unfounded is the popular theory of the Russo-Jewish
Question is shown by the fact that, whenever the Jews
in Russia were politically unrestricted, they exerted a
distinctly beneficial influence on the country. Their
history is, indeed, at every step a refutation of the
charges now brought against them.

About the year 726 Leo the Isaurian, Emperor of
Byzantium, published at Constantinople his celebrated
Edict against Image Worship. The clergy and monks
rebelled, and the Emperor was on all sides denounced
as a Jew. In order to show that, notwithstanding his
enlightened opposition to miracle-working fetishes he
was in other respects a good Christian, Leo attempted
to persecute the Jews into embracing the Cross. Many

conversions were effected ; but a large number of the
Hebrews, whose ancestors had established themselves
in the land long before Christianity, fled further afield,
to seek an asylum among the more tolerant pagans.
Thus it came about that Jewish settlements were
formed in the Cimmerian Peninsula of Tauris (the
modern Crimea), and Hebrew communities were
founded at Theodosia (now Kaffa), Kareonpolis (Eski
Krim), Phanegoria (Taman), and Bosphorus (Kertch).
From the Crimea these Græco-Jewish communities
spread to the Caucasus, the Caspian Sea, and the
Mouth of the Volga. These are the first authentic
appearances of the Jews on Russian soil.

The inhabitants of the region thus invaded were the
Khozars, or Togarmi (as they subsequently called
themselves), a Finnish tribe, who, after the break-up
of the Empire of the Huns, had established themselves
in the neighbourhood of Astrachan, whence they had
gradually extended a powerful dominion. Successful
in a war with the Persians, they disputed the
sovereignty of the East with the Byzantine Emperors,
and both the Bulgars and Russins paid them tribute.
Upon this semi-barbarous people the Jews exercised
the happiest influence, and ultimately one of their
sages, Isaac Sangari, converted their King, Bulan, and
a large portion of the nation, to Judaism. In a subsequent reign, that of a King named Obadiah, Judaism
was formally acknowledged as the religion of the State.
Learned Jews crowded the Court ; synagogues were
built and public colleges established for the study of

the Bible and Talmud. While the West and South were distracted by an anarchy of sectarian wrangling, and the North and East were shrouded in an impenetrable shadow of barbarism, the shores of the Caspian and the Euxine flourished in the benignant light of a Jewish civilization.

The Jews persuaded the Khozars to abolish slavery, to tolerate all races and religions, to acknowledge the sanctity of family ties, and to cultivate literature and the sciences. One of their Kings, Joseph, corresponded with Chasdai Ibn-Shaprut, the famous Jewish Vizier of the Caliph Abderrahman III., of Cordova. The power of this Jewish State increased rapidly. Even the Byzantine Emperors paid tribute to it, and there was at one time a chance of Khozar-Judaism spreading all over Russia. The country was, however, saved to Christianity by Sviatoslav of Kiev, the Charles Martel of Muscovy, who in 965, on the field of Sarkel, inflicted a severe check on the power of the Togarmi. From this date the importance of the Khozars gradually declined. Under the influence of Judaism they had become a peaceful people, and they were no longer able to withstand the inroads of the martial Slavs and Russins by whom they were surrounded. The kingdom shrunk until it became confined to the Crimea. In the reign of a King named David they made a last effort to re-establish Judaism in the provinces they had lost by sending Jewish Rabbis to convert the Russin Prince, Vladimir the Great, but he, under the influence of his wife, a sister of the Emperor of Constantinople, preferred the doctrines of the Greek Church, and was baptised. David was the last of the Khozar kings. In 1016 the Crimea was seized by the Russins, and the Jewish State was suppressed. The Khozar princes and nobles fled to Spain, where many of their descendants became distinguished for Talmudic learning. The people, equally true to their Judaism, held aloof from the conquerors, and gradually merged themselves with the Karaites, who had become numerous in Taurida. The modern Karaites of the Crimea, with their fair complexions and un-Jewish features, are descendants of this intermixture of Jewish Khozars and Karaite Jews.

In the meantime other Jews had effected an entrance into Russia [*] from the West. The circumstances were curiously similar to the Southern immigration. Christianity had been introduced into Germany, and one of its first results was a persecution of the Hebrews, who, like their brethren in the Byzantine Empire, had preceded by some centuries the arrival of the new faith. Compelled once more to take in hand the wanderer's staff, the German Jews sent a deputation to the Pagan Leszek, Prince of Poland, asking to be permitted to take refuge in his dominions. The names and condition of the members of this embassy throw an interesting light on the degree of culture attained by the Jews of Central Europe at this early epoch.

---

[*] The Russo-Jewish Question being largely a Polish-Jewish question, the term "Russia" is used here in its most extended geographical sense.

They were Rabbi Hezekiah Sephardi, Rabbi Akiba Estramaduri, the mathematician Emanuel Ascaloni, the rhetorician Rabbi Levi Baccari, and Rabbi Nathaniel Barcelloni. At Gnesen, in the year 893, they interviewed the Polish Prince. Rabbi Levi was the spokesman of the party, and delivered a short address in Latin, describing the persecutions to which his brethren were subjected in Germany. He prayed that they might be allowed to find an asylum in Poland, and, anticipating some anti-Jewish prejudice among the subjects of Leszek, suggested that a remote and unpopulated district might be assigned to them to inhabit and cultivate in peace. Leszek enquired what were the tenets of Judaism, and then promised to take counsel with the national priesthood on the petition. Three days later Rabbi Levi and his companions were summoned into the presence of the Polish potentate to hear his decision. Christian Russia of to-day might learn a lesson from the liberality of this pagan and semi-barbarous prince of nearly a thousand years ago. Not only did he open his dominions freely to the persecuted Hebrews, but he declined to accept their humble suggestion to limit their rights of residence. He permitted them to settle freely all over Poland, and to follow agricultural, industrial, commercial, or any useful avocations without let or hindrance. In the following year, 894, a great concourse of Jews settled in Poland.

According to the theories of the modern persecutors of the Jews, Leszek's liberal policy should have resulted

in disaster to the whole country. Strange to say the
very contrary was the case. We have seen how beneficial was the Jewish settlement in the South while it
lasted; in the West it proved equally advantageous.
For nearly seven hundred years the Jews managed,
with but slight intermission, to preserve the privileges
granted to them in 894, and we have it on the testimony of countless chronicles that they deserved the
liberty they enjoyed. This period, marked by the
dynasties of Piast and Jagellon, was the golden age of
Polish history, and the Jews contributed not a little to
the reigning prosperity. It is one of the creeds of
modern anti-semitism that Jews in large numbers must
be injurious to a country, while a few may be economically useful; and yet at this period the Jews were
proportionately more numerous in Poland than at the
present day. The tolerance of the Polish rulers
attracted them from all parts of Europe. They flew
thither from the restrictive laws of the Hungarian and
Bohemian rulers, and from the popular outbursts in
Germany and France. The expulsion from England
in 1290 furnished a large contingent. Albertrandy
states that in 1264, in some of the Polish provinces,
they constituted one-eighth of the population.

Can it be because Anti-Semitism had not then
become a scientific movement, that men of intelligence congratulated the country on the numerous-
ness of its Hebrews? Hardly. A large number
of Jews forced to ply a few not very wealth-making
trades may be an undesirable element in a country,

but when this large number is unhampered by in-
vidious legislation, and distributed in every depart-
ment of industry, it is valuable in proportion to
the intensity of the inherent energy and skill of
its individuals. The Jews in Poland, between the
eighth and sixteenth centuries, were unrestricted in
their avocations, and their industry and intelligence
constituted them a mainstay of the agricultural and
mercantile prosperity of the land. The foreign trade
was entirely in their hands, and their transactions
extended even to Asia and Africa. A work, published
in 1539, states that while handicrafts were almost
unknown among the Polish Christians, and there were
not more than 500 Christian merchants in the country,
the Jewish merchants numbered 3,200 and the Jewish
mechanics three times as many. Casimir the Great
was, probably, the wisest monarch that ever reigned in
Poland, and he ostentatiously recognised the utility of
the Jews by confirming and extending their privileges.
It was principally with Jewish money that he built the
seventy towns with which he endowed Poland. The
historian Mickiewicz, reviewing the influence of the
Jews, says truly:—" Ce n'est pas sans une raison
providentielle que plusieurs millions d'Israélites existent
depuis tant de siècles au milieu des Polonais et que
leur sort se lie intimement avec celui de la nation
polonaise." Indeed, so obvious was the value of the
Jews in Poland that, towards the end of the eleventh
century, the Russian monarch, Sviatopolk, invited a
number of them to Kiev, and granted them important

privileges with a view to the promotion of the trade of the city.

The best proof, however, that the Jews did not constitute a pernicious element in Russia in the days of their freedom, is afforded by the estimation in which they were held by their native fellow-countrymen. Mr. Freeman's theory of the mediæval Jew, protected by nobles but hated by the people, would not find a shadow of confirmation in Russian history. Czacki, writing of the reign of Casimir the Great, says : " The Christian in his Church and the Jew in his Synagogue offered up thanks to Heaven for their happiness in living in the same country, and for their enjoyment of equal rights." Cardinal Commandoni, Papal Nuncio at the Court of Sigismund Augustus, at the time when Roman Catholic influences were just beginning to darken the political horizon, expresses astonishment at the favourable position of the Jews. " There are," he says, " a large number of Hebrews in these provinces who are not held in contempt as in other countries. They do not live on the ignoble profits of usury and brokerages, but they possess lands, are engaged in commerce, and devote themselves to literature and science. They are rich, and enjoy a reputation for honesty. No badges are worn by them to distinguish them from Christians, but, on the contrary, they carry swords and possess equal rights with other citizens." The Cardinal was not disposed to paint a favourable picture of the Jews, for, in the same document, he inveighs fiercely against the Poles for their indulgence to such "infidels." The *Jus militare* held the Jews equally liable to military service with other Poles, and instances of their valour are noted more than once in Polish history.

Judaism itself was held in high esteem, and at one time, when the country was distracted with sectarian jealousies, the Jews proselytised with such success that for a moment the whole edifice of Polish and Russian Christianity trembled at its base. In Poland the uncompromising attitude of Peter Gamrat, Bishop of Cracow, who condemned several of the converts to the stake, damped the proselytising ardour of the Jews ; but in Russia their success was most remarkable. The soul of the movement was a Jew of Kiev named Scharja or Zacharias, a learned and accomplished man, well versed in the literature and sciences of his day. In 1471 he came to Novgorod in the train of the Prince Michael Olelkovich, and his reputation as a *savant* brought him into contact with a distinguished circle. The first converts he made were two priests named Dionysius and Alexius, Gabriel, the proto-papas of the Cathedral of Novgorod, and the Bojar Tutchin, a layman of high rank. With the assistance of several learned Jews from Lithuania secret communities of converts were organised at Novgorod and Pskov, and the propaganda was proceeded with industriously. When Novgorod became a portion of the Grand Duchy of Moscow, Dionysius and Alexius were appointed proto-papas of the two principal churches in the capital. Here they succeeded in making the most extraordinary conversions. Kooritzin, the secretary of the Grand Duke, his brother, Ivan, the Princess Helena, and Zozimus, abbot of the convent of St. Simeon, were among the converts; and on the latter being elevated in 1490 to the dignity of Archbishop of Moscow, a circumcised believer in Judaism became the head of the Russian Church. There was every likelihood of the history of the Khozars being repeated on a larger scale in Russia proper, when the heresy was discovered by Gennadius, Bishop of Novgorod. Its spread was promptly stopped. Dionysius and Gabriel were imprisoned for life, Zozimus resigned his high position and retired to a convent, and Kooritzin was burnt alive. The moment was, however, critical for Russian Christianity. It is said that not a single town in the whole country was free from a taint of Judaism. The movement split up into many sects, of which the modern Molokani and Subotniki are the remains.

In Poland the Jews continued for a hundred years longer to enjoy their ancient privileges, but in Russia their doom was sealed. Christianity recognised in them its direst foes, and persecuted them unmercifully. Very gradually the hostile feeling spread to Poland; but it assumed no tangible form until the rise of the Jesuit power towards the end of the Jagellon dynasty. Then, one by one, all the restrictions of Ghetto life were introduced. The oppression was avowedly religious; no pernicious influences of an economical kind were alleged. With a full conviction of the

righteousness of their conduct, and in the name of a
merciful God, the representatives of Latin and Greek
Christianity set themselves to the task of demoralising
a million human beings.

If, then, to-day there is anything objectionable in
the character of the Polish Jew, who is to blame ? Do
the Russians expect a people to emerge from a seclusion of three centuries undazed, uncramped, familiar
with the progress achieved in their absence ? The
wonder is that the Jews are not infinitely worse than
they really are. It is marvellous that throughout
their oppression they should have so completely conserved their moral purity, and their intellectual power.
To-day they are nearly four millions in number, and
are still enchained by odious disabilities. Over and
over again in modern times they have proved their
capacity for progress, and demonstrated the falsity of
the charges brought against them. But, apart from all
controversies as to their character, they are human
beings, and this surely should be sufficient to enlist
the sympathy of the boasted humanity of the century
in their behalf. It will read curiously in the pages
of some future historian that the age which gloried in
having freed the Negro, silently acquiesced in the
oppression of the people, to whom the world is indebted
for the Decalogue.

CHAPTER XI.

The Board of Deputies and the Russo-Jewish Question—Sir Moses
Montefiore invited to St. Petersburg by the Russian Government to confer with the Minister of Education on the condition
of the Jews—Policy of the Czar Nicholas towards the Jews—The
persecuting Ukaze of 1843—Jewish appeals to Sir Moses Montefiore—Temporary suspension of the Ukaze—David Urquhart on
Russian persecutions—Re-issue of the Ukaze—Sir Moses Montefiore appeals to Lord Aberdeen to intercede with the Czar—The
Ukaze is again suspended—Promulgated once more in 1845
—A deputation of Russian Jews arrives in England—Diplomatic
representations to the Russian Government are ineffectual—Sir
Moses Montefiore deputed to proceed to St. Petersburg—Dangers
of the journey—Flattering reception in the Russian capital—The
Ukaze suspended for a third time—Interview with the Czar—Sir
Moses proceeds on a tour of the Western provinces—Adventures
on the journey—Willingness of the Jews to follow his advice—
Triumphant progress through Jewish Russia—Sir Moses Montefiore and Prince Paskievitch—Revocation of the Ukaze—Return
to England—Enthusiasm of the English Jews—Royal appreciation of the mission—A baronetcy conferred on Sir Moses
Montefiore.

AT a meeting of the Board of Deputies, held on
the 12th September, 1842, Sir Moses Montefiore
announced that he had received an important communication from the Russian Government, inviting
him to St. Petersburg to confer with Count Ouvarov,
Minister of Education, on the condition of the Russian

Jews. The letter, which was couched in very complimentary terms, stated that the Jews were in so retrograde a state, that it would be impossible for some time " to pronounce the word ' Emancipation ;' " but that with a view to their ultimate affranchisement the Emperor desired to introduce among them an advanced system of education. Unfortunately the Government had found in the " bigotry and ignorance " of the Jews an invincible obstacle to the realisation of their benevolent desires. They therefore appealed to Sir Moses for his co-operation. " You, Sir," declared the letter, " enjoy the fullest confidence of the Russian Jews : your name is uttered with the most profound veneration by them." The Government, therefore, hoped that, with his assistance, the scheme they had in contemplation might be made acceptable to his co-religionists. At the same time other letters were received by Sir Moses from several of the Jewish communities, urging him to seize the opportunity of pleading their cause before the Czar.

Sir Moses was unable for private reasons to accept this invitation ; but had he proceeded to St. Petersburg, it is doubtful whether he would have found the Russian Government as anxious as they professed to be to ameliorate the lot of his brethren in faith. The real history of the remarkable invitation of Count Ouvarov has yet to be written. Read in the light of the cruel and arbitrary policy pursued by the Emperor Nicholas towards the Jews since his accession to the throne in 1825, it cannot but suggest some *arrière-*

pensée at issue with its well-intentioned tone. No
section of the Russian population had felt the weight
of the Czar's iron hand more heavily than the Jews.
In 1827, when he was engaged in the organisation of
a navy, it was suggested to him that the serfs were
too clumsy and loosely knit to make good sailors, but
that the Jews, with their lithe and active figures,
might be very advantageously employed, especially if
trained for the purpose in their youth. The Emperor
acted upon the suggestion with the literal and reckless promptness that always characterised him. In
one night 30,000 young Jewish children were torn
from their mothers' arms, and carried away to the
shores of the Black Sea to be inducted into the
mysteries of seamanship. From the moment of their
seizure they were submitted to the most rigorous discipline, and were so cruelly treated, that not more
than 10,000 of them survived to enter the navy. Shut
out from communication with their families, the Czar
also closed against them the portals of their religion,
and had them brought up in the tenets of the Russo-
Greek Church. This was not the only occasion on
which his Majesty showed that his attitude towards
the Jews was biassed by religious considerations; for
in 1828 he tried to have all the Jews in the Russian
army forcibly baptized.

But, besides isolated instances of persecution such
as these, the Emperor Nicholas had made himself specially conspicuous in Russo-Jewish history,
by codifying on a comprehensive scale the laws for

the oppression of the Jews, which had been formu-
lated at different times by his Russian and Polish
predecessors. The ostensible object of the new
code, which was promulgated in April, 1835, consisted "in a regulation of the position of the Jews,
which, while enabling them to earn their livelihood
by agriculture, and industrial occupations, as also to
educate their children, would at the same time remove
all inducements to indolence and illegal pursuits."
Their effect was, however, very different. Prince
Demidoff San-Donato, in his admirable work on "The
Jewish Question in Russia," which has recently been
translated into English, under the auspices of Sir
Moses Montefiore's nephew, Mr. H. Guedalla, says of
this code :—"From the sense of its enactments it
would appear that, according to the views of the
Legislature, the Jews, *per se,* do not possess any of
the rights inherent to all men and citizens. Thus,
for instance, with regard to all Russian subjects, with
the exception of Jews, the fundamental legal principle
is that everything not prohibited by law is allowed ;
whereas for the Jews the maxim is that everything
which is not positively allowed by law, is to be considered prohibited." This is the legislation by which
the Jews of Russia are governed to-day. Well might
Baron Henry de Worms exclaim, on a recent occasion,
that it was tantamount to a ban of excommunication !

The only recognisable explanation of Count
Ouvarov's invitation to Sir Moses Montefiore was,
that the Russian Government had seen the error of its

ways in respect to the Jews, and had resolved to mend
them.   This theory was, however, rudely dispelled in
the following year.   In consequence of the smuggling
which took place on the Western frontiers, and in
which a few Jews were thought to participate, the
Czar, with his usual drastic precipitancy, issued a
Ukaze, on the 20th April, 1843, ordering the removal
into the interior of *all* Jews domiciled within a zone
of 50 versts (close upon 35 English miles) along
the German and Austrian frontiers.   This reckless
measure was worthy of the man who, heedless of
engineering difficulties, commanded his railways to be
built in mathematically straight lines.   It was calculated to break up no less than a thousand Jewish
congregations, and ruin over three hundred towns and
villages.   Its effect on the commerce of the Empire
would have been disastrous in the extreme.   To the
communities at which it was levelled, it was of terrible
significance.   It meant the destruction of all their little
property, and their means of livelihood; it meant the
break-up of homes which, however miserable, were still
brightened by loving domestic reminiscences, and hallowed by the recollection of ancestors whose ashes re-
posed in the immediate vicinity.   For wanton cruelty,
the whole legislation even of autocratic Russia may be
searched in vain for the equal of this decree.

Nearly three months elapsed before any intelligence
of the new persecution reached Western Europe.   One
morning in July, Sir Moses Montefiore was shocked to
receive a letter from the Jews of Königsberg describing

what had taken place, and appealing for help. With his customary promptness he called upon Baron Brunnow, the Russian Ambassador at the Court of St. James, and urged him to inform his Government how dire were the hardships the Ukaze was calculated to inflict. At the same time he wrote a friendly letter to Count Ouvarov, soliciting his good offices to obtain an abrogation of the decree. The effect of these representations was, that the Ukaze was suspended for some months.

In January, 1844, an intimation was forwarded to the Jewish communities, that the Ukaze would shortly be enforced, and agonizing appeals were again addressed to Sir Moses Montefiore. The cause of the persecuted Jews was, on this occasion, generously taken up by the whole European press. In England, David Urquhart, then in the acutest throes of his Russophobia, thus wrote in the *Portfolio* :—

" Hitherto there was one People who, obedient Beasts of Burthen, could excite neither the Fears nor the Antipathies of Russia, who presented neither a political nor religious Bond, or Hold, or Opposition to Her. These were the Jews. Suddenly they too are added to the number of the sufferers. First, came a Ukaze, subjecting them to Military, not Service, but Conscription; and now an Imperial Command converts them into homeless and destitute Wanderers. Half a Million of Human Beings are thus smitten, but the very Option is not left to them of what was the Doom

of the Jews of Spain. They dare not even fly from
their Oppressor and seek a Refuge in less inhospitable
lands, or that Mercy from the Mussulman that the
Christian denied. They are expatriated yet firmly
grasped, Hopelessness of Refuge is added to Destitu-
tion—their Fate is completed in the Words, *to move
fifty versts into the interior of Russia.* . . . .
Russia, who had outraged every Commandment of
God, and every Law of Man, fills up with this last
Atrocity the Measure of Iniquity. Russia having
already, by such Crimes committed with Impunity,
steeped the Nations of Europe in Infamy, by this
last fills up the Measure and the Proof of their
Degradation."

Convinced this time that direct appeals to the Russian Authorities would be useless, Sir Moses Montefiore resolved on public and organised action. In
consultation with the Board of Deputies, he determined to lay the facts of the persecution before the
British Government. Accompanied by his nephew,
Baron Lionel de Rothschild, he accordingly waited on
the Earl of Aberdeen, who, on behalf of Her Majesty's
Ministers, promised to use his friendly offices with the
Czar. A couple of months later, the Emperor himself
appeared in England on a visit to the Queen. Sir
Moses sought an interview with His Majesty, but in
vain. He prevailed upon him, however, to receive and
consider a memorial, and again it was notified that the
operation of the edict would be suspended.

Not for long, however. The Emperor's heart was apparently set on the execution of his grim scheme, and, towards the end of 1845, he resolved on the re-issue of the Ukaze. This determination, after twenty months of tranquillity, took the Jews of Europe by surprise. For a time they hesitated as to the course they should pursue. Their apparent inactivity drew upon them the scornful reproaches of David Urquhart, expressed with his usual array of italics and capital letters. Writing in the *Portfolio*, he thus contrasted the energy they had displayed in the Damascus affair with their seeming apathy in face of the Russian persecution :—

" How Can this Indifference of a Body so proverbially attached to each other, and which have recently manifested that Attachment in so signal a Manner, be accounted for under this, the heaviest Blow that for Centuries has fallen on their Head ? This there is no Difficulty in accounting for. *The Persecutor is Russia.* That says all ! Who dares to question, aye, or even to wince, when he knows that it is her hand that applies the Lash ? That Moment, those who were heard the loudest, and who looked the fiercest, are heard no more, and their Eye is on the Ground. It is all one, Jew or Gentile, Stockbroker or Field-Marshal, Clothesman or Sovereign, Montefiore or Gordon, Rothschild or Guelf, they are all Servants to the same Master, and Beasts of Burden— there is Pasture for them in the same Valley, Harness

L

for them in the Stall; they feed, and perform their
Task!"

Urquhart was mistaken.   Soon after the publication
of this article, a deputation of Russian Jews arrived
in England to lay their grievances before Sir Moses
Montefiore, and he once more endeavoured to interest
the British Government in their behalf.   At the same
time, at Vienna, Baron Solomon de Rothschild publicly
called upon the Russian Ambassador to intercede with
his Government.   These representations proved fruit-
less.   The Jews of Western Europe now became
thoroughly aroused.   Supported by the leading
journals, Dr. Fränkel, the learned Chief Rabbi of
Dresden, published a vigorous appeal to the world for
help.   The Russian Government mockingly answered
with an expulsion of foreign Jews.   Notwithstanding
the irritation caused by this last measure, no European
Power ventured on a remonstrance.   To avert the
impending disaster the Jews evidently had only themselves to rely upon.   In this crisis Sir Moses Montefiore
gallantly came forward and offered to proceed to St.
Petersburg to plead the cause of his brethren
personally with the Czar.

This proposal was received by the Jews with
enthusiasm.   As soon as the necessary preparations
were completed, special prayers for the success of the
Mission were offered up in all the synagogues of the
British Empire by order of the Chief Rabbi, and even
the Reform Congregation in Burton Crescent sent

forth an applauding " God speed " from its proscribed
pulpit.   On the 26th February, 1846, Sir Moses
Montefiore, accompanied by Lady Montefiore and
Dr. Loewe, and attended by a numerous suite, set out
on his second important expedition.   The wintry
weather was exceedingly severe, and the journey long
and tedious.   On the snow-bound roads the travellers
were frequently alarmed by the howling of hungry
packs of wolves, and they had to keep a gong
perpetually sounding to frighten them away.   St.
Petersburg was not reached until the 31st March.

The reception accorded to Sir Moses in the Russian
capital was very flattering.   Apart from the recommendations with which he had been furnished by the
British Government, and which, under any circumstances, would have secured him ceremonious attention, the political whirligig had brought about a modi-
fication in the Czar's view of the obnoxious Ukaze
which enabled him to be more gracious to the
Jewish champion than might have otherwise been
possible.   Sir Moses was treated not merely as a
distinguished private individual, but as the representative of a people.   He was asked to consider himself
the guest of the Emperor ; State carriages were placed
at his disposal, and a Government official was ordered
to be in constant attendance on him.   During the
Passover holidays he worshipped in the synagogues
used by the Jewish soldiers of the garrison, which, for
the occasion, were handsomely decorated at the expense
of the Czar.

The presentation of the Memorial of which he was the bearer took place on the 9th April. Previous to the arrival of the Hebrew philanthropist in St. Petersburg, the counsellors of the Czar had ventured to point out that, while it was doubtful whether the proposed removal of the Jews into the interior would have the contemplated effect of checking smuggling, it was certain that so sudden a change in the social condition of the Western Provinces would bring about grave economical evils which would re-act upon the entire Empire. The Czar had listened to these representations with more attention than he usually bestowed on advice opposed to his preconceived opinions, and on the 22nd March the operation of the Ukaze had been suspended for four years. This action had not, however, removed the *raison d'être* of Sir Moses Montefiore's Mission. He was charged to procure, if possible, the entire revocation of the decree, and also to obtain a general reform of the laws affecting the Russian Jews.

Sir Moses gave the following account in one of his letters of his audience with the Emperor :—

"I have the pleasure to inform you that, with the blessing of God, I have had the opportunity of pleading the cause of our brethren in this Empire before the mighty monarch. On Thursday I was honoured with an audience by the Emperor, was most graciously received, and all my statements listened to most patiently. His Majesty said I should have the satis-

faction of taking with me his assurance and the
assurances of his Ministers, that he was most desirous
for the improvement of my co-religionists in his
Empire, and that object engaged his attention at
present. His Majesty intimated a desire that I should
visit my brethren in those towns in which they were
the most numerous, and he would put me in communication with his Ministers."

The conversation here referred to occupied half-
an-hour, and was conducted without witnesses. In
honour of the occasion the Palace guard for the day
was composed of Jewish soldiers. After the Emperor
had read the Memorial he turned to Sir Moses and
said, in the most affable manner, "*A présent causons.*"
He then chattily descanted on the difficulties of the
Russo-Jewish problem, gave his visitor some details
of alleged Jewish demoralization, which, Sir Moses
subsequently declared, "made every hair of my head
stand on end," and expressed a desire to deal liberally
with the Jews, if only the ancient laws of the Empire
would allow him. "But your Majesty might alter
these laws," interposed Montefiore. "I hope I may
succeed," answered the Emperor. Referring to the
Jewish sentries on duty, Nicholas said he had 100,000
brave Israelites in his army, and complimentarily
described them as "veritable Maccabees." It appeared
to Sir Moses that, in spite of the Czar's liberal protes-
tations, he was strongly possessed by a perverted
estimate of Jewish character. In concluding the

interview, the Emperor made the suggestion, referred to in Sir Moses' letter, that he should himself visit the Jewish communities in the West, and he advised him to counsel his co-religionists to lay aside their old-fashioned dress and mediæval customs. In taking his leave, Sir Moses observed, " Sire, I commend my Jewish brethren to your protection." " They shall have it if they resemble you," courteously answered the Czar.

Sir Moses lost no time in acting upon the Emperor's suggestion that he should visit his Russian brethren in their homes. The earnest spirit in which he undertook this important investigation is indicated in a letter he addressed to a friend in London. He wrote :—

" To-morrow, please God, I proceed on my visit, in compliance with the desire of his Imperial Majesty, to several towns in which the Jews principally reside. After witnessing their situation, I have the assurance of the Ministers that any report or suggestion that I may think proper to make shall have their earnest attention, and a promise that my letter shall be placed in the hands of the Emperor himself. I have had long and frequent intercourse with the principal Ministers on the subject of the unfortunate condition of our co-religionists in this Empire ; and I feel confident that there is a great desire for their improvement, but I fear there is the greatest poverty among them. The most likely remedy for this evil would be their

employment in the cultivation of land and the establishment of manufactories; these pursuits require
capital, which, I apprehend, it will be difficult to raise
in this country. I have been much pleased with two
Synagogues, which I have had the gratification of
attending during the holidays, with the consent of His
Majesty, who was graciously pleased afterwards to
enquire if I was satisfied with them. Both buildings
were crowded with Jewish soldiers; and it was a
gratifying sight to witness their orderly conduct and
great devotion. The *Hazanim* were soldiers, and the
prayers, *Parasa*, &c., were extremely well read, and
would have done credit to any Synagogue in London."

Armed with letters to the provincial authorities and
with the privilege of using the Government relays, Sir
Moses left St. Petersburg on the 21st April. His
journey is said to have resembled a royal progress.
At Wilna, the capital of Jewish Russia,—one-third of
the population are Jews—he spent eleven days. Immediately on his arrival he was waited upon by the
Military Commandant, General von Mirkowicz, while
the wives and daughters of the principal officials paid
their respects to Lady Montefiore. A round of festivi-
ties was proposed by the authorities, but declined by
Sir Moses. He found the Jews willing to follow his
advice in every particular. They expressed their
readiness to engage in agriculture, and the adminis-
trators of the communal schools undertook to have the
boys instructed in the vernacular and in branches of

useful secular knowledge. At every town at which he stopped he gave largely to the poor of all denominations, and at Wilna left 10,000 silver roubles for the Jewish poor alone. The journey was not without its adventures. In crossing the Dwina the ice gave way, and one of the servants was drowned. The Montefiores themselves narrowly escaped with their lives. The general results of Sir Moses' observations are tersely described in one of his letters to London. Writing from Warsaw, under date of the 20th May, he says :—

" There is much to be done in Poland. I have already received the promise of many of the *Hasidim* to change their fur caps for hats, and to adopt the German costume generally. I think this change will have a happy effect on their position, and be the means of producing a good feeling between their fellow-subjects and themselves. I have received the assurance of many that they would willingly engage themselves in agriculture if they could procure land; and his Highness the Viceroy is desirous that they should do so. I therefore hope that those Jews in this kingdom who have the ability will purchase land (which I am told is very cheap), and will employ their brethren in its cultivation. Our co-religionists are most willing to work; they are good masons, bricklayers, carpenters, &c., and of course tailors, shoemakers, bootmakers, weavers, &c. I was pained to witness how some labour for a bit of bread : there were thousands of them on the roads breaking stones; and truly

happy when they could get even that humiliating
employment. The Jewish schools are most deserving
of commendation; the females are quite equal in
talent to the males."

At Warsaw Sir Moses was somewhat rudely reminded of the insincerity of the Russian authorities
in their assumed benevolence towards the Jews. In
an interview with Prince Paskiewitch, the Governor-
General of Poland, he represented how advantageous
it would be to admit Jewish pupils to the public
schools. " God forbid!" cynically replied the Prince.
" The Jews are already too clever for us. How would
it be if they got good schooling?" This remark,
spoken probably in jest, throws a flood of light on the
Russian policy towards the Jews. The opinion is not
new in Russian history. It reminds us of a remarkable letter written some sixty years before by the
Empress Catherine to the Governor of Moscow, who
had complained of the difficulties he experienced in
establishing schools. " Mon cher Prince," wrote the
Empress, "vous vous plaignez de ce que les Russes
n'ont pas le désir de s'instruire. Si j'institue des
écoles, ce n'est pas pour nous, c'est pour l'Europe
où il faut maintenir notre rang dans l'opinion; mais
du jour où nos paysans voudraient s'éclairer, ni vous
ni moi, nous ne resterions à nos places."

His tour of the Jewish communities completed, Sir
Moses Montefiore returned to England by rapid stages,
bringing with him the news that the Ukaze which

had occasioned his journey had been finally abrogated. As a further result of his mission, an Imperial rescript was subsequently issued, granting Jews the right to acquire land, and to enrol themselves in commercial corporations. The conditions attached to this permission were, however, not sufficiently favourable to admit of the Jews availing themselves very extensively of its provisions. The personal advice and example of Sir Moses did more to stimulate the Russian Hebrews to an improvement of their condition than all the grudging concessions of the Government. If the Jews are to-day better off than they were in 1846, it is only in a very small measure due to the exertions of the authorities.

In England Sir Moses Montefiore's co-religionists received him with an enthusiasm hardly inferior to that which greeted him on his triumphant return from the East in 1840. His efforts on behalf of his persecuted brethren were graciously appreciated, too, by the highest personages in the realm. An entertainment in his honour, given by his sister-in-law, the then Dowager Baroness de Rothschild, at Gunnersbury Park, was attended by more than one member of the royal family; and the Queen testified her interest in his humanitarian work by conferring upon him his baronetcy.

CHAPTER XII.

A BUSY DECADE.

THE meridian of Sir Moses Montefiore's career was reached in the period we are now approaching. At an age when with most men "the years have stolen fire from the mind, and vigour from the limb," he was in the prime of life. Time had dealt its gentlest with him. Almost within sight of the Psalmist's limit of age, his appetite for work was unslaked, and his energies unexhausted. The ten years ending on his seventy-third birthday were the busiest in his whole career.

The session following his return from Russia found him again hard at work in the President's chair of the Board of Deputies. One of the first questions he was called upon to consider was the resumption of the Emancipation struggle in England. Strange as it may seem, it is nevertheless a fact that Sir Moses Montefiore, a Baronet of the United Kingdom, ex-sheriff of London and Middlesex, and high sheriff for the county of Kent, a Commissioner of Lieutenancy for London, and a Magistrate of Middlesex, Deputy Lieutenant for Kent, and a Magistrate for the Cinque Ports, who had been twice honoured by his sovereign for his labours in the cause of oppressed humanity, and whose example had taught his co-religionists in the remotest countries to regard England as the home of liberty, was himself in 1847 still a victim of political disabilities. Two years before he had initiated, after a lull of eight years, a new campaign against the disqualifications under which the English Jews laboured; but he had not been able to achieve more than the opening to them of Corporation offices. The occasion of this campaign was the annulment of the election of his brother-in-law, Mr. David Salomons, as Alderman for the ward of Portsoken in the City of London, in consequence of his inability to subscribe to the declaration " On the true faith of a Christian," with which the oath of office concluded. At a meeting of the Board of Deputies held on the 23rd of January,

1845, Sir Moses Montefiore brought the circumstance
officially under the notice of his colleagues, and moved
" that the time is now fitting for a recommencement of
the agitation for Jewish emancipation." The resolution was adopted, and a special committee appointed to
act upon it.

This body met frequently at the chambers in
Capel Court, occupied by its chairman in his capacity as President of the Alliance Insurance Company. At one of these meetings (10th February) it
was resolved to seek a conference with Her Majesty's
Government, and, accordingly, on the 19th February,
Sir Moses Montefiore, accompanied by his nephew,
the late Baron Lionel de Rothschild, had an interview
with Sir Robert Peel at Downing Street. The Premier
stated that a measure for the partial repeal of Jewish
Disabilities was under his consideration, but that he
was not then prepared to disclose it. On the 4th
March another interview took place, when the Minister
showed Sir Moses Montefiore a Bill enabling Jews to
fill Corporation offices. This, he said, was the extent
to which the Government was inclined to go. Sir
Moses expressed his regret that no larger measure of
repeal was contemplated, but hoped that in a subsequent session the Ministry would present the Jews
with a final instalment of relief.

The Bill was introduced into Parliament, and passed
both Houses without opposition. In the Lords it was
warmly commended by the Duke of Cambridge, uncle
to the Queen, and a patron of the Jews' Hospital, who,

in the course of his speech, made some interesting references to Sir Moses Montefiore. His Royal Highness said :—

"I have had occasion for some time to know the good which persons professing the Jewish religion have done, and particularly with reference to the different charities to which I belong; and I can certainly say that it is to them that we owe a great deal, and that they contribute a very large portion of the funds of all the charities over which I have the honour of presiding. Two of the individuals whose names were mentioned in the speech of my noble and learned friend on the Woolsack are personally known to myself. One was formerly High Sheriff of the county of Kent (Mr. Salomons), and I can bear witness to the good which he has done. Also, there was Sir Moses Montefiore, who, about five years ago, was Sheriff of London, and I must state, in justice to him, what occurred between him and me whilst he held that office. I happened to be requested by the Bishop of Winchester to preside at a meeting for the purpose of increasing the number of churches in that diocese. I went down to Winchester, and I happened to be walking in the garden, when I met Sir Moses Montefiore, who had come down on a very melancholy occasion, to attend the deathbed of a favourite niece. He came up to me, and learning what was the object of the meeting which I was about to attend, he gave me a very handsome sum which he desired me to present. I will not mention what the sum was, for it would be a violation of good taste to do so; but I think it only just to mention his name, and to show that I really feel that we owe a great debt of gratitude to gentlemen professing his persuasion for the good which they have done."

During Sir Moses Montefiore's absence in Russia, an important change took place in the direction of political affairs at home. On the 25th June, 1846, Sir Robert Peel was defeated on the Irish Coercion Bill, and two days later his Ministry resigned. The hopes of the Jews rose high when Lord John Russell, the author of the repeal of the Test and Corporation Acts, and a prominent sympathiser with the cause of Jewish emancipation, was invited by the Queen to form a new administration. At the very first meeting of the 1846—47 session of the Board of Deputies, Sir Moses Montefiore, who enjoyed the personal friendship of the new Premier, promised to use his influence to obtain the repeal of the remaining disabilities. Unfortunately other urgent political questions so completely absorbed the time of the new Ministry that they were unable to give any immediate attention to the Jewish question.

On May 22nd, 1847, however, Parliament was dissolved, and at the general election which followed, Baron Lionel de Rothschild was elected one of the members for the City of London. Being unable to take his seat in consequence of the obnoxious wording of the oath, the Government were forced to take action in accordance with their well-known proclivities.

On the 16th December Lord John Russell, in an able and exhaustive speech, moved in the House of Commons, "That this House resolve itself into a Committee on the Removal of Civil and Religious Disabilities affecting Her Majesty's Jewish subjects." An interesting debate ensued, and the motion was carried by 256 to 186 votes. A Bill was introduced on the 20th December. The unimpeachable conduct of the Jews in the municipal offices they had filled afforded their parliamentary friends a new argument in their favour; and the high character of Sir Moses Montefiore, Sir David Salomons, and Baron de Rothschild was quoted more than once by the partisans of the Bill. The Prime Minister in his opening speech made very dexterous use of this argument. He said :—

"We have been told also, that there is a very solemn denunciation in the prophecies which should prevent our granting to the Jews the rights they claim. But, I would ask, where it is that those who use this argument would draw the line? In this country we have much relaxed the rigour of our enactments respecting them. A Jew has been a magistrate; a Jew has been a sheriff. By a late statute, which was introduced by the Right Honourable member for Tamworth, Jews may hold offices in corporations; and it was but the other day that a Jew was admitted to the office of Alderman in the Corporation of the City of London. I ask you what right or business have you to interpret a prophecy so as to draw the line between an Alderman and a Commissioner of Customs, between a Justice of the Peace and a person having a right to sit in Parliament ? ''

These observations derived especial force from the circumstance that " the Right Honourable member for Tamworth," Sir Robert Peel, had at first declared himself against the Bill. On the second reading, to the great surprise of the House, the ex-Premier announced that he had changed his mind, and both spoke and voted in its favour. In this speech Sir Robert several times referred to Sir Moses Montefiore. The following passage may be quoted :—

" I have other motives that weigh with me. There are countries in which the Jews are still subject to persecution and oppression. Twice within the last three or four years has a British subject, distinguished for his benevolence and philanthropy, Sir Moses Montefiore, repaired to distant lands, in the hope of mitigating the hard lot of the suffering Jews. He repaired to St. Petersburg for the purpose of imploring mercy towards the Jews in Poland. He repaired to the East for the purpose of relieving, if possible, the Jews in Palestine, from shameful wrongs, perpetrated on the pretext that they murdered Christian children in order that their blood might be available for the Passover. He carried with him letters of recommen-

M

dation from British Ministers, certifying his high character for integrity and honour, and the purity of the motives by which he was actuated. How much more persuasive would those letters have been if they could have announced the fact that every ancient prejudice against the Jews had been extinguished here, and that the Jew was on a perfect equality, as to civil rights, with his Christian fellow-citizen."

The Bill was passed ; but on reaching the Lords it shared the fate of its predecessors, and was defeated by 163 to 128 votes. Baron de Rothschild hereupon resigned his seat.

As soon as the result of the deliberations of the Upper Chamber was made known, Sir Moses Montefiore convened a meeting of the Board of Deputies to consider by what means the agitation should be continued. It was resolved to confide it to a special committee, the chairmanship of which was offered to the President of the Board. Sir Moses accepted the honour, and began forthwith to organise a formidable movement. He secured the co-operation of the Goldsmids, who had already distinguished themselves by their exertions in the cause, and drew up a form of petition which he distributed among all the metropolitan and provincial Jewish congregations for signature. In January, 1848, he was enabled to send up a large number of memorials to the House of Lords in favour of Lord John Russell's Bill. His committee met three times a week during something more than a year at Baron Rothschild's offices in New Court, St. Swithin's Lane. The Lords, however, again threw out the measure, and the Jews, disheartened by their want of success, gradually dropped their agitation.

From this time until 1858, when, through the personal exertions. of Baron de Rothschild and Sir David Salomons, the Jewish Disabilities were at last repealed, Sir Moses Montefiore was but little concerned in the agitation. He remained, however, to the end Chairman of the Special Committee of the Deputies charged with its organisation, and when eventually his nephew was permitted to take his seat in the Commons, he was the first to offer him his congratulations. Baron de Rothschild, in the course of his reply, expressed a hope which to-day reads almost like a prophecy. " Permit me," he wrote, " to felicitate you, upon an event in which we have a strong common interest, and to reciprocate the hope that you, too, may long live to enjoy the advantages and to witness the ulterior results which may be expected to flow from it."

Sir Moses had no Parliamentary ambition, although, had he desired it, he could have been returned without opposition, on more than one occasion for the division of the county of Kent in which he resides. His family has, however, never ceased to be represented in St. Stephen's, and at the present time a nephew (Mr. Arthur Cohen, Q.C.) and a grand-nephew (Sir Nathaniel de Rothschild) occupy seats in the Commons. The wish

has often been expressed that the last shadow of
Jewish disability might be removed from the British
Constitution by the admission of a Jew to the House
of Lords; and Sir Moses Montefiore has been, not
unreasonably, indicated as the man upon whom such
a distinction should fall. There are those, both within and without the Jewish community, who still hope
to see this wish fulfilled.

Throughout the Emancipation struggle Sir Moses
Montefiore's heart remained as heretofore with his
foreign brethren. This will account for his not taking
so prominent a part in the solution of the great political
question at home as his less travelled relatives and
colleagues. The foreign Jews, particularly those in
the East, remained in a distressing state, a prey not
only to persecuting laws, but persecuting popular
passion. The negative indignity of political disability,
that had been the great trouble of the British Jews,
was happiness in comparison with the positive hardships, the misery, and insecurity, which beset the
lives of thousands of their brethren in Eastern Europe
and Western Asia. It was well for them that Sir
Moses Montefiore *did* interest himself in their welfare.

A revival of the Blood Accusation at Damascus
engaged his attention towards the middle of 1847. In
April of that year, a Christian child had disappeared,
and the Jews had been charged with murdering it in
order to employ its blood for ritual purposes. The
wretched superstition was supported by the French

Consulate, the chief of which represented to the
Ottoman Governor, Sefata Pasha, that it was credibly
established that the Jews used Christian blood in the
celebration of their Passover. Sefata Pasha does not
seem to have been acquainted with the famous Firman
of the 12th Ramazan, which vindicated the Jews from
this accusation under the hand and seal of the Padishah
himself, for he ordered a strict search to be instituted
in the Jewish quarter, and, although nothing of an in-
criminating nature was found, imprisoned several Jews
on suspicion. Ultimately the missing boy, who had
been staying at Baalbec, reappeared in good health,
but the Jewish prisoners were not released.

On these facts being brought under the notice of
Sir Moses Montefiore, he determined to seek an interview with the French King, in order to assure his co-
religionists in future against the extraordinary male-
volence of the French diplomatic agents in the East.
Accompanied by Lady Montefiore and Dr. Loewe, he
proceeded to Paris, where M. Guizot lent a ready ear
to his complaint, and obtained for him an audience of
Louis Philippe. His Majesty, more cordial than in
1840, assured his Jewish visitor that he regarded the
Blood Accusation as a gross calumny on the Jews.
He expressed his indignation that it should have been
countenanced by any person employed by his Government, and promised that every necessary step should
be taken to prevent a repetition of the outrage. This
promise His Majesty did not forget. Sir Moses, a
short time after his return to England, had the

satisfaction of receiving the following letter from
M. Guizot :—   PARIS, *August 25th*, 1847.

"Sir,—The King has sent to me a letter,
addressed by you to him on the 9th of this month, on
the subject of the prejudice which unhappily prevails
against the Israelites in the East, and which accuses
them of using human blood in their sacrifices. You
express a wish that the agents of His Majesty in the
Levant shall not only be restrained from contributing
in any way to uphold such a prejudice, but that they
shall employ every means in their power to dis-
countenance and refute it.

"The King's Government regards the imputation
in question as false and calumnious, and its agents are
generally too enlightened to make themselves the
organs of it. The Government regrets and censures
it in the most express terms. This it is eager to do
in the case to which you refer, relative to a Christian
child at Damascus, who had disappeared in April
last, and the accusation which the agent of the French
Consulate did not scruple to prefer on that subject to
the Pasha against the Jews. No direct information
having been received on that subject, I have called for
explanations from the King's consul at Damascus,
directing him, if the case as reported to you be correct,
to express on my part the severest censure of the conduct of the individual, who, on a mere report, should
cast such imputations on a whole people.

"Accept, sir, the assurance of my most distinguished
consideration.   "GUIZOT."

The consular officers were subsequently censured, but it was only after very great difficulty and a long correspondence with the Turkish authorities that the imprisoned Jews were set free.

In 1854 Sir Moses was again at work in the interests of the Turkish Jews. He directed the attention of the Earl of Clarendon to their condition, and memorialised the British Government to include them in their schemes for the benefit of the Turkish *rayahs*. He also corresponded with Lord Stratford de Redcliffe, and obtained through him several important decisions, which helped to, protect the provincial Jews against the rapacity of local officials.

A vast amount of miscellaneous business—both foreign and domestic—was transacted by Sir Moses at this period at the Board of Deputies. Among other interesting matters, we find him, in 1854, corresponding with several Spanish noblemen on the readmission of the Jews to Spain. M. Furtado, of the Consistoire Israelite de St. Esprit, first wrote to him on the subject, and, on the recommendation of that gentleman, he formed a committee to take the matter in hand. The proposal was brought before the Cortes at Madrid some months later, but was lost by seventeen votes. After the dissolution of the Committee, Sir Moses' nephew, Mr. H. Guedalla, gave a great deal of attention to the question, and it was mainly through his exertions in 1868 and 1880, that General Prim and Senor Sagasta, eventually announced the revocation of the Edict of Expulsion of 1492.

In home affairs Sir Moses zealously continued to watch the work of Parliament in so far as it affected the interests of his co-religionists. He procured the insertion of clauses protecting Jewish marriages in the Marriage Act, corresponded with Sir George Grey on the bearing of the law on Jewish Friendly Societies, and induced the Lord Advocate of Scotland to make considerable alterations in a Bill for the Registration of Births in Scotland in order to satisfy Jewish requirements.

By far the largest portion of his time was, however, given to his brethren in the Holy Land. His labours during this busy decade include no less than three pilgrimages to Palestine. In January, 1849, the cholera broke out at Tiberias. As soon as the intelligence reached England, Sir Moses Montefiore issued an appeal to the Anglo-Jewish community. The period was one of great commercial depression, and the appeal was not successful. The subscriptions fell short of £200. Meanwhile the distress spread in all directions. The Christian Conversionist Societies availed themselves of the opportunity to push forward their propaganda, and, being well supplied with funds, were for a time exceptionally fortunate in making converts. This only added to the distress of the remaining faithful, and in March they addressed a letter to Sir Moses Montefiore, pressing him to come to their assistance. The benevolent Baronet lost no time in responding to this prayer. Accompanied by Lady Montefiore and Colonel Gawler (an ex-Governor

of South Australia, who had gone deep into schemes
for the colonization of Palestine), he started for Jerusalem early in May. He did not go further on this
occasion than the Holy City, and confined himself to
the distribution of money to the needy of all confessions. The amount he gave away is said to have
exceeded £5,000.

The second journey took place in 1855, under much
graver circumstances. The outbreak of the Russian
war in 1853 had stopped the influx of charitable contributions from Poland upon which a large number of
the Jews of Palestine depended for their daily bread.
This misfortune was aggravated by a failure of the
crops, followed by one of the severest winters ever
experienced in the Holy Land. Neither food nor
fuel was procurable, and, to crown the misery, a
severe epidemic of small-pox appeared in Jerusalem
itself. The Chief Rabbi set out for Europe to collect
funds, but died on his way at Alexandria. In England, Dr. Adler, and Sir Moses Montefiore, issued an
appeal, and succeeded in collecting nearly £20,000.
Remittances amounting to £8,000 were made to the
distressed communities, and a scheme was drawn up
to expend the balance on works of more permanent
usefulness than a mere eleemosynary distribution.
About this time a wealthy and charitable Israelite of
New Orleans, named Judah Touro, died, and, although
perfectly unknown to Sir Moses, bequeathed to him
50,000 dollars, to be applied, as he might think fit, for
the benefit of his co-religionists in Palestine. Sir

Moses resolved to proceed once more to the East to
ascertain personally the best means of expending this
legacy, as well as the remainder of the London Fund.
Accompanied by his devoted wife, Mr. and Mrs. H.
Guedalla, Dr. Loewe, and Mr. G. Kursheedt, one of
the executors of Touro's will, he set out in May, 1855.
The party journeyed *viâ* Hanover, Prague, Trieste,
Corfu, and Constantinople.   In the Turkish capital a
Firman, permitting purchases of land in Palestine,
was obtained from the Sultan by the aid of Lord
Stratford de Redcliffe.   Arrived at Jerusalem, Sir
Moses encountered considerable opposition to his
determination to devote the funds in his hands to
reproductive enterprises.   The Jews considered that
it was no part of their duty to work or to learn to
earn their living, and protested that their task in life
was sufficiently fulfilled by prayer and religious exercises.   With his usual good sense, Sir Moses persisted
in his wise resolution.   He laid the foundation-stone
of a hospital, planned the Touro Almshouses outside
the Jaffa Gate, gave orders for the erection of a wind-
mill, opened a girls' school and an industrial school,
had the public slaughtering place removed from the
Jewish quarter, where offal had been allowed to accumulate since the days of the Caliph Omar, to a place
without the city, and established agricultural colonies
at Jaffa, Safed, and Tiberias.

On his way home he stopped for a few days at
Alexandria, where he was royally entertained by the
Viceroy, Said Pasha, who in 1852 had been his guest

at Park Lane. A palace was placed at his disposal, and his meals were sent to him daily by the Pasha. Said was then full of his scheme for a canal through the Isthmus of Suez, and at his farewell interview with Sir Moses he asked him to use his influence to raise capital for the enterprise in England. Sir Moses explained how unpopular the project was, but expressed his opinion that if the Khedive would guarantee a dividend of five per cent. English money might still be forthcoming. His Highness' answer was worthy of his exalted position. "If that is the only way in which it can be obtained," he answered, "I will do without it. I have already sunk two millions of my own money in the undertaking, and that should be a sufficient guarantee for any investor."

The third Mission of this series took place in 1857, but it had no public significance.

CHAPTER XIII.

THE MORTARA CASE, ETC.

Lady Montefiore's health gives cause for anxiety—A winter in Italy
—Sad condition of the Italian Jews—Return to England—
The Mortara Case—Abduction of a Jewish boy by the Roman
Inquisition on the ground that he had been secretly baptised—
The Pope refuses to surrender him—Appeal to Sir Moses Monte-
fiore—Excitement in Europe—Another attempted secret baptism
—The pretensions of the Papacy—Action of Christian public
bodies in England—Indignation meetings—Consternation among
the Jews of the Papal States—Sir Moses Montefiore interviews
Lord Malmesbury — Representations to Napoleon III. — The
Powers remonstrate with the Papal Government—*Non Possumus*
—Sir Moses Montefiore proceeds to Rome—Negotiations with
Cardinal Antonelli—The Pope refuses to see Sir Moses or to
surrender the child—Subsequent efforts unavailing—The labours
of 1859, 1860, and 1861—Miscellaneous foreign business—The
Morocco Relief Fund—Persecution of the Syrian Christians—
Appeals of Sir Moses Montefiore and M. Crémieux—The " Blood
Accusation " tablet at Damascus.

Towards the end of 1857, Lady Montefiore's health
gave cause for much anxiety. Since the trying journey
to Russia, in the depth of the winter of 1846, she had
been more or less ailing, and her indisposition had,
unhappily, shown but little sign of yielding to medical
skill. The physicians now advised that it would be
dangerous to winter in England, and she accordingly
repaired with her husband to Italy. Here, during

several months, the affectionate pair roamed from town
to town, seeking health in change of scene and the
geniality of the climate, and finding happiness in
renewed efforts to relieve the misery of their Italian
co-religionists, still in a sad and degraded condition.
Many passages in Lady Montefiore's diaries—some
have been quoted in a preceding chapter—testify to
her deep sympathy with the Italian Hebrews. Their
oppression touched her nearly. The name she bore
had been adopted in an Italian Ghetto, and she must
have frequently thought with gratitude of the circumstance that had naturalised it in a freer clime. The
dawn of a new era for Italy was, however, already
perceptible on the political horizon. At the very
moment that Sir Moses and Lady Montefiore were
celebrating the Passover—the Jewish feast of Freedom
—at Florence, Mazzini was maturing his plans at
Genoa for another of the insurrections upon which,
but a few years later, the structure of Italian Liberty
was reared.

In July the Montefiores were again in England. A
few weeks after their return, the newspapers gave
currency to a story which re-directed their attention to
the woes of their Italian co-religionists. Quoting from
the Bologna correspondence of a Turin journal, the
Jewish Chronicle, of August 15th, 1858, published the
following intelligence :—

"On Wednesday evening, the 23rd of June, an
officer of the Papal police, accompanied by *gens d'armes*,

presented himself at the residence of Signor Mortara, an Israelite, and demanded, in the name of the Holy Office, the surrender of one of his boys. The same had been secretly baptised by the Christian servant-maid in the house, which had been betrayed to the Holy Office. The terror and consternation of the Jewish family can easily be imagined, when, despite all remonstrance, the order was executed, and the boy, on the evening of the 24th, was transferred to the Convent of the Dominicans, in order to be brought up there as a Christian."

At the ensuing meeting of the Board of Deputies on the 17th, the President's attention was called to this extraordinary story by Mr. Henry Harris—at present the Treasurer, and, we believe, the senior member of the Board. Sir Moses Montefiore replied, that he had already seen the paragraph, but that it had not taken him by surprise, as during his recent stay in Italy, he had been much saddened to observe the oppressed condition of many of the Jewish communities. He suggested that enquiries should be made, with a view to ascertaining whether the paragraph was true, and if so, what were the full details. The suggestion was agreed to, and enquiries were immediately set on foot. The story they disclosed was startling in the extreme.

On the date given in the extract quoted by the Jewish newspaper, a number of officers of the Roman Inquisition had appeared at the house of Momolo, or Solomon, Mortara, a Jew of Bologna, and without

assigning any reason, had forcibly carried off Edgar
Levi Mortara, his infant son, aged six years. Several
applications were made to the Holy Office for an
explanation of the outrage, and eventually the parents
of the abducted boy were informed, that he had been
secretly baptised when one year old by his nurse, Mina
Morisi, and that he was consequently the property of
the Church. The child, it was further stated, was ill
at the time, and the nurse, anxious for its welfare, had
consulted a druggist named Lepori, who had piously
suggested that it should be baptised. For five years
Mina had kept the story secret, but it had recently
come to the knowledge of the Inquisition through her
confessor, and the Church had determined to claim its
own. Mortara urged upon the consideration of the
Holy Office several circumstances which seemed to
indicate that the narrative of Mina Morisi had been
concocted, and that no baptism had taken place at all.
For reply, he was informed, that the tribunal of the
Inquisition had thoroughly sifted the case, and had
established the right of the Church to the child. He
then addressed himself to Cardinal Antonelli, but with
no better result, and finally he petitioned the Pope.
The Holy Father informed him that there was only
one means of recovering his son, and that, by following him into his new faith. During these unhappy
negotiations, the mother of the stolen child died of
grief.

   Together with these details came an appeal to Sir
Moses Montefiore for assistance, signed by the represen-

tatives of twenty-one Sardinian Jewish congregations. A special meeting of the Deputies was summoned, to consider this appeal and the new information. The result of their deliberations was, that a sub-committee was appointed, under the Chairmanship of Sir Moses Montefiore, to concert action with foreign Jewish bodies. In the meantime, the Italian papers circulated the story all over Europe, and a very painful sensation was caused by it, even in Catholic countries.

No action of the Papal Government more distinctly marked the abandonment of the liberal principles, by which Pius IX. had appeared to be actuated before the flight to Gaëta. Even the friends of the Papacy who had formerly regarded the Pontiff as hardly sufficiently orthodox, felt that this revival of the mediæval rights of the Inquisition was a grave error. The prevailing indignation was increased by another and similar story, reported about the same time from Genoa. A Catholic nurse, having charge of a Jewish infant, secretly took it to her confessor for baptism. The priest regretfully explained to the woman, that in Piedmont the mere act of baptism would not, as in the Papal territories, ensure the child being brought up as a Christian, but he advised her to deprive the infant of sustenance, and when it was on the point of death to bring it to him, and he would baptise it and save its soul. The conspiracy was discovered by the doctor attending the child, and, the nurse having confessed, the priest was prosecuted.

The liberal journals throughout Europe severely

commented on this and the Mortara case. The official
Government paper at Turin called on every civilised
country to demand the restitution of the boy Mortara;
the *Journal des Débats* counselled the withdrawal of
the French Ambassador at the Papal Court; and the
Siècle, the organ of Prince Napoleon, considered that
such outrages had rendered the abolition of the
Papacy a European duty. Public bodies also took
the matter in hand. At the Annual Conference of
the Evangelical Alliance, a vote of sympathy with the
Jews was unanimously agreed to on the motion of Sir
Culling Eardley, who communicated it to Sir Moses
Montefiore. The Committees of the Protestant Association,   and   the   Scottish   Reformation   Society,
petitioned for the intervention of the British Government, and indignation meetings were held in London,
New York, Philadelphia, and many other cities.

The excitement was much aggravated when the
uncompromising attitude of the Papacy was made
known through its organs in the Press. No single
detail of the story was denied: on the contrary,
the Ultramontanes congratulated themselves on what
had taken place. The *Volksblatt*, of Wurtemburg, a
clerical journal, thus frankly expounded the views of
Rome :—" The world, and all Christendom, might put
on sackcloth, yet the child, having received baptism,
must remain Catholic. Rome, after all, only wishes
to keep open to the child the path to salvation, and in
any case, the authority of the parents over their child
has to yield to the authority of the Church, and that

N

of the Pope." The Roman correspondent of the
Journal de Bruxelles, a kind of Belgian *Univers,*
affected to see the hand of God in the iniquitous proceedings. "The knowledge of what has occurred at
Bologna," he wrote, "will only exhibit in stronger
relief the wisdom of the Church, the paternal vigilance
of the Roman Government in regard to its Israelitish
subjects, and the mysterious prodigies of Grace, which
sometimes employs the means most unexpected and
most extraordinary in the eyes of the world to
manifest its force." The most shameless stories were
invented to apologise for the conduct of the Holy
Office. A favourite theory was, that by a miracle the
infant Mortara had become a convinced Catholic even
before his abduction. One of the clerical papers
related, that when he entered the institution of the
Catechumens, he perceived a statue of Our Lady of
Tears. "Why does she cry?" he asked. "She is
weeping," answered his attendants, "because the
Jews do not become converted, and are not willing
to acknowledge her divine son." "Then she is
weeping for my father and mother," replied the child.

Meanwhile the utmost consternation seized the
Jewish communities in the Papal States. Scores of
children were hurriedly sent away to the guardianship
of friends in Modena and Tuscany. A day of humiliation was publicly proclaimed by the Rabbis in the
Roman Ghetto, and appeals innumerable were addressed
to the foreign communities. Dr. Philippson, the
able and eloquent Rabbi of Magdeburg, impatient of

the diplomatic and reserved action of the eminent Jews in England and France, obtained the signatures of forty eminent German Rabbis to a memorial to the Pope, which he forwarded direct to the Vatican. About the same time the London Board of Deputies, flushed with its Damascus and Russian successes, proposed that a Jewish mission should proceed to Rome. Sir Moses Montefiore declined to entertain the suggestion, while the ordinary means of expostulating with a foreign Government were unexhausted, and it consequently fell to the ground. On the 4th October Sir Moses had an important interview with the Foreign Secretary. Lord Malmesbury assured him that Her Majesty's Government was fully alive to the importance of the question involved in the abduction of young Mortara, " as Protestants were as much exposed to such acts of injustice as Jews," and promised to make strong representations to Rome. At the same time the Central Jewish Consistory of France presented a petition to the Emperor Napoleon III., who also expressed his sympathy with the Jews, and promised to use his good offices with the Pope. The result of these negotiations was that on the 17th November all the Great European Powers—Austria not excepted—addressed private remonstrances to the Papal Government, and strongly advised the surrender of Mortara. The reply was a firm *Non possumus*.

The project of a Jewish Mission to the Pope was now revived, and at a meeting of the Board of Deputies held on the 22nd December Sir Moses Montefiore was

asked to undertake it. With his usual alacrity he
consented, although it seemed to many a forlorn
hope. The veteran Jewish champion was more sanguine than his colleagues, and in his hopefulness was
encouraged by his kind-hearted wife, who insisted on
rising from her bed of sickness to bear him company
on his new errand of mercy. By the advice of her
physicians the journey was postponed for a few weeks,
and, when ultimately it was undertaken, she was only
permitted to travel by short stages. On the Sabbath,
February 5th, special prayers to prosper the mission
were read in all the synagogues, and on the 27th,
accompanied by Dr. Hodgkin, their medical attendant,
and Mr. Kursheedt, on behalf of the American Israelites,
Sir Moses and Lady Montefiore left London. In
consequence of Lady Montefiore's continued indisposition the journey was a protracted one, and Rome
was not reached until April 5th.

Prior to his departure Sir Moses Montefiore had
been assured of the sympathy of the late Prince
Consort, and had been provided with cordial letters
of recommendation to the British diplomatic agent
at Rome. The Emperor Napoleon III. had also
promised him the unofficial support of the French
representative, the Duc de Gramont. The delicate
semi-official position of British agent at the Papal
capital was at this period filled by the late Lord
Ampthill, then Mr. Odo Russell. Sir Moses Montefiore had already met Mr. Russell at Constantinople
in 1855 when he was first *attaché* under Lord Stratford

de Redcliffe, and it was with pleasure that he renewed
the acquaintance of a young man of so charming
a presence and so liberal a disposition. Mr. Russell
proved indefatigable in his exertions to forward the
object of the Jewish mission and to procure an interview for Sir Moses with the Pope; but the greater the
pressure he brought to bear on the Holy See the
greater seemed the resistance it offered. At first a
somewhat humorous disposition to temporise was
shown. Cardinal Antonelli, doubtful as to whether
anything could be done, referred Mr. Russell to
Monsignore Talbot. In his turn Monsignore Talbot
was hopeful, thought that the Pope would receive Sir
Moses, but recommended an application to Monsignore
Paca, the Papal " Maestro di Camera." The suggested
application was made, but no reply was received. After
waiting a few days an explanation of Monsignore Paca's
silence was asked for, when it was unofficially intimated
to Sir Moses that it was not usual for the Papal
" Maestro di Camera" to enter into correspondence
with private individuals on public matters. In this
ill-timed joke some twenty days were wasted.

Another application was now made to Cardinal
Antonelli, and Mr. Russell was informed that the
Pope, considering the case terminated, had finally resolved not to see Sir Moses, but that he (the Cardinal)
was willing to receive the Jewish emissary and to
convey to His Holiness the petition he was so desirous of presenting. Accordingly, on the 28th April,
Sir Moses Montefiore had an interview with the Car-

dinal, who listened courteously to all he had to say, and promised to lay his memorial before the Holy Father. A few days later Mr. Odo Russell was requested to notify to Sir Moses that the Pope remained immoveable; that it had been determined that Edgar Mortara should be educated in the Romish faith, but that when he attained his sixteenth or seventeenth year he would be "free to follow his own judgment." In communicating this decision Mr. Russell gave sympathetic expression to his disappointment: "I fear," he wrote, "you were but too right in saying that our only hope now rests with that great God whose most holy laws have in this melancholy case been violated by the hand of man."

Sir Moses himself was deeply chagrined at his failure; but he did not despair of eventual success. He remained some ten days in Rome, in the hope of inducing the Pope to reverse his decision. Even after his return to England he frequently renewed his efforts. On the establishment of the "Alliance Israelite Universelle" in 1860 he endeavoured to concert measures with that body to induce the Pope to re-open the question; and in 1861, when Victor Emanuel was proclaimed King of Italy, he tried to interest the new monarch in the case. All, however, to no avail. Edgar Mortara remained Catholic.

How deeply the susceptibilities of the Papacy were wounded by the agitation to which this abduction had given rise is shown by a speech which the Pope delivered eight years later to the assembled canons of

the Lateran and of the Basilica of St. Peter, on the
occasion of the sixteenth anniversary of the return to
Rome from Gaëta. Among the students entered for
education as Catholics in the Lateran was Mortara,
whom Pius incidentally addressed thus :—

"You are very much endeared to me, my son,
because I have obtained you for Christ at a great
price. I have paid a very large ransom on your
account. A universal invective has broken out against
me and the Apostolic Chair. Governments and nations,
the mighty of the world, and the men of the Press,
who are also the power of the day, have declared war
against me. Even the kings have placed themselves
at the head of the campaign, and caused their Ministers
to write me diplomatic notes on your account. But I
do not wish to complain of kings. All I wish is to
refer to the outrages, calumnies, and maledictions pronounced by many individuals who appear to feel indignation that the good God should have made to you the
gift of the true faith, by removing you from the darkness of death, the same in which your family is still
immured. They complain chiefly of the misfortune
suffered by your parents because you have been
regenerated by the holy baptism, and because you have
received that instruction which God was pleased to
grant you."

Since then nothing has been heard of young Mortara,
except that in due course he was formally ordained a
priest.

One effect—fortunately only transitory—of the ill-success of the Mission to Rome appears to have been that the doughty philanthropist began to distrust his own powers to support the benevolent enterprises in which he was engaged. On his re-election to the Presidency of the Board of Deputies, at the opening of the new session in 1859, he addressed a letter to his colleagues, the burden of which was contained in the following paragraph:—

"I am constrained to add that I fear increasing years may ere long impair such efficiency as I may be able, at present, to exhibit in the performance of my duties, and I would, therefore, venture to hope that it may be agreeable to the Board to permit me to retire from the office (the presidency) at no distant date."

The feeling that prompted this letter was only momentary, and the minute-books of the Deputies contain ample evidence that their President's "efficiency in the performance of his duties" was still far from being impaired. The years 1859, 1860, and 1861 found him as busy as ever. A revival of the Blood Accusation at Galatz directed his attention to the down-trodden condition of the Roumanian Jews, and he induced Lord John Russell to make repeated representations to both Constantinople and Bucharest on the subject. He also prevailed upon the Government to use their influence to stop a brutal persecution of the Jews of Persia, who addressed a touching appeal to him, in

which they styled him " Our Prince and Father."
Through his exertions, too, Musurus Pacha obtained
redress for the Jews of Bagdad, who had been molested
in their possession of the tomb of the Prophet Ezekiel,
and some improvement was effected in the condition of
the Jews of the Ionian Islands, in consequence of his
timely representations to Mr. Gladstone on his appointment as High Commissioner to the Islands. In 1860
he raised a fund of over £12,000 for the relief of the
Jewish refugees from Morocco, who, in consequence of
the outbreak of the war with Spain, and the fanaticism
to which it gave rise among the Moors, had fled to
Gibraltar, Algesiras, and Tarifa. The condition of
these fugitives, numbering close upon 5,000, was
pitiable in the extreme, but they were received with
generous hospitality by the late General Sir William
Codrington, Governor of Gibraltar, and son of Sir
Moses Montefiore's old friend, the hero of Navarino,
and by the Spanish authorities, both ecclesiastical and
lay. The fund raised more than sufficed for their relief
and repatriation, and with the balance schools were
established at Tetuan, Tangier, and Mogador.

A more notable instance of Sir Moses Montefiore's
active benevolence occurred later in the same year,
when the Christians of Syria were attacked by the
Druses of Mount Lebanon. The disaster was terrible ;
20,000 Christians who had escaped massacre were
wandering in the open country without food or fuel,
and in peril of their lives. Immediately on reading
the news in the *Times,* Sir Moses hurried up to town,

and called personally at Printing House Square, at one
o'clock in the morning, bearing the following letter,
which he requested might be inserted :—

" SIR,—I have noticed with the deepest sympathy
the statement made last week in the House of Lords
that, owing to the recent outbreak in Syria, there are
20,000 of the Christian inhabitants, women and
children, wandering over its mountains, exposed to
the utmost peril. Being intimately acquainted with
the nature of that country and the condition of its
people, I appreciate, I am sorry to say, but too pain-
fully, the vast amount of misery that must have been
endured and which is still prevalent.

" I believe that private benevolence may do something towards the alleviation of the distress of the
unhappy multitudes now defenceless, homeless, and
destitute.

" I well know from experience the philanthropy of
my fellow-countrymen, and I venture to think that the
public would gladly and without delay contribute to
the raising of a fund to be applied, as circumstances
may require and under judicious management, for the
relief of these unfortunate objects of persecution.

" I would suggest, therefore, a small, active, and
influential Committee be at once formed, with the view
of raising subscriptions and of placing themselves in
communication with the British Consul-General at
Beyrout, and the other British Consular authorities
throughout Syria, so that assistance may be rendered

by the remittance of money and the transmission of necessary supplies ; and I take the liberty of enclosing my cheque for £200 towards the proposed fund.

"Your recent eloquent and judicious advocacy of the cause of the Syrian Christians has encouraged me to address you, and will, I trust, be a sufficient excuse for my so doing.

"I have the honour to be, Sir,

"Yours faithfully,

"MOSES MONTEFIORE.

"EAST CLIFF LODGE, RAMSGATE, *July* 10."

Curiously enough, the very next day an appeal on the same subject was addressed to the Jews of France by M. Crémieux, who called upon his co-religionists to be the first to fly to the assistance of their persecuted Christian brethren. Both appeals were very successful. Sir Moses Montefiore's Committee alone raised £22,500.

This action of the two men who, nineteen years before, had had so much difficulty in rescuing their brethren from the fanaticism of the same Syrian Christians who were now persecuted in their turn, affords a splendid illustration of the generous and forgiving spirit which Christianity is generally supposed to monopolise. But it was on broader grounds than mere generosity or magnanimity that these noble Jews took up this movement—the grounds of humanity and religious toleration. Their feelings received eloquent expression in the stirring farewell verses which a

Jewish poet, Léon Halevy, brother of the composer, addressed to the French expeditionary corps on its departure for the scene of the disorders :—

> " Pour punir des meutres infâmes,
> Vous courez aux bords syriens.
> Vengez les enfants et les femmes,
> Sauvez des frères, des chrétiens !
> Croisade du Dieu qui console,
> Tu réunis tous les croyants :
> Le juif a donné son obole
> Comme il donnera ses enfants."

And still there were fanatical hearts in Europe which this action of the Jews could not soften. One journal publicly insinuated that they were actuated by a desire to expiate the ritual murder of Father Thomas in 1840. The Jews reaped, however, an unexpected reward. During the disturbances at Damascus the Church of the Capuchins was destroyed, and with it the notorious " Blood Accusation " tablet, imputing the alleged murder of Father Thomas to the Jews, which Sir Moses Montefiore had made so many unsuccessful efforts to have removed.

CHAPTER XIV.

LADY MONTEFIORE.

Death of Lady Montefiore — Her early years — Education —
Marriage—Participation in her husband's humanitarian work
— Accompanies Sir Moses on his foreign missions — Diaries
of the journeys to Palestine—Extracts from her journals—Home
life — Anecdote illustrative of her benevolence — Communal
labours—The Funeral at Ramsgate—Memorial foundations—
The tomb on the East Cliff.

On the 24th September, 1862—the eve of the Jewish
New Year 5623—Sir Moses Montefiore experienced
the great sorrow of his life, in the death of his dear
help-mate of fifty years. The Continental tours
advised by the doctors had proved only of slight avail,
and since the return from Rome in 1859 so visibly
had her health declined that even these had had
to be abandoned. Lady Montefiore spent the last
year of her life alternately in London and Ramsgate, the object of the unceasing solicitude of her
affectionate husband. During the summer of 1862,
when the Jubilee of her married life was celebrated, a slight improvement in her health inspired
her friends with hope. "Providence," as one of her
biographers* sympathetically remarked, "restored,

* *Jewish Chronicle*, Oct. 3rd, 1862.

before the final extinction of the lamp, a portion of the
brightness which it once shed around." She was
even able to take some carriage exercise with seeming
benefit, and on the very day that she was attacked by
the sickness which finally consigned her to the grave,
arrangements had been made to take her to the Inter-
national Exhibition.

This was on the 19th September. The following
Tuesday prayers for her recovery were offered up
during morning service in Bevis Marks, and in the
afternoon in the Great Synagogue. The next day
was the Eve of the New Year, and again re-assur-
ing symptoms showed themselves. Hopes for the
prolongation of her life were entertained. She conversed with her usual serenity and pious resignation,
and even expressed some anxiety on the score of the
hospitable reception of her visitors. As the setting
sun announced the commencement of the Jewish
Festival, Sir Moses repaired to the room adjoining
hers, which formed a kind of domestic oratory, and
offered up in her hearing the prayers prescribed for
the solemn occasion. These devotions over, he re-
entered her room, and, laying his hands on her head,
pronounced the benediction, which he had never
missed for fifty years on Sabbaths and Festivals, and
then bowed his head to receive her blessing in his
turn. Re-inspired with hope, he descended to his own
room, where he cheerfully conversed with the friends
and relatives assembled round his hospitable board.
When, however, the physician came to pay his evening

visit he found the patient so weak and her pulse so low that he deemed it necessary to inform Sir Moses that the end was near. At half-past eleven Lady Montefiore peacefully breathed her last. "Her death," said the sympathetic necrologer from whom we have quoted, "was like her life—calm. She did not die—she fell asleep. She expired without a struggle, as our sages say of Moses—by a kiss."

"Good Lady Montefiore," as she was lovingly called by all who knew her, was a perfect daughter of Israel. "The woman who feareth the Eternal," said the wisest of kings, "deserveth to be praised;" and no woman's life was ever more completely or more happily governed by the fear of God than that of Judith Montefiore. Born two years before the death of Moses Mendelssohn, when the influence of the great "Regenerator of Judaism" had made itself felt upon Jewish women, to the extent of raising them to pre-side over some of the most brilliant of the continental *Salons*, Judith Montefiore readily assimilated all the culture of that restless period. At the same time she conserved the inherent sympathy with the historic aspirations of her race which constitutes the true Jewess, and which was so conspicuously absent in the characters of the brilliant circle of Hebrew women — Dorothea Mendelssohn, Henriette Herz, Rahel Levin, &c.—who were the high priestesses of German culture in her youth. Her father, Levy Barent Cohen, was already a wealthy London merchant, and a man of consequence in his Synagogue, when the first Montefiore and D'Israeli emigrated to this country; when the elder Rothschild was still a money-changer in the Frankfort Ghetto; and the London money-market was ruled by Sampson Gideon, the ancestor of the Eardley family. Levy Barent Cohen was a man whose mind had been widened by an extensive intercourse with men; but this, instead of weakening his allegiance to his faith, had enlarged his conception of his duty to it. The spirit that reigned in his home, situated in the heart of the Jewish quarter of London, was a happy combination of the religious idealism of Judea, and the cultivated spirit of the age of Gibbon and Hume, Walpole and Burke. No pains were spared to place his children on the highest mental level of the day, and the highest moral level of the Jewish Law. Taught by the best masters, and trained by the loving care of pious parents, they grew up to be accomplished and religious men and women. One of the daughters, Hannah, became the first Baroness Rothschild; Judith married Moses Montefiore on June 10, 1812.

The young couple went into house-keeping in New Court, St. Swithin's Lane, close to the home of their relatives, Mr. and Mrs. N. M. Rothschild. Here they lived happily for thirteen years, undisturbed by distracting ambitions, and prospering steadily year by year. The wife idolised her noble-minded and handsome husband; he reverenced her beautiful womanly nature. Her prudence and intelligence ruled all his undertakings; and he has never ceased to ascribe his success in life to the wisdom of her advice and her sympathy with his labours. When he retired from business her humanitarian instincts largely directed the spending of the fortune she had thus helped to accumulate. But it is impossible to write a separate account of her participation in her husband's life-work, she was so completely identified with it. A few years ago an admiring stranger expressed to Sir Moses his gratification at having been permitted to converse with the man "whose glory is engraved on the heart of every Israelite." "I am no great man," modestly answered the philanthropist. "The little good that I have accomplished, or rather that I intended to accomplish, I am indebted for it to my never-to-be-forgotten wife, whose enthusiasm for everything that is noble and whose religiousness sustained me in my career."

Lady Montefiore accompanied her husband in all his foreign missions up to 1859, and was the beneficent genius of these memorable expeditions. A thousand little incidents illustrate the enthusiasm with which she seconded her husband's labours. When in the Holy Land, in 1838, she took part personally in the ceremony of receiving a new Scroll of the Law in the Synagogue at Safed; in another Synagogue she decorated the Scroll during divine service; and at one of the Jerusalem houses of worship she piously lit the lamps in front of the altar, and before the whole congregation. In the latter city she promoted the formation of a

Ladies' Charity for the relief of the sick.   How often she officiated as godmother in the course of this tour it is difficult to say.   A farewell address, presented to Sir Moses by the Portuguese and German congregations of Jerusalem, concludes with a reference to Lady Montefiore which indicates how thoroughly she had engaged the affections of the people of the Holy City:—

"Blessed be the Eternal Lord of Hosts, who failed not to send a Redeemer to his land, and succour, from the Majesty of his power, to the offspring of his righteous servants.   On the head of his people he has placed a helmet, and in his great mercy has appointed his servant Moses to exalt the light of his resplendent might, and to make it a wonder before all the nations of the earth.   By the blessing of the Almighty did Moses obtain the accomplished, honoured, and most virtuous Lady Yehoodit (Judith).   May all the blessings of ladies in their tents rest upon her ! "

During the journey to Russia in 1846, when her health was already breaking, she was indefatigable in her efforts to alleviate the misery she saw everywhere around her.   A Polish Jew, writing from Wilna to Mr. Councillor Barnett, of Birmingham, shortly after Sir Moses' visit, said:—"His Lady (long may her life be spared !) had not a dry eye for weeping over the extreme distress she here beheld."   The wife and daughters of the Russian Governor paid her a ceremonious visit, and expressed in handsome terms the admiration she had inspired among all classes.   At Berlin, on the

homeward journey, seventeen young maidens, some
dressed in white and others in blue, presented her
with a laurel crown wreathed with white roses, on an
embroidered velvet cushion. To her conduct during
the eventful mission to Mehemet Ali in 1840 her
husband paid a public tribute in a speech he delivered
on his return home. " To Lady Montefiore," he said,
" I owe a debt of gratitude ; her counsels and zeal for
our religion and love to our brethren were at all times
conspicuous. They animated me under difficulties
and consoled me under disappointments." In the
earlier journeys Sir Moses had frequent occasion to
marvel at her quiet courage. Lady Montefiore relates
in her diaries that when crossing the Alps in 1827 he
admiringly dubbed her " a little Napoleon." Also
during the severe weather which they encountered in 1838
between Alexandria and Malta her fearlessness was so
conspicuous that he playfully declared she was "a little
Admiral."

Lady Montefiore's diaries, two of which were printed
some years ago for private circulation, afford a sufficient insight into the manifold beauties of her nature.
They are charming reading, and illustrate every side
of a richly varied character. The first is a record of
the journey to the East in 1827. It seems to be the
less studied work of the two, and is full of delicious
little peep-holes to her mind. The following passage
written at Naples delightfully illustrates the gaiety
and thorough womanliness of her disposition :—

" We landed opposite the *Hotel della Victoria,* and

having been welcomed on our return by Mr. Martigny,
we inquired if the apartments we occupied on our late
visit were disengaged; he answered that they were
occupied by a lady and gentleman. 'Their names?'
'The Baroness and Baron Anselme de Rothschild!'
In an instant we were together. What a delightful
surprise! How handsome she looks! and the baby,
what a fine fat boy! We dined with them, and Baron
Charles engaged us to go to the Opera. It was a
grand night, in honour of the Duke of Calabria's natal
day: and all the company were in full dress. Returned
from San Carlo: a brilliant spectacle, all the royal
family were present. The ladies in diamonds and
feathers had a fine effect in this handsome theatre."

After a stormy day on the road Lady Montefiore's
spirit of domesticity peeps out in this pretty word-
picture :—

"Now seated by a comfortable fire with an affectionate companion, the table nicely prepared for tea,
and kettle boiling, the rattling of the windows and
boisterous sounds make me the more sensible of
present enjoyments and the storm we have just
escaped. Surely the German saying is true, '*Getheilte
Freude' ist ganze Freude ; getheilter Schmerz ist halber
Schmerz !* "

Lady Montefiore was an excellent whist-player.
There is a touch of humour in the following reference
to this *penchant* of hers :—

"The firmament presented a more than usually

majestic appearance : the golden and bright tinted
clouds, Sicily bordering the horizon on the right, on
the left Malta, and Gozo opposite. A chilly atmosphere, however, made me hasten to quit this varied
scene for the more domestic and comfortable one of a
game at cards, though I confess not quite so sublime
and rational. Dr. Madden joined us in the rubber."

Her observations on the Holy Land are conceived
in a spirit of singular loftiness. Kayserling, in his
" Jüdischen Frauen," compares their style to that of
Schubert's "Reise in das Morgenland." Of Jerusalem
she thus wrote in 1827 :—

" There is no city in the world which can bear comparison in point of interest with Jerusalem,—fallen,
desolate, and abject, even as it appears—changed as it
has been since the days of its glory. The capitals of
the ancient world inspire us, at the sight of their
decaying monuments, with thoughts that lead us far
back into the history of our race, with feelings that
enlarge the sphere of our sympathies, by uniting our
recollections of the past with the substantial forms of
things present; but there is a power in the human
mind by which it is capable of renewing scenes as
vividly without external aids, as when they are most
abundant. There are no marble records on the plain
of Marathon, to aid the enthusiasm of the traveller,
but he feels no want of them : and thus it is, whenever any strong and definite feeling of our moral
nature is concerned, we need but be present on the
spot where great events occurred, and if they were

intimately connected with the fate of multitudes, or
with the history of our religion, we shall experience a
sentiment of veneration and interest amounting to
awe, and one above all comparison nobler than that
which is excited chiefly by the pomp or wonders of
antiquity. It is hence that Jerusalem, notwithstanding
the ploughshare of the heathen, infinitely exceeds in
interest Rome, Athens, and even the cities of Egypt,
still abounding, as they do, in monuments of their
former grandeur, and wonderful and venerable as they
are above all other places on which the mere temporal
history of mankind can bestow a sanctity. No place
has ever suffered like Jerusalem :—it is more than
probable that not a single relic exists of the city that
was the joy of the whole earth : but the most careful
and enthusiastic of travellers confess, that when they
have endeavoured to find particular marks for their
footsteps, there was little to encourage them in the
investigation. But it depends not for its power of
inspiring veneration on the remains of temples and
palaces ; and were there even a less chance of speculating with success respecting the sites of its ancient
edifices, it would still be the city towards which every
religious and meditative mind would turn with the
deepest longing. It is with Jerusalem as it would be
with the home of our youth, were it levelled with the
earth, and we returned after many years, and found
the spot on which it stood a ploughed field, or a deserted
waste : the same thoughts would arise in our hearts as
if the building was still before us, and would probably

be rendered still more impressive from the very circumstance that the ruin which had taken place was complete."

In reference to the Pyramids, Lady Montefiore has some remarks which are equally notable :—

" Time has been longer conquered by the Pyramids than by any other production of human art. They lift their strange forms above that sea of ages which holds in its bosom all other relics of that hoar antiquity to which they belong : they were old in days which are the remotest in authentic history ; and instead of their crumbling down to the earth, like other monuments of men's labour, it appears as if they are only doomed to disappear when the earth shall have gradually accumulated its own dust and ashes around them. They truly merit the appellation of one of the seven wonders of the world ; and it is next to impossible to contemplate them without experiencing a keen desire to determine the motives of those who built them, and the object for which they were erected."

Lady Montefiore's theory on this subject illustrates the religious side of her character :—

" There is every reason to believe that religion furnished both the motives and the design from which they sprang ; and the most rational antiquaries agree in considering them in the light of temples, certain portions of which were appropriated for the burial of the dead. The numerous idols still to be found in them, and the splendid mausoleums of their chambers, afford the strongest proof of the correctness of this idea. There is, however, a general principle which affords, it may be observed without presumption, a still more powerful proof of their sacred origin. Religion is the only motive sufficiently strong, and sufficiently enduring, to inspire men with such vast designs; and in the early ages of the world this was especially the case. A few great principles of thought governed all their actions; and among these, as it must ever be when the economy of society is simple, the fear or the love, the desire to propitiate, or the hope of pleasing, the Deity, will always be found predominant over the rest."

On the way home Dr. Madden was among the fellow-travellers of the Montefiores, and contributed not a little to their enjoyments of the voyage. He composed a song on the storm, and wrote a poem on the New Year, to which Lady Montefiore added a verse. Dr. Madden's poem ran thus :—

> " It is a wayward, strange delight,
>   That mankind feel to part with time—
>   To fix upon the old year's flight
>   For festive joys in every clime.
>
> " To me this season's not of joy,
>   But sadness more, for it doth seem,
>   In its brief passage, to destroy
>   Another trace of life's short dream.
>
> " The old year passes, and the flow
>   Of youthful feeling sinks apace,
>   The new advances, and the glow
>   Of early ardour yields its place.

> " Each year the hand of age falls cold
> And colder on the heart ; and all
> Our fondest hopes, as we grow old,
> Flit by, like phantoms past recall."

The verse added by Lady Montefiore was characteristic :—

> " But is there not one cheering hope yet left ?
> That which should animate succeeding years ?
> For if of transient joys we are bereft,
> Our trust in heaven will chase away our tears."

The second diary is a record of the journey of 1838. That expedition, it will be remembered, had a distinctly Jewish and humanitarian aim, and Lady Montefiore's journal fully reflects its *quasi*-public character. It is less of a personal diary, and more of a serious narrative of travel than the former work. Full of important memoranda on Jewish questions, it forms a really useful book of reference on the condition of the Continental and Eastern Jewish communities forty-five years ago. The facts mentioned by Lady Montefiore have already been summarised in a preceding chapter. There remains, however, several interesting passages that may be quoted here.

On the way to Ghent the diarist amused herself with reading Bulwer's last new novel, " Leila, or the Siege of Granada," a work in which there is a strong Jewish element. These are Lady Montefiore's shrewd reflections on the book :—

" I admire Mr. Bulwer's delineations, but not his sentiments, which give a colouring to the character of a people tending to support prejudices, so galling to the feelings of those who are as sensible to honour, generosity, and virtue, as those of more prosperous nations. It may be policy to exaggerate faults, but is it justice to create them solely to gratify opponents? It is too much the practice of authors engaged in the production of light literature, to utter sentiments existing only in their own imaginations, and, by ascribing them to others, to disseminate a baneful prejudice against multitudes who feel indignant at finding themselves the subjects of unjust suspicion."

The condition of the Jews at Nice evokes the following sympathetic remarks :—

"In the course of conversation we learned that this country was greatly wanting in liberality, and that the members of our community are subject to much oppression, and many disadvantages. How long will the powerful oppress the weak, and endeavour to stifle the energies of their fellow beings? One consolation remains under such a state of things. Conscientious feelings, well maintained under oppression, ever excite the sympathy and admiration of independent and virtuous minds."

At Rome, where the orthodox Jewess was delighted to find that divine service was conducted " without the introduction of modern airs in the chanting," she was a witness, among other sights, of the ceremony of the Pope's benediction of the people. On the inconsistencies of this ceremony she reflects very pointedly :—

" His Holiness washed the feet of twelve pilgrims, each of whom received a new suit of clothes and a medal. His Holiness then waited on them at dinner, assisted by several Cardinals, who knelt to the Pope when handing him the dishes to serve to the poor men. These acts of humiliation may be well intended, and doubtless have some good tendency, teaching the individual, however exalted in rank, the virtue of a humble spirit, and that religion surpasses every other distinction ; but, on the other hand, the accompanying pomp and display may be regarded as somewhat lessening the merit of the action. The table was decorated with all the magnificence of regal state ; and the pilgrims, after regaling themselves with every luxury, were permitted to take away the remains of everything that was served to them."

The arrival in Egypt is sketched with great animation :—

" It was at an early hour that I heard the call to make ready the anchor—a most satisfactory sound. At seven o'clock we dressed and went on deck to have a sight of Pompey's Pillar and Cleopatra's Needle, objects bright and familiar to our memory. The pilot now came on board, and we were soon surrounded by Turkish boats, turbans, and divers-coloured costumes. The quarantine boat then approached, and our bill of health was demanded. Captain G——, on handing it out, said that it might be taken with the hand; but no! a long pair of scissors, more resembling a pair of tongs, were stretched forth, and by these the document was held till perused by the janissary. When it had been ascertained that all were healthy, this singular instrument was laid down, and the paper taken by the hand. A corpulent Turk, the British Consul's head dragoman, came on board, and the letter-bags were handed out; while, amidst the vociferations and unintelligible jargon of the Arabs, numerous boats surrounded the ship, the anxious masters of which, pleading for themselves, or the hotels for which they were employed, could only be kept off so as to afford a free passage from the vessel by a copious sprinkling of water."

Lady Montefiore is particularly happy in her description of Scriptural scenes. On reaching Beyrout she writes :—

"At an early hour the land of Syria was in view, and at seven o'clock the anchor was cast in the Bay of Beyrout. We were soon on deck, and magnificent was the scene presented to our view. Immediately before us rose the lofty mountains of Lebanon, precipitous, and crowned with snow, in strange contrast with the yellow barren shore, and in stranger still the glowing sky, and the dazzling rays of the sun, which threw their effulgence far and wide over every object that the eye could reach, wrapping the town of Sidon itself in a blaze of morning splendour."

A still more picturesque passage is written after leaving Safed :—

" At a short distance forward, the beautiful lake of Tiberias, part of which some of our suite called Beer Miriam, presented itself to view. A delicious valley then appeared to our right, extending to the famous village Akbara, mentioned in the Talmud. After a continued ascent for some distance, we began to descend, and noticed to our left the rock called Akebi, in which are extensive caves, where the inhabitants took refuge during a former attack on Safed by the Druses. The rock is also famous for its number of bees ; and when we witnessed the honey exuding from it, and filling the air with its fragrance, how forcibly did the words of the Psalmist recur to our minds. ' And with honey out of the rock would I have satisfied thee.' We then passed the cross-roads, of which the right leads to Acre, the left to Damascus ; and soon after, several villages and valleys, filled with luxuriant corn, interspersed with fig, olive, mulberry, and pomegranate trees, covered with bright blossoms, delighted the sight. On the road lay some pieces of stone, which our mukkarries amused themselves with striking ; the sound returned was like that of a fine bell, verifying the saying of Scripture—' A land whose stones are iron, and out of whose hills thou mayest dig brass.' "

Again on reaching Gilead :—

" Having seated ourselves in a small cavern, formed

in the rocks of Mount Djalood, the ancient Gilead,
how many solemn though pleasurable thoughts floated
through our minds! 'Is there no balm in Gilead?
Is there no physician there? Why then is not the
health of the daughter of my people recovered?'
Jer. viii. 22. So sighed the prophet in times when
the sorrows of Israel were as yet but beginning. Oh,
how does the heart of the pilgrim cling to and yearn
over the later words of the same prophet, 'I will bring
Israel again to his habitation, and he shall feed on
Carmel and Bashan, and his soul shall be satisfied
upon Mount Ephraim and Gilead. In those days, and
in that time, saith the Lord, the iniquity of Israel
shall be sought for, and there shall be none; and the
sins of Judah, and they shall not be found; for I will
pardon them whom I reserve.'"

Approaching Jerusalem the narrative becomes very
striking:—

"What the feelings of a traveller are, when among
the mountains on which the awful power of the
Almighty once visibly rested, and when approaching
the city where he placed his name; whence his law
was to go forth to all the world; where the beauty of
holiness shone in its morning splendour; and to which,
even in its sorrow and captivity, even in its desolation,
the very Gentiles, the people of all nations of the
earth, as well as its own children, look with profound
awe and admiration.—Oh! what the feelings of the
traveller are on such a spot, and when listening to the

enraptured tones of Israel's own inspired king, none
can imagine but those who have had the privilege and
the felicity to experience them.   As we drew nearer to
Jerusalem the aspect of the surrounding country
became more and more sterile and gloomy.   The land
was covered with thorns and briars, and sadly did the
words of the Psalmist rise to the thoughts—' He
turneth rivers into a wilderness, and the water-springs
into dry ground ; a fruitful land into barrenness, for
the wickedness of them that dwell therein ! ' (Ps. cvii.
33, 34).   But solemn as were the feelings excited by
the melancholy desolateness of the rocky hills and
valleys through which we were passing, they were
suddenly lost in a sense of rapture and indescribable
joy—for now the Holy City itself rose full into view,
with all its cupolas and minarets reflecting the splen
dour of the heavens.   Dismounting from our horses,
we sat down and poured forth the sentiments which so
strongly animated our hearts in devout praises to Him
whose mercy and providence alone had thus brought
us, in health and safety, to the city of our fathers.
Pursuing our path, we soon passed the tomb of Nabi
Shemuel (the Prophet Samuel), and at about five
o'clock reached the gates of the Holy City.   Khassan
having dismounted, his mule instantly ran off, and
notwithstanding the efforts of his master, of Ibrahim,
Armstrong, and Bekhór, kept them in chase till he
stopped on the Mount of Olives.   There Dr. Loewe
proposed we should encamp ; but Montefiore, being
greatly fatigued, considered that it would be better to

select a less elevated situation.   We accordingly
proceeded to the valley fixed on by the mukkarries;
but soon discovered that we had committed a serious
error in choosing a spot whence the air was excluded,
and which the contagious atmosphere of the town was
so much more likely to infect; we, therefore, ascended
a steep path, cut out of the mountain, almost like a
flight of stairs, but which our horses scaled with their
customary ease and safety.   The pure air of the Mount
of Olives breathed around us with the most refreshing
fragrance; and as we directed our attention to the
surrounding view, Jerusalem was seen in its entire
extent at our feet, the Valley of Jehoshaphat to our
left, and in the distance the dark misty waves of the
Dead Sea."

Before leaving the Holy Land the travellers visited
the tomb of King David and the remnant of Solomon's
temple.   Both subjects Lady Montefiore treats with
sympathetic dignity.   The first she thus describes:—

"Having entered a spacious vaulted chamber,
painted in Turkish fashion, we saw at the further end
a trellised door, and being led to the spot, we beheld
through the lattice the sacred and royal deposit of the
best and noblest of kings.   Yes! there we contemplated the resting-place of all that was mortal of him
whom the electing wisdom of the Almighty had placed
on the throne of a kingdom, which had, at first, but
the Lord himself for its king: of him who, resplendent
as he was in royal dignity, was still more glorious for

those gifts of wisdom, of holiness, and heavenly genius, in the sublime power of which he moulded the thoughts of countless generations to forms of celestial beauty, and still furnishes worshippers of every clime and nation with the purest and noblest language of devotion. In the records of his experience, whether tried by affliction and humbled by the weight of conscious sin, or filled with the gladdening feelings of hope, the heart never fails to read revelations of its deepest secrets, to discover more of its state and nature, and to learn better how to adore the eternal Spirit, who spoke by the mouth of this kingly prophet."

The reference to the remnant of the Temple concludes with a beautiful aspiration :—

"We yesterday went to inspect the western wall of the temple of Solomon. How wonderful that it should have so long defied the ravages of time ! The huge stones seem to cling together; to be cemented by a power mightier than decay, that they may be a memorial of Israel's past glory ; and, oh! may they not be regarded as a sign of future greatness, when Israel shall be redeemed, and the whole world shall, with one accord, sing praises to Israel's God ! "

Many more extracts might be made from these charming volumes, but we have quoted enough to justify the highest estimate of Judith Montefiore's character. The experience of those who knew her is that her soul walked out in these pages.

P

With her literary powers she united other attain-
ments of a high order.   She spoke French, German,
and Italian with ease, and much of her leisure during
the voyage of 1838 she devoted to the study of Arabic
under Dr. Loewe, with whom she likewise read Hebrew
literature.   She was also an accomplished musician,
playing the piano and guitar, and singing sweetly.
It was her delight to join with her melodious voice in
the hymns which on Sabbaths and festivals resounded
in her house. Her home life was a pattern. "Possessed
of a refined mind," said the Chief Rabbi in his dis-
course over her grave, " of the most cultivated taste,
she still, in a quiet unassuming way, devoutly fulfilled
the duties of a Jewish wife.   To mention only one of
these, never, not even during severe illness, did she
neglect to light the Sabbath lamp—she who herself
was the light of her home."   Her generosity knew no
bounds ; no one ever sought help of her and was
denied.   Her husband still tells a story illustrative
of her large hearted benevolence.   Among those who
had frequently received money from him was a co-
religionist of the most undeserving kind.   Again and
again had Sir Moses sent him cheques, and again and
again had the irrepressible beggar applied for assistance.   Sir Moses, having discovered that his money was
spent in gambling, informed his wife that he should give
the ne'er-do-well no more help; whereupon Lady Montefiore opened her own cheque-book, and wrote a cheque,
remarking, " My dear, I think we had better send him
something; I am sure nobody else will, if we do not."

In communal affairs she was by no means inactive. At school prize distributions she was a familiar figure, and she worked, together with her sister the Baroness de Rothschild and her niece, Baroness Lionel de Rothschild, in the organisation and administration of many philanthropic enterprises. At the Jews' Free School and the schools of the Sephardic community she was a frequent visitor. The Jewish Ladies Loan and Visiting Society was started partly under her auspices.

On the Fast of Guedaliah—three days after her death—the remains of this pious daughter of Israel were laid to their eternal rest, close by the Synagogue which she and her husband had founded and endowed thirty-two years before, near their Ramsgate home. A large gathering of Christians and Jews testified in sympathetic silence to the affection in which she was held. The day being Sunday, the shops in the adjoining town were closed as a matter of course; but in all the churches the ministers feelingly alluded to the sad event, while the vessels in the harbour had their flags at half-mast.

The sorrowing husband gave large sums in her name to every synagogue in the United Kingdom, and to the inmates of the Jewish orphan asylums. He built in her memory a College at Ramsgate where aged Rabbis study and expound the Law, and he also founded prizes and scholarships for girls and boys at the several Jewish public schools. The Jewish community perpetuated her name by establishing the

Judith Lady Montefiore Convalescent Home at South Norwood. At East Cliff Lodge her memory is still fondly cherished. None of the old-fashioned furniture has been altered since she superintended the household, and the same damask curtains hang at the windows and surround the beds. Portraits of her hang in many of the rooms, and every scrap of linen used in the house is marked with a Hebrew *in memoriam* inscription. Even her custom of feeding the wild birds and encouraging them to frequent the dense shrubberies round the Lodge is still maintained with scrupulous exactitude. In fact it may be said that all the wishes she expressed while living are faithfully observed now she is dead.

On the road between Bethlehem and Jerusalem is a small white-domed structure which the guides point out as the tomb of Rachel. The pilgrim who enters the building may yet read on the walls the inscription " Judith Montefiore," traced there fifty-seven years ago by a hand now twenty-two years stilled in death. On the landward side of the ridge of a high cliff in the county of Kent, embowered in the evergreen foliage of cypress and arbor-vitæ, and within sound of the restless waves of the North Sea, is a fac-simile of this historic tomb. It covers the earthly remains of Judith Montefiore.

CHAPTER XV.

THE bereaved husband spent the winter of 1862—
63 in seclusion at Nice. He was meditating another
pilgrimage to the Holy Land, when letters reached
him expressing fears lest the death of the Sultan
Abdul-Medjid might change the benevolent attitude
of the Turkish Government towards its Jewish subjects. This rendered an alteration in his plans
necessary, and he proceeded to Constantinople instead
of Jerusalem. The new Sultan Abdul-Aziz, received

him graciously in audience, and confirmed the Firmans granted by his late brother. His Majesty spontaneously assured his visitor, that his Jewish subjects should have his full protection, the same as all other religious denominations in his realm. Sir Moses had also several interviews with the Grand Vizier, who gave him an official letter to the Pasha of Jerusalem, acquainting him with the Sultan's confirmation of the Firmans. Returning to England towards the end of June, the venerable baronet retired to his seat near Ramsgate, where he passed his time superintending the important works he had planned in memory of his beloved consort. The events of the latter part of the year, however, called him from his sorrowing retirement.

Among the letters received at East Cliff Lodge on the last day of October, 1863—ten days after Sir Moses' eightieth birthday—was a bulky packet bearing the seal of the Gibraltar Jewish congregation. The day being Sabbath, it was not opened till sundown. Its contents were, however, of pressing importance. At Saffi, a seaport on the West coast of Morocco, a Spaniard had died suddenly, and suspicions of foul play, probably poisoning, had been aroused in the mind of the Spanish Consul. In his official capacity he called upon the Moorish authorities to investigate the case, and they, in great trepidation, cast about for a convenient scapegoat. The procedure was singular. No steps were taken to ascertain whether there were any facts to establish the cause of death, or to show

that it had a connection with crime; but the most
convenient person was forthwith arrested and examined
under the scourge and other kinds of torture.
Israelites being the least protected of the population,
the culprit was sought among their body, and it being
discovered that a Jewish lad, about fourteen years of
age, Jacob Wizeman by name, had resided in the
family of the deceased, he was seized and " examined."
There is little variation in the methods of human
brutality; and from this point the story recounted by
the chiefs of the Gibraltar Jewish congregation, bore
a close resemblance to many other narratives of
Eastern persecution, which had in previous years
engaged Sir Moses Montefiore's sympathies. After
persisting for a long time in the assertion of his
innocence, Wizeman yielded to the pressure of protracted agony, and acquiesced in the suggestion that
poison had been used. Further instalments of torture
induced him to denounce, one by one, eleven persons
whose names were mentioned to him. These were
arrested, and one, Eliahu Lalouche, was also subjected to examination by torture, but without wringing
any confession from him. The lad, when released,
re-asserted his innocence; this, however, did not save
him. His confession being on record, he was condemned to death by the Moorish authorities and
publicly executed, the Spanish Consul acquiescing in
the sentence, notwithstanding the irregular manner in
which the conviction had been obtained. Of the other
prisoners eight were thrown into prison, and three

sent to Tangier, where one of them, Eliahu Lalouche, was executed. These events had produced
the greatest dismay among the Jewish population,
and from Tangier urgent appeals for help had been
despatched to Gibraltar, whence they were forwarded
to England.

This shocking story aroused Sir Moses Montefiore's
active benevolence to a high pitch. Early the next
morning he was on his way to London, and by noon was
hunting up the Secretary and Under Secretary of State
for Foreign Affairs. Earl Russell was out of town,
but, though it was Sunday, Sir Moses succeeded in
gaining an interview with the Under Secretary, Mr.,
afterwards Sir Austin H. Layard. Telegraphic communication was resorted to, and in a very short time
the continental wires were at work, conveying the
instructions of the Foreign Office to Sir John
Drummond Hay, the British Ambassador at Tangier,
to use all the influence of his position, to obtain at
least a temporary suspension of further executions.
Such was the cordial alacrity with which the British
Government gave its important assistance, that this
despatch anticipated a telegram previously sent by Sir
Moses Montefiore by some hours.

In the course of the following week, Sir Moses
Montefiore laid the facts that had come to his knowledge before the Board of Deputies, and an active
correspondence was set on foot with Gibraltar and
Tangier. It was ascertained that both the Moorish
and Spanish authorities were averse to the release of

the prisoners, although their innocence seemed to be completely established. Beyond this, the correspondence revealed an extremely sad state of affairs among the Jews of Morocco, and a terrible condition of lawlessness in the whole country. Sir Moses rightly judged that something more was necessary to assure the well-being of the Jews than the mere rescue of the prisoners of the moment. He came to the conclusion that outrages such as had been enacted at Saffi were inevitable in a country where the Jews were unprotected by law. He consequently intimated to the Board of Deputies his readiness, notwithstanding his advanced years, to proceed to Morocco, and to endeavour to obtain at the hands of the Sultan, a definite legal status for his co-religionists. Needless to say, the offer was gratefully accepted.

Preparations for the new expedition were rapidly made, and on the 15th November the veteran champion of Israel was ready to leave England. His suite consisted of his nephew, Mr. H. Guedalla, whose father was a native of Morocco and extensively known as a merchant in the country, Mr. Sampson Samuel, the solicitor and secretary to the Board of Deputies, and Dr. Hodgkin, his physician and attached friend, whose feelings were warmly engaged in the undertaking. Besides these gentlemen he was accompanied by an experienced courier and two trusty servants. On the Sabbath preceding the departure of the Mission Sir Moses visited the principal London Synagogues, where special prayers to " crown his efforts with success,"

and to "'cause him to return in safety to his beloved
home " were offered up by order of the Chief Rabbi.
Two days later the party assembled at Dover, and the
venerable baronet having piously deposited a new
scroll of the Law in the local synagogue, they crossed
over to Calais in the steamer. Tuesday evening they
spent at Paris, and the following morning before daybreak were again *en route.* At Bordeaux Sir Moses
inspected the works of the Imperial Continental Gas
Association, of which he is still President, and then
proceeded to Bayonne, where he halted for the Sabbath.
The next day the party pursued their journey, partly
by rail and partly by diligence, across the Pyrenees to
St. Sebastian, whence they journeyed *viâ* Burgos to
Madrid.

Here Sir Moses placed himself at once in communication with Sir J. F. Crampton, the British Ambassador
to the Court of Spain, to whom he carried letters of
introduction from the Home Government. The
Minister received him cordially, and frequent interviews took place between them, both at the British
Embassy and the Hotel de los Principes, where Sir
Moses had taken up his abode. Visits were also paid
to and received from the Marquis of Miraflores, the
Prime Minister, the Duke of Tetuan, General Prim,
and other persons of distinction to whom he was
introduced both by the British Ambassador and his
friend and relative, M. Weisweiller, who had long
resided in Madrid, and whose high position as a
banker and the Consul of more than one foreign Power

rendered him highly influential even with the Court. Although these introductions were the means of procuring for Sir Moses the most friendly feeling on the part of the Queen's Ministers and distinct assurances that the proceedings at Saffi had not been dictated by any unkindness or prejudice on their part, as well as letters to the Spanish Minister at Tangier, written to facilitate his object, he was naturally unwilling to quit Madrid until he had had an interview with Queen Isabella herself. This took place on the 30th November. Sir Moses was introduced by Sir J. F. Crampton, and the audience, which was private, lasted a considerable time. Sir Moses wrote home that he was highly gratified with the gracious and kind manner of his reception.

During the stay in the Spanish capital it had transpired that M. Weisweiller was intimately acquainted with Don Antonio Merry, father of the Spanish Minister at Tangier, and Sir Moses consequently stopped at Seville on his way to the coast, saw Don Antonio, and obtained a friendly letter of introduction to his son. At Cadiz the fatigue of incessant travelling began to tell on the energetic philanthropist's health, and he was obliged to keep his bed. His vigorous constitution, however, soon enabled him to overcome his indisposition, and the 10th December saw him on board the French steam frigate *Gorgone*, on his way to Tangier. The arrival at the Moorish port is amusingly sketched by Dr. Hodgkin, who wrote an account of the tour :—

" Our kind captain and his officers had ingeniously

contrived, on the spur of the occasion, by the help of a mattress and cordage, a kind of portable couch or car, in which, for want of a suitable landing-place, Sir Moses might be borne over a considerable extent of shallow water between the boat and the shore. His porters and a great many of the labouring class of Israelites were wading, and his superior size thus conspicuously moving over the water, surrounded by a shabby amphibious group, appeared to me like a travestied representation of Neptune among the Tritons."

The Jews of the town received Sir Moses with enthusiasm. M. Pariente, a prominent Israelite, vacated and expressly fitted up his commodious residence for the occupation of the Hebrew Embassy, and no sooner were they housed than deputations waited upon them from the communities of Tetuan, Alcazar, Arzila, Laraish, Mequinez, Mogador, Azamor, and Fez. The following day they attended divine service in a new Synagogue erected by M. Joseph Eshriguy, who dedicated the sacred edifice for the benefit of the poor in commemoration of the Mission. Visits were then paid to Sir John D. Hay, the British representative; his Spanish colleague, Don Francisco Merry y Colon; and the Moorish Minister of Foreign Affairs, Sid Mohammed Bargash. The result of these interviews was the release of the two Israelites in prison at Tangier, and a promise that representations should be made to the Saffi local authorities in reference to the remaining prisoners within their jurisdiction.

Sir Moses did not confine his attention to the Jews. During his stay at Tangier he was one day visited by a large deputation of Moors, about fifty in number, who, with their chiefs, had come from a distant part of the country to appeal to him to intercede for the release of one of their tribe, who had been imprisoned during two years and a half on suspicion of having murdered two Israelties, but had not been brought to trial. Gratified at this display of confidence in his sense of justice on the part of the native population, generally so hostile to Jews, Sir Moses made careful inquiries into the case, and, finding that the man's guilt had not been proved, promptly interceded with the authorities. In a few hours the prisoner's chains were removed, and he was brought by the members of his tribe to return thanks to his deliverer. Sir Moses availed himself of the opportunity to urge the grateful Moors to show kindness and afford protection to his co-religionists ; and they readily gave their solemn promise that all Jews travelling in their district should be safe.

Having determined to proceed into the interior, to the City of Morocco, in order to thank the Sultan for his release of the Tangier prisoners, and to petition His Majesty to grant to his Jewish and Christian subjects the same protection and privileges as were enjoyed by their Moorish co-citizens, Sir Moses now returned to Gibraltar, in order to take shipping round the West coast to Saffi or Mogador. Before leaving Tangier he made a careful examination of the condition of the Jewish community, gave a great deal of good advice to its chiefs, and subscribed largely to its several charities.   Noticing that the means of educating Jewish girls of the poorer class were very inadequate, he gave a sum of £300 to found a new girls' school in memory of Lady Montefiore.   At Gibraltar Sir Moses was cordially received by the Governor, General Sir William Codrington, with whom he had been in correspondence four years before in relation to the Jewish refugees from Morocco.   As a mark of respect, a military band was ordered to play before his house in the evening, and the Governor gave a banquet in his honour.   A gratifying proof of the benevolent interest of the Home Government in the Mission was afforded by H.M.S. *Magicienne* being placed at Sir Moses Montefiore's disposal by Earl Russell, who telegraphed his instructions to Malta, where the frigate was staying.

On the 6th January the party again embarked, and three days later, in the teeth of contrary winds, arrived off Saffi.   Here, as at almost every port on the West African coast, the landing is very difficult, and the surf ran so high that all idea of going on shore had to be abandoned.   The *Magicienne* saluted the fort with several guns, and the compliment was promptly returned.   A conversation was carried on with the town by signals, when, to Sir Moses Montefiore's great satisfaction, he was informed that the Saffi prisoners had been liberated.   The arrival of the Sultan's escort, destined to accompany the venerable

Jew to the capital, was also announced. On the
following day a safe landing was effected at Mogador;
and during the afternoon of Sunday, the 17th January,
the octogenarian philanthropist, with a numerous
escort, set out on his difficult journey across the desert
of the Atlas to the City of Morocco.

Sir Moses Montefiore has himself briefly described
this interesting excursion in his letters to his nephew,
Mr. J. M. Montefiore, who acted as President of the
Board of Deputies during his uncle's absence. In a
letter dated " Morocco, the 26th January," he
writes :—

" Were I to attempt even an outline of each day's
events I should greatly exceed the limits of a letter;
suffice it, therefore, to say that we happily accomplished our journey from Mogador to this city in eight
days, resting on the Sabbath. During this period we
were subjected to a broiling sun by day, and cold and
occasionally heavy dews and high winds by night;
nevertheless, we have borne our fatigues well; fortunately we escaped rain, otherwise, apart from every
other inconvenience, we might have been detained for
days in staying to pass rivers; as it was, happily no
such impediment arose. . . . The distance from
Mogador to Morocco (city) is said to be about 110
miles; we have, therefore, travelled upon an average
of sixteen miles a day. This may occasion a smile to
those who are accustomed to railway speed; but it
should be borne in mind that there are no roads in

this Empire, that we had to encamp each day some
hours before darkness to enable our camels, &c., to
reach the resting-place, and for the erection of our
tents, &c., &c., and it was absolutely necessary that we
should stop at the margin of some stream or river, an
ample supply of water being indispensable. After our
first day's journey we kept the snow-clad Atlas mountains constantly in view; our encampments and the
surrounding scenery each day of our pilgrimage would
have offered a series of charming scenes for an artist.
You may judge of the importance of our numbers:
Our encampment consisted of from thirteen to fifteen
camels, several baggage mules, about 100 camp
followers, including soldiers, &c.; indeed, on Friday
afternoon, after we had been met by the deputation
from Morocco, Mr. Samuel counted about eighteen
camels and sixty horses and mules, with a few donkeys
in addition."

At every town and village on their route the travellers, being guests of the Sultan, were received with
hospitality and respect. Each night the Moors in the
locality made "mona" for them and their retinue,
an entertainment, provided gratis by the people,
and subtracted from the taxes, which they afterwards
pay in kind to the Sultan. One of these "monas,"
presented by a generous Basha, consisted of four
sheep, a large number of fowls, a thousand eggs,
melons, a stupendous gourd, honey, ten pounds of
loaf-sugar, wax candles, vegetables, &c. Sir Moses,

of course, made suitable presents in return. The aged traveller finding himself unequal to keeping the saddle, travelled in a *chaise-à-porteur*, lent him by Sr. Jose Daniel Colaço, the Portuguese Minister at Tangier. Long before the arrival at the City of Morocco, deputations of Jews, and further escorts of the Sultan's troops reached Sir Moses, and outside the walls twelve officers of distinction waited to conduct him to the Palace which the Sultan had appointed for his residence. Dr. Hodgkin's description of this Moorish dwelling is very interesting :—

" It consists of two storeys, with an imperfect third. In the basement is an inner court, with a small fount in the middle, surrounded by apartments, which served as day-rooms, eating-rooms, and bed-rooms. The court is not open to the sky, as is common in Moorish houses; and its roof forms the floor to the court of the storey above. A narrow staircase near the entrance leads to the next storey, consisting of a larger and smaller hall, both of which are open to the sky, and partially surrounded by apartments, devoted to the personal service of Sir Moses Montefiore, and also of his official attendants. From this floor another staircase leads to the roof, which is surrounded by a parapet. The openings to the halls below are similarly protected. Two small rooms taken out of the apartments on one side form the partial third storey. The first impression we received on entering this imperial residence was not very pleasing. There was

Q

a degree of dampness, with a close and musty odour, which convinced us that it had not been recently tenanted; but a little observation sufficed to show us that it had been diligently put into something like order, and beautified, though still very deficient in furniture, and most of those things we regard as comforts; but there was a good deal of finery and effect in inferior workmanship. For example, there were pilasters and arches in plaster, and the capitals of the latter picked out in coloured wash. Paint, and white and yellow washes had been employed within and without. New Brussels carpets had been laid down on some of the floors; beds and ornamental pillows, either placed on European bedsteads, or immediately on the floor, were prepared in the sleeping apartments. Tumblers of cut glass, gilt, for use at dinner; large earthen jars, capable of holding nearly twenty gallons, stood in the halls; but tables, chairs, and other seats were nearly, if not altogether, absent. The windows were not glazed; but they might be closed by jalousies or shutters, which, though they would serve to keep out light and rain, were ineffectual defences against the cold, which, owing to the proximity of the snowy Atlas range, made the nights of so low a temperature, that we stood in more need of warm clothing in that part of the twenty-four hours than I have almost ever done in England. There were no fire-places, so we used the kitchen chafing-dishes to give us a little warmth in the evening."

Five days were occupied in listening to Jewish deputations, and conferring with Moorish Ministers. On the 31st January an official intimation was conveyed to Sir Moses Montefiore that the Sultan would receive him publicly on the next day. We cannot do better than give Sir Moses' own account of this memorable interview :—

" On Monday, the 1st instant, long before dawn, we could distinguish the sounds of martial music, indicating the muster of the troops, in and about the environs of the Sultan's palace. At the early hour of seven A.M., I had the honour to receive a visit from Sid Saib El Yamany, the good and intelligent Oozier, or Chief Minister of His Sheriffian Majesty, Sidi Mohamed Ben Abderahman Ben Hisham, the present Sultan of Morocco. He expressed the pleasure of the Sultan to receive us at his Court, and His Majesty's desire to make our visit to his capital an agreeable one. Shortly after the departure of the Oozier, the Royal Vice-Chamberlain, with a *cortège* of cavalry, arrived at our palace to convey us to the audience. You may recollect that our party, in addition to myself, consisted of Mr. Thomas Fellowes Reade, Consul to Her Britannic Majesty at Tangier; Captain William Armytage, of *H.M.S. Magicienne;* two of his officers, Dr. James Gibson, Thomas Forbes, and Lieutenant Francis Durant, my fellow-travellers Dr. Thomas Hodgkin and Mr. Sampson Samuel, and Mr. Moses Nahon, of Tangier, who had volunteered to accompany us to

Morocco, and to whom we are all deeply indebted.
. . . . A quarter of an hour's ride brought us to the
gates opening upon an avenue leading to the courtyard,
or open space before the palace. This avenue, which
is of very considerable length, was lined on both sides
by infantry troops, of great variety of hue and accoutre-
ments. They were standing in closely serried ranks,
and we must have passed several hundreds before
emerging into the open plain. There a magnificent
sight opened upon us; we beheld in every direction
masses of troops, consisting of cavalry and foot soldiers.
I should estimate the total number assembled on this
occasion at not less than six thousand. We went
forward some little distance into the plain, and saw
approaching us the Oozier, the Grand Chamberlain,
and other dignitaries of the Court. I descended from
my vehicle, and my companions alighted from their
steeds to meet them. We were cordially welcomed.
We arranged ourselves in a line to await the appearance of the Sultan. This was preceded by a
string of led white horses, and the Sultan's carriage
covered with green cloth. His Majesty's approach
was announced by a flourish of trumpets; then His
Majesty appeared, mounted on a superb white charger,
the spirited movements of which were controlled by
him with consummate skill. The colour of the
charger intimated that we were welcomed with the
highest distinction. The countenance of his Majesty
is expressive of great intelligence and benevolence.
The Sultan expressed his pleasure at seeing me at his

Court; he said my name was well known to him, as
well as my desire to improve the condition of my
brethren; he hoped that my sojourn in his capital
would be agreeable; he dwelt with great emphasis on
his long-existing amicable relations with our country;
he also said it was gratifying to him to see two of the
officers in its service at his Court. I had the honour,
at this audience, to place in the hands of His Majesty
my Memorial on behalf of the Jewish and Christian
subjects of his Empire. After the interview we were
escorted back to our garden palace with the same
honours as had been paid to us on our way to the
Court, my chair having a white horse led before it, as
well on my going as on my returning, which is a high
and distinguished mark of honour. The Oozier had
invited us to his palace for the evening of the same
day; we were entertained with true Oriental hospitality. In the course of the evening's conversation, we
elicited from the Oozier the assurance of the Sultan's
desire, as well as his own, to protect the Jews of
Morocco. He took notes of some particular grievances
which we brought to his knowledge, and promised to
institute the necessary inquiries, with a view to their
being redressed. Other measures were discussed, such
as the enlargement of the crowded Jewish quarters in
Mogador, the grant of a house for a hospital at
Tangier, all of which the Oozier assured us should
receive his favourable consideration."

On the following Friday the Sultan's reply to Sir

Moses Montefiore's Memorial was received in the shape
of an important edict commanding that the Jews and
all other subjects " shall be treated in manner con-
formable with the evenly balanced scales of justice,
and that they shall occupy a position of perfect equality
with all other people." The next day he paid a farewell
visit to the Moorish sovereign, who received him in
state in a Kiosk in the Palace Gardens. His Majesty's
manner was extremely courteous, and, in a conversation of some length, he renewed his assurance of
welcome, expressed a hope that Sir Moses had been
happy and comfortable during his stay in the capital,
and repeated his declaration that it was his intention
and desire to protect his Jewish subjects. An inspection of the Jewish quarter followed, and on the 8th
February—the objects of the Mission having been accomplished—Sir Moses Montefiore, accompanied by a
brilliant military escort, bade-farewell to the city and
proceeded towards Mazagran, where it had been arranged that the *Magicienne* should meet him. The
journey back to the coast occupied seven days, ex-
clusive of the Sabbath, and was marked by even greater
cordiality on the part of the native population than the
march from Mogador into the interior.

At Gibraltar Sir Moses again spent several days,
receiving deputations, paying visits, and getting
through a vast amount of correspondence, which
the business of his mission had entailed upon him.
Thence he took the French steam packet to Malaga,
and the railway to Madrid, where he had a second

interview with Queen Isabella, who congratulated him
on the success of his embassy. From Madrid he
travelled, partly by carriage road and partly by railway,
to Paris, stopping at Bayonne for a day to celebrate
the Jewish feast of Purim. In the French capital he
had a private audience of the Emperor Napoleon III.,
who welcomed him most graciously, and to whom he
presented a copy of the Imperial Edict of the Sultan
of Morocco. Two days later he was receiving the
felicitations of his friends at East Cliff Lodge.

Congratulatory addresses were showered upon the
venerable baronet from all parts of England and the
Continent. In the House of Commons the Under
Secretary of State for Foreign Affairs (Mr. Layard)
gave an interesting account of the mission. "When
it is recollected," said the honourable gentleman,
"that there are 500,000 Jews in Morocco, some idea
may be formed of the great service rendered by Sir
Moses Montefiore; and having had the honour of
acting with him on various occasions, I can bear
testimony to the noble and generous spirit of humanity
and philanthropy which actuates him, without reference to any sect or creed, which extends to the people
of every nation who are suffering wrong and injustice."
The Court of Common Council took the opportunity
of publicly according him the thanks of the citizens of
London " for the signal services he had rendered by
missions to various countries for the relief of persons
oppressed for their religious convictions, and more
especially by a journey to Morocco, undertaken to

solicit the Emperor to relieve his Jewish and Christian subjects from all civil and religious disabilities." It may be mentioned here that at a later date the Fishmongers' Company offered him their freedom, and the Master, Mr. Venning, and other members of the Court, proceeded to East Cliff to invest him.

The mission to Morocco was a notable achievement; and although it did not altogether stop persecution, it must be ranked among the most remarkable of Sir Moses Montefiore's works. Whatever the local acts of oppression by irresponsible officials, the Edict obtained by the venerable Hebrew remains a charter to which his co-religionists can always appeal; and when, one of these days, there may be more cohesion in the machinery of Moorish Government, it will be a power in the land. But power or no power, law or dead-letter, the spirit which inspired its silver-haired author, under the weight of four-score years, to undertake a long and perilous journey to obtain it, can never cease to do honour to his name.

CHAPTER XVI.

ANOTHER BUSY DECADE.

Drought in the Holy Land—A new Relief Fund—The ,sixth journey
to Palestine—The locust pest in Palestine—Sir Moses investigates
the condition of the Jerusalem Jewish community—Promotes
public works in the Holy City—Holds an inquiry respecting a
charge brought against the Safed Jews by the Rev. Dr. Macleod
—Suggestions for the application of the balance of the Relief
Fund—Death of Dr. Hodgkin—Persecution of Jews in Roumania
—Mission to Bucharest—Interviews with Prince Charles—The
Prince's assurances—Home labours—A second journey to Russia
—Reception at St. Petersburg—Audience with the Czar Alexander
II.—Improved condition of the Russian Jews—Resignation of
the Presidency of the Board of Deputies—The Montefiore
Testimonial Fund.

VERY few examples of activity in public affairs after
the eighth decade are afforded in biographical literature.
The spectacle of Lord Brougham at eighty-two heading
a great social gathering like that which took place at
Glasgow in September, 1860, or of Lord Lyndhurst at
eighty-eight pouring out the words of experience and
sagacity in the House of Lords for four hours at a
time, stands almost alone. These octogenarian feats
have, however, been eclipsed by Sir Moses Montefiore.
In the most characteristic business of his public career
—missions to foreign countries in the interests of his

brethren—his eighth and ninth decade have been the busiest of his life. If the reader will turn back the pages of this work he will find that while Sir Moses undertook only one journey during his fifth decade, and two in his sixth and seventh respectively, he performed four in his eighth. During his ninth decade he also undertook four journeys—two to Jerusalem, one to Roumania, and one to Russia.

The year 1865 found the Holy Land again suffering from drought and disease. A pest of locusts covered the country, and in Jerusalem the cholera raged with such fierceness that within a short time fifteen per cent. of the population were cut off by it. The usual appeal was addressed to Sir Moses Montefiore, and he, in conjunction with the Board of Deputies, started another Holy Land Relief Fund. About £3000 were sent out to meet the necessities of the moment, and early in 1866, Sir Moses proceeded to the East with the object of personally applying the balance of the Fund. He was accompanied by Dr. Hodgkin, his Quaker physician; Captain Henry Moore, brother of the British Consul at Jerusalem; his relatives, Mr. and Mrs. Sebag and his old friend, Dr. Loewe.

Of this tour, as of the succeeding journey to Palestine, Sir Moses Montefiore has himself written an account. It is in the shape of a report to the Board of Deputies, but in style and matter it is far more interesting than official documents usually are. He tells us how on his arrival in Egypt, he repaired to the Synagogue Kinees Elieyahoo, "which is built on the spot where it is said the celebrated Temple of Alexandria, or Onias, once stood." He graphically describes his landing at Jaffa, when he was ceremoniously received by the governor of the town, the judges, the commander of the troops, and the representatives of the various religious denominations. He relates how his friends immediately on his arrival gave him descriptions of the sufferings and loss of life occasioned by the recent calamities. " Very frequently," he adds, " these afflicting narratives were interrupted by the appearance upon our windows of the new and still green locusts, which we were informed were the much dreaded forerunners of another bad season. Many a morning before sunrise we heard the rattling of the drum to awaken the inhabitants of Jaffa to the fulfilment of their duty, each to collect a measure of locusts before daybreak, so that the threatening enemy might be destroyed. The appearance of these locusts is the more dreaded on account of the belief that it always brings in its train some epidemic disease, the woeful consequence of which had so recently been experienced."   On the road to Jerusalem he was hospitably entertained in the mountain home of the chief of Aboo-Goosh, " supposed to be the Kiryat-Yearim of Scripture, where Abinadab dwelt, in whose house, on the top of the hill, the ark of the Lord had been placed when taken from the Philistines of Beth-Shemesh."

At Jerusalem Sir Moses was, as usual, received with distinction, and during his stay the Governor stationed a guard of honour at his dwelling. He visited the various institutions of the city, and his own special foundations, and was pleased to find them well administered. During his stay he not only enquired minutely into the condition of the Jewish community, and distributed large sums among the poor, but he also promoted several works of importance to the general population. He concerted measures with the Governor to improve the water supply of Jerusalem, and had the gratification of seeing water reflowing into the city from the pools of Solomon; he contributed to the building of a hospital for leprosy, and he erected an awning at the "Wailing Place," near the western wall of the Temple, in order to afford shelter to the pious persons visiting the sacred spot for meditation and prayer.

An interesting incident of his stay in the Holy City was a quasi-judicial enquiry he held respecting an accusation published by *Good Words* against the spiritual heads of the Safed congregation. The Rev. Dr. Macleod, who had visited Palestine in 1864, wrote to that journal charging the Safed Jews with having inflicted the punishment of death on a Spanish Jewess who had been convicted of adultery. Sir Moses sent to Safed for the Rabbis, the members of the Jewish Ecclesiastical Court, and a number of other persons capable of giving evidence in the case, and satisfied himself that there was no truth in the accusation.

The result of his enquiries as to the best means of

expending the balance of the Relief Fund, he thus sets forth in his Report :—

" There now remains for me to present to you my humble opinion as to the most practicable remedies which can be applied for the mitigation of the evils under which our brethren in the Holy Land labour, and to state to you the result of that investigation. Let me remind you, in the first place, that in our own country it seems to have become the settled opinion of those to whom England would point as the men of the highest intellect, and the greatest experience and zeal in the cause of humanity, that the wisest scheme for being at the same time useful and charitable to the poor, is to be found in the erection, maintenance, and improvement of dwelling-houses. The reasons on which this opinion is founded, have been of late so often and so ably expounded, that any attempt to enlarge upon them here would be out of place. But if these reasons apply to the condition of the poor of England, I am convinced, by the information I received from the most intelligent persons in the East, and by a careful and anxious study of those circumstances which surround the Jews of Palestine — circumstances which I have attempted to foreshadow in this Report—that the same reasons apply with tenfold force to the poverty and distress which prevail amongst our co-religionists in the Holy Land. I am therefore of opinion, that the balance of the Relief Fund cannot be better employed than in the erection

of dwellings, as far as the means will admit, on the
ground already selected by me—a ground which, for
its healthy position, and many other reasons, I deem
best adapted for the desired object. I would further
suggest to my co-religionists, that with a view of
removing existing evils, and of promoting the well-
being of the Jews in the Holy Land, a general collection should be made, so as to constitute a fund, as
well for the encouragement of agricultural pursuits, as
for the erection of additional dwellings outside the
walls of the Holy City. I am quite aware that your
honourable Board could not impose on itself so heavy
and responsible an undertaking; but I hope and
believe, that the Jews at large may direct their attention thereto, and conjointly, by means of Building
Societies, or otherwise, organise the necessary
arrangements."

During this tour, Sir Moses Montefiore had the
misfortune to lose his attached and highly valued
friend, Dr. Hodgkin, who expired after a short illness
at Jaffa. For forty years he had been intimately
associated with the Jewish philanthropist, in whose
benevolent schemes he had always taken an ardent
interest. Sir Moses made a touching reference to his
loss in his Report to the Board of Deputies:—

"It has pleased the Almighty to take him (Dr.
Hodgkin) from us, and that he should not again
behold his loving consort and beloved relatives. He
breathed his last in a land endeared to him by

hallowed reminiscences. To one so guileless, so
pious, so amiable in private life, so respected in his
public career, and so desirous to assist, with all his
heart, in the amelioration of the condition of the
human race, death could not have had any terror.
His soul has ascended to appear before the throne of
glory, there to receive that heavenly recompense which
is awarded to the good and righteous of all nations.
I trust I may be pardoned for this heartfelt but
inadequate tribute to the memory of my late friend.
His long and intimate association with me and my late
dearly-beloved wife, his companionship in our travels,
and the vivid recollection of his many virtues, make
me anxious to blend his name, and the record of his
virtues, with the narrative of these events."

Over his grave at Jaffa Sir Moses erected an obelisk
inscribed with a feeling tribute to his scientific attain-
ments and " self-sacrificing philanthropy."

The next journey was to Roumania, and was undertaken in the following year. The persecution and
oppression of the Jews in this Principality arise very
curiously from an abuse of the constitutional form of
government which the Western Powers conferred on
Moldo-Wallachia in 1856. Although to-day the Roumanian Jews are held by law to be aliens, they were,
as a matter of fact, established in the country long
before the present composite people, or even the race
which gave its name to the land. From the soil of
ancient Dacia prayers were offered up to the God

of Abraham, Isaac, and Jacob, at a time when altars
dedicated to Mars and Venus were yet unknown.   But
what in after years particularly attracted the Jews to
the country was the absence there of any great trading
class.   Agriculturists were many, and landed pro-
prietors were also numerous ; but a mercantile and
industrial class, capable of turning the resources of the
land to commercial account, did not exist.   For a
long period the Jews were the only mechanics, manu-
facturers, and merchants in Roumania.   When, in
course of time, the Roumans themselves engaged in
these occupations, the rivalry between them and the
Hebrews became intense, and bitter jealousies arose.
The Roumans, assuming a history and an ethnography
that did not exist, murmured that the " stranger "
was stealing the national birthright.   It was not, however, until 1856 that this rivalry assumed a dangerous
form.   Then, when the people, under a constitutional
government, superseded the powers of the Hospodars
and Boyars, who had formerly protected the Jews,
they set themselves to oppress their too active com-
petitors.   They commenced by ignoring them in their
franchise scheme, and afterwards, one by one, closed
against them various branches of trade.   Constitutional government, in fact, enabled an ignorant and
selfish people to give expression to their selfishness
and intolerance, where a wise autocracy had formerly
kept such passions in check.   It is truly a curious
page in the history of politics.

Popular feeling once unmuzzled, the anti-Jewish

movement took a wide scope. From legal oppression
in the Council Chamber to violent persecution in the
streets is but a step; and from 1864 to the end of
1866 not a month passed but some dreadful outrage
upon the Jews was chronicled. M. Crémieux paid a
visit to Bucharest in 1866, and secured a large number
of promises from members of the Chamber of Deputies
to support a measure emancipating the Jews; but no
sooner had he left, than the people rose, threatened
Parliament, maltreated a number of Jews, and destroyed
their Synagogue, which was the finest building in the
capital.

In 1867 the persecutions became more cruel.
No sooner had Sir Moses Montefiore returned from
Jerusalem, than he found himself compelled to open
a correspondence with the British Government on the
subject. At his request Lord Stanley telegraphed a
vigorous remonstrance to the Roumanian Government, but still the persecutions continued. In June
serious anti-Jewish riots took place at Jassy and
other places; and about the middle of July public
opinion in Europe was shocked by an exceptionally
terrible outrage at Galatz, called in the consular
despatches the "*Noyades* of Galatz." Ten Jews, who
were alleged by the Roumanian Government to be
vagabonds from Turkey, but who were in reality
natives of Roumania, were ordered to be expelled
the country. A file of soldiers escorted them from
Galatz, half-way across the Danube, and landed them,
without food or fuel, on a marshy island. During the

R

night one of them perished in the mud. The survivors were rescued by the Turks, and taken back to Galatz; but on attempting to reland, a scuffle took place, and the Roumanian soldiers drove the poor Hebrews, at the point of the bayonet, into the river, where they were drowned.

The incident caused great indignation in Western Europe, and Sir Moses Montefiore, as President of the Board of Deputies, set out immediately for Bucharest, to make personal representations to Prince (now King) Charles on the whole question of the treatment of the Roumanian Jews. At Paris he was received by the Emperor Napoleon III., who assured him of his best wishes and support, and attached a French officer to his suite as a mark of his sympathy. Notwithstanding his great age, Sir Moses travelled very rapidly, engaging special trains when the ordinary service did not ensure sufficient despatch, and at Donauwerth hiring a special steamer to take him down the Danube *viâ* Vienna into Roumania. Immediately on arriving at Bucharest, he was cordially welcomed by the Corps Diplomatique, who assured him that, under the instructions of their respective Governments, he might rely on their best services being placed at his disposal for the accomplishment of the object of his Mission.

Sir Moses had several interviews with the Prince, and the members of his Government, and succeeded in obtaining from his Highness the most gratifying assurances. Before his departure he received the following note from the Prince :—

" MONSIEUR LE BARONNET,

"J'ai reçu votre lettre du 27 Août dernier,
et j'en ai pris connaissance avec un vif intérêt. Comme
j'ai eu l'occasion de vous le dire de vive voix, les
vœux que vous formez pour vos co-religionnaires sont
déjà accomplis. Les Israélites sont l'objet de toute
ma sollicitude et de toute celle de mon Gouvernement,
et je suis bien aise que vous soyez venu en Roumanie
pour vous convaincre que la persécution religieuse, dont
la malveillance a fait tant de bruit, n'existe point. S'il
est arrivé que des Israélites fussent inquiétés, ce sont
là des faits isolés dont mon Gouvernement ne peut
pas assumer la responsabilité. Je tiendra toujours à
honneur de faire respecter la liberté religieuse, et je
veillerai sans cesse à l'exécution des lois qui protégent
les Israélites, comme tous les autres Roumains dans
leur personne, et dans leurs biens.

"Veuillez recevoir, Monsieur le Baronnet, l'assurance de ma considération très distinguée.

" CHARLES."

"COTROCENI, *le* 18/30 *Août*, 1867."

To what extent Prince Charles was hoodwinked by
his own Ministers it is impossible to say ; but notwithstanding the professions contained in this letter—
the sincerity of which there is no reason to doubt—
he has been powerless to stop the persecutions. The
vicious national sentiment has been too strong for him,
and the Jews of Roumania are still unemancipated,
and are periodically persecuted by both the Government
and the people.

R 2

The third journey in this decade was to Russia, and took place in 1872. The intervening years were spent in labours in connection with the home community. In 1870 Sir Moses assisted at the consecration of the Central Synagogue in London. In 1871 he opened a subscription for the relief of a famine among the Jews of Persia, in whose political condition he had formerly taken much interest. A considerable fund was raised, and £17,973 was distributed through Mr. Alison, the British Minister at Teheran.

In 1872, on the occasion of the 200th anniversary of the birth of Peter the Great, the Board of Deputies adopted an address of congratulation to the Czar Alexander II., and Sir Moses Montefiore was deputed to journey to St. Petersburg to present it. *En route* every one tried to dissuade him from proceeding to his destination on account of the cholera which raged there with great severity ; but impelled by a sense of duty he determined to persevere even if left alone. " The journals," he wrote home, " gave an alarming account of the unsatisfactory state of health in St. Petersburg, and it being the opinion of some of those who accompanied me that it would be imprudent on my part to proceed any further, I considered it my duty to gather around me those who appeared to fear the approach to the Russian frontier, counselling their return to England (it being well established that persons who entertain the fear of infection are more liable to be attacked by the epidemic), but after due consideration all decided to resume the journey with me."

On his arrival in the Russian capital Sir Moses presented to the English Ambassador and M. de Westmann the letters of introduction with which he had been furnished by Earl Granville and Count de Brunnow. By the Russian Minister he was received with marked kindness and urbanity. After some conversation, M. de Westmann observed :—"We were acquainted with the object of your visit to our city before your arrival; the Emperor will receive you, and we shall endeavour to render everything as easy and agreeable to you as possible. His Imperial Majesty is at present absent from St. Petersburg at the military manœuvres, but I shall seek His Imperial Majesty's orders regarding the day and place when and where the Emperor will receive you." In recording this conversation Sir Moses wrote :—"I need scarcely say how grateful I felt to our Heavenly Father for having thus, a few hours only after my arrival in St. Petersburg, enabled me to receive from the Russian Minister such kind and assuring expressions, and, deeply sensible of the goodness of the Almighty who had succoured and protected me and my companions, I prepared with gladness for the holy Sabbath."

The interview with the Czar, which took place on the following Wednesday, Sir Moses thus describes :—

"At the appointed hour, I proceeded to the Winter Palace, accompanied by Dr. Loewe. Instead of having the fatigue of ascending the Grand Staircase, we were elevated by means of a lift to the Grande Salle d'Attente of the Emperor, into which we were immediately ushered. There we found His Excellency Monsieur de Westmann, the Imperial Lord Chamberlain, the Imperial Grand Maître des Cérémonies, and several other distinguished personages, who entered into conversation with me on various subjects of importance to our co-religionists. After an interval thus agreeably passed, His Excellency, the Minister for Foreign Affairs, was summoned before the Czar, and soon afterwards I was conducted into the presence of His Imperial Majesty, to whom, in the name of your Board and its several constituent congregations, I presented the Address. His Imperial Majesty, who conversed most fluently in the English language, received me with the utmost grace and kindness ; he adverted to the circumstance of my having had the honour of an audience with his august father in the year 1846, and expressed himself most graciously on every subject having reference to my mission. His Imperial Majesty also graciously received Dr. Loewe. Nor can I here omit to record my grateful appreciation of His Imperial Majesty's consideration in having come from the seat of the summer manœuvres to the Winter Palace—expressly to spare me fatigue, in consequence of my advanced age—and having there received the Address of which I was the bearer. I quitted the Palace with a heart overflowing with gratitude, for indeed I am at a loss for words in which adequately to describe the gracious sentiments which His Imperial Majesty, and the members of his Government, evinced towards me.

On my way to the hotel I was enthusiastically greeted by hundreds of our brethren who were awaiting my return from the Palace, and whose faces were illumined by joy."

During his short stay in St. Petersburg Sir Moses was gratified to find a remarkable improvement in the position of the Jews since his earlier visit. He saw a considerable number of Jews who had been distinguished by decorations of different grades by the Emperor, and conversed with Jewish merchants, literary men, editors of Russian periodicals, artisans, and persons who had formerly served in the Imperial army, all of whom expressed satisfaction with their position. He found Synagogues in which sermons were preached in Russian and German, and obtained copies of "beautiful maps with all the modern improvements in which the cities, villages, mountains, rivers, railways, &c., all appear in Hebrew, and several educational works on history, geography, grammar, natural philosophy, and physics, also published in the Hebrew language, to enable those who are yet unacquainted with the national language to advance their education in all useful secular subjects." Summing up his observations on the condition of the Russian Hebrews, Sir Moses wrote:—

" The Jews now dress like any gentlemen in England, France, or Germany, their schools are well attended, and they are foremost in every honourable enterprise. During my journey, I had frequent opportunities of receiving from our brethren assurances of the rapid increase of their Synagogues, schools, and charitable institutions ; and, as indicative of the improved spiritual and social condition of our co-religionists abroad, I may notice, that amongst the many thousands of Jews with whom I came in contact, I observed the most charitable and benevolent dispositions, an insatiable thirst for knowledge, a pure and religious zeal, and a high degree of prosperity. Looking back to what the condition of our co-religionists in Russia was twenty-six years ago, and having regard to their present position, they have now indeed abundant reason to cherish grateful feelings towards the Emperor, to whom their prosperity is in so great a measure attributable ; and if there yet remain some few restrictions, the hope may surely be entertained, that, with the advance of secular education among them, these disabilities may be gradually removed."

A hope, unfortunately, not destined to be realised. Ten years later it was Sir Moses Montefiore's grief to read of popular persecutions and official intolerance in the Empire of the Czars, carried out on as large a scale as during the darkest period of the reign of Nicholas.

Sir Moses Montefiore was now nearly ninety years of age, and he began to feel that the time had arrived when he might resign to younger hands his office in connection with the Board of Deputies. The members of the Board returned at the General Election of April,

1874, met for the first time on the 7th May. Sir
Moses was re-elected to the presidency, but declined the
office on the ground of the uncertain state of his health.
The Board urged him to reconsider his decision, and
a deputation from its body having waited on him at
Ramsgate, he was at length prevailed upon to accede
to its wishes. Later in the session, however, his colleagues were pained to receive a letter again pressing
his resignation both of the presidency and of his seat.
Earnest efforts were made to induce him to alter his
determination but without avail, and, bearing in mind
his advanced age, it was felt that it would not be right
to persuade him further to retain an office involving
arduous and responsible duties. In parting with its
venerated President, the Board expressed its high
estimate of his labours in a series of eloquent resolutions which, engrossed on vellum and emblazoned,
were signed by every deputy and presented to the
worthy Baronet. Sir Moses acknowledged the resolutions in the following characteristic letter to his nephew,
who had been elected to succeed him :—

"GROSVENOR GATE, PARK LANE,
" 24th November, 5635—1874.

" MY DEAR JOSEPH MAYER MONTEFIORE,
        " I have the honour to acknowledge the
receipt from your hands of a copy of resolutions,
beautifully engrossed on vellum and emblazoned,
adopted by the London Committee of Deputies of
British Jews at a meeting held on the 6th October,

ultimo, on the occasion of my resignation of the office
of President of the Board. The sentiments conveyed
by these resolutions are so highly gratifying, and the
language in which they are couched so extremely
cordial, that I can but very inadequately assure the
Board and yourself how profound an impression they
have made on my heart. It has been my oft-
recurring and much-valued privilege to receive mani-
festations of the Board's approbation and regard, but
never have I experienced more perfect satisfaction
than I derive from the resolutions now before me ;
satisfaction enhanced, indeed, by the circumstance of
their being signed by every Member of the Board. In
my retirement from the Board of Deputies, over which
I have had the distinguished honour to preside for
upwards of thirty years, and with which I have been
connected from a very early period, I carry with me
the unfading recollection of the sympathy and encouragement it has invariably afforded me at those
important moments of my life, when, moved by the
murmur of the oppressed or the cry of the afflicted,
the Board deputed me to plead on its behalf, in distant
lands, the cause of toleration and humanity. The
Board may, indeed, discern the best reward of its
active labours in the amelioration of the condition of
our co-religionists, that has resulted from those just
and enlightened measures, which, by God's blessing,
are attributable to its wise and temperate intervention.
Long may the Members of the Community of Israel,
who rejoice in the benignant sway of our Gracious

Sovereign, find the promotion of their welfare, and the
preservation of our Holy Religion, the objects of the
zealous care of the London Committee of Deputies
of British Jews. Long may our brethren in foreign
countries receive from the Board a ready response
when appealed to for aid or intercession. I am
sensible that I have given but feeble expression to
that which, however, I deeply feel. But I may rely
on that indulgent consideration which has been ever
extended to me. And I feel assured that you will
kindly make known to my former esteemed colleagues,
far better than any words of mine can acquaint them,
how heartfelt is my gratitude for the resolutions with
which they have presented me, and how fervent is my
prayer for the long life and enduring happiness of
themselves and their families, for the lasting prosperity
of the Board of Deputies, and for the speedy restoration of the Glory of Zion.

" I have the honour to be, my dear Joseph Mayer
Montefiore,

" Yours most faithfully,

" MOSES MONTEFIORE."

The Board elected its late President an honorary
member of its body, and raised a fund of over £12,000
as a testimonial to his high character and public services.
On being consulted as to the application of this money,
Sir Moses expressed a wish that it should be devoted
to public works for the improvement of the condition
of the Jews in the Holy Land, in accordance with

the suggestions made in his report on the Mission of 1866.

In July, 1874, Sir Moses Montefiore, still active, notwithstanding his four-score-and-ten years, set out on his seventh journey to Palestine—the fourth foreign Mission in his ninth decade.

CHAPTER XVII.

" FORTY DAYS' SOJOURN IN THE HOLY LAND."

ALTHOUGH undertaken after his retirement from
public life, this seventh journey to Palestine by Sir
Moses Montefiore was no mere holiday tour. Its
history illustrates interestingly the energy and public
spirit that continued to animate the warm-hearted
nonagenarian. Soon after he was released from his
labours in connection with the Board of Deputies, he
commenced anew to study the problems connected
with the condition of the Jews of the Holy Land,
which for nearly fifty years had baffled all attempts at
solution. On the 29th July, 1874, he addressed a
Hebrew circular letter to the Jewish congregations,
asking for suggestions as to the best means of im-

proving their condition. The following is a translation
of this interesting letter :—

"I have set the Lord always before me."

"GROSVENOR GATE, PARK LANE,
"LONDON, *Wednesday*, 15*th of Ab*, 5634.

"Peace, peace to the chosen of the people, whose
delight is in the law of the Lord; my soul loves them
according to their worth and dignity. May the Eternal
bless them. May their reward be complete from the
Lord, the God of Israel, and may their eyes and ours
behold the glory of the rebuilding of Aree-él.

"To the REV. the HAHAM BASHI, and the representatives of the several Hebrew Congregations in
the Holy City of * * *.

"GENTLEMEN,
"It has ever been my earnest desire, since I
first had the opportunity of becoming acquainted with
the state of great poverty and distress that prevailed
among you, to ameliorate your condition and cause
salvation to spring forth in the Holy Land by means
of industrial pursuits, such as agriculture, mechanical
work, or some suitable business, so as to enable both
the man who is not qualified to study, but is fully able
(by his physical strength) to work, as well as the
student, who, prompted by a desire to maintain himself by the labour of his hands, may be willing to
devote the day to the work necessary for the support
of his family, and the night to the study of the Law

of God, to find the means of an honourable living.
Already, in the years 5599 and 5626, I entreated you
to assist me with your wise and judicious counsel, and
begged of you to point out to me the right path. I
then forwarded to you statistical and agricultural
forms, to enable you to record therein all the information required, and you most cheerfully complied with
my request, and gave me all the particulars referring
to these subjects. I, on my part, made known to all
my friends and acquaintances the information I received from you; but, unfortunately, from various
unaccountable causes, I met with little success, and
your condition remained the same as before. Having
again this year noticed all the troubles and hardships
you had to undergo from scarcity of bread, and from
want of means to procure it, I thought I would try
again, now for the third time, to ascertain whether
any of your suggestions regarding the best mode of
ameliorating your condition, either by agriculture or
by mechanical work, within or without the house, or
some suitable business pursuits, if clearly and distinctly set forth to our brethren, might not, under
present circumstances, be more favourably received,
and induce them more readily to hasten with their
succour to a most deserving class of people, so as to
procure lasting comfort among you. Let me, therefore, entreat you to fully acquaint me with your views
on this subject; point out to me what I am to do in
order to hasten thereby the cause of bringing salvation into the land. Consider well which is the proper

path, appearing most clearly to you, to produce the
remedy you stand in need of. By doing so you will
comply with the wishes of your brethren, who love
and kiss, as it were, the dust of the Holy Land. Be
strong and of good courage. Do not say, ' Our words
are of no avail,' but send speedily a reply to him who
holds you in great esteem, and prays for the welfare of
his people.

" MOSES MONTEFIORE."

The replies received by Sir Moses Montefiore were
presented by him to the Palestine Committee of the
Board of Deputies. They expressed a willingness to
work, and suggested large purchases of land for the
foundation of agricultural colonies. The Board did
not accede to the proposals of Sir Moses' correspondents, and some of the members seemed to be of the
opinion that the Jews of the Holy Land were not the
honest and willing people that Sir Moses believed
them to be. Objections were especially urged against
the system that prevailed in Palestine of maintaining
by the bounty of the foreign communities such Jews
as might elect to pass their time in religious exercises.
These opinions being communicated to Sir Moses
Montefiore, he resolved once more to proceed to
Palestine to see for himself whether he had been de-
ceived in the estimate he had formed of his co-religionists in that hallowed region.

This journey Sir Moses has described in a diary,
privately circulated, under the title of " Forty Days'

Sojourn in the Holy Land." It is an interesting pendant to the journals of the earlier Missions written by his lamented wife. The same religious spirit serenely illumines its pages, and, in the course of its unaffected chronicle, many an insight is afforded into the workings of a character, the mainspring of which is reliance on the eternal bounty of God.

Having offered up his prayers "in the mausoleum of her who, like a guardian angel, so often sustained me on my journeys with her loving affection and judicious counsel," he left East Cliff on the 15th June. By the advice of his physician he only travelled by short stages, but this restriction he utilised, to enable him to communicate with the Jewish congregations on his route, with a view of ascertaining their opinions regarding the Jews of Jerusalem.

On arriving at Venice he was met by Admiral Sir James Drummond, to whom he presented a letter of introduction, with which he had been furnished by the British Government. The Admiral assured him of his desire to do anything he might require to facilitate his journey, but informed him that his old enemy the cholera had broken out at Damascus, and that the spread of the epidemic along the coast was apprehended. Sir Moses writes :—

" This unexpected news at first somewhat startled me, for I well knew the danger to which we should be exposed in a hot climate, in the most unhealthy season, but I soon recovered my former resolution. It

S

appeared to me that I had a certain duty to perform—
a duty, owing to our religion, to our beloved brethren
in the Holy Land; nothing therefore, I made up my
mind, should prevent me proceeding on my journey.
I communicated my resolution to the Admiral, who
kindly expressed his hope for my safe return.   Returning to the hotel, I heard that the sad news of the
cholera being in Syria, and the necessity of remaining
in quarantine on leaving that country, had also reached
my *compagnons de voyage*, and they all entreated me
to give up the idea of going to the Holy Land, but I
would not yield; indeed, with every persuasive word
of theirs to make me return, my resolution became
stronger and stronger to proceed."

The Jews of Venice received Sir Moses with
enthusiasm.   A service in his honour was held in the
Synagogue, and so numerous was the attendance, that
the whole square around the sacred edifice and the
adjoining streets, were filled with those who could not
obtain seats.   On leaving the Synagogue and stepping
into his gondola, a choir which lined the street
chanted the prayer of the congregation for his safe
journey.   During his stay, Signor Soave, a Jewish
professor, brought under his notice an interesting
document which had been found in the archives of the
Venetian congregation.   This was a letter addressed
to the treasurer of the Jewish association called the
" Caisse for the Redemption of Captives," by the
Portuguese congregation of London, in May, 1705.

The writer of the letter, Mr. Mosse de Medina, Warden of the English congregation, made a remittance of 60 ducados de banco towards the redemption of three Hebrew slaves, brought to Venice in a Maltese vessel. On this Sir Moses pointedly remarks :—

"The sympathy which Hebrew communities have at all times evinced towards their suffering brethren has always been proverbial; it is one of the noblest traits in the character of Israel, and we have every reason to hope that our communities will continue to retain that characteristic, especially when it concerns the aid of those who sacrifice all their worldly interest to the service of God, and the glorification of our holy religion."

After a short visit to Alexandria Sir Moses embarked on the Austrian steamer *Ettore* for Jaffa. The day after his departure was the Sabbath, and he did not fail to celebrate the holy day with all the minutiæ prescribed by the Jewish ritual. He tells us :—

"That day has always been a particular object of delight to me. By the kindness and civility of the people on board I was never interrupted in any way in the performance of my religious duties. Every Friday, as the Sabbath was about setting in, I could light my Sabbath-lamp, which I always carried with me, and I often had the gratification of seeing the seven lights (emblems of the six days of creation, and the seventh day of rest,) burn as late as midnight, undisturbed by the motion of the vessel, even when going at the rate

of ten to eleven knots an hour. We recited our
prayers and 'Kidoosh,' the blessings of which were
responded to by the sincere 'Amen' of those who
joined me in prayer, and enjoyed our Sabbath meal.
On the Sabbath morning I had always the satisfaction
of hearing, after the usual prayer, one of our Commen-
taries on the portion of the week expounded to me by
Dr. Loewe, and the rest of the day passed in pleasing
conversation on all that concerns our brethren in the
Holy Land. On board of the *Ettore*, that happiness
became greatly enhanced by the contemplation of the
short distance which now only separated me from the
hallowed goal I had in view."

A characteristic and graphic passage describes the
night before the arrival in the Holy Land :—

"Myriads of celestial luminaries, each of them as
large and bright almost as any of the radiant planets
in the Western horizon, were now emitting their silvery
rays of light in the spangled canopy over us.   Sure
and steady our ship steered towards the coast of the
land so dearly beloved, summoning all to sleep, but
few of the passengers retired that night. Every one of
them appeared to be in meditation. It was silent all
around us—silent, so that the palpitation of the heart
might almost be heard. It was, as if everyone had the
words on his lips, 'Ah, when will our eyes be gladdened
by the first glance of the Holy Land? When shall
we be able to set foot on the spot which was the long-
wished for goal of our meditations!' Such were that

night the feelings of every Gentile passenger on board. And what other thoughts, I ask, could have engrossed the mind of an Israelite ? The words of R. Yehooda Halevi, which he uttered when entering the gates of Jerusalem, now came into my mind :—' The kingdoms of idolatry will all change and disappear ; thy glory alone, O Zion, will last for ever ; for the Eternal has chosen thee for His abode. Happy the man who is now waiting in confiding hope to behold the rising glory of Thy light.' "

At Jaffa, Sir Moses was received by the authorities with the usual ceremonies. As he stepped from his boat a detachment of soldiers drawn up in two lines, commanded by the Kaimekam, presented arms, and a large concourse of people cheered enthusiastically. Deputations read addresses of welcome from the congregations of Jerusalem, Jaffa, and Hebron, and the British Vice-Consul invited him to accept the accommodation of his country residence, situated a little way outside the town on the Jerusalem road. Staying here for a few days, Sir Moses examined minutely the garden he had established in the neigh- bourhood some years before. He found that it con- tained 900 fruit trees, and that it required some repairs, but he refused to supply a steam-engine to work the water-wheel in place of the ordinary mules, because of the cost of fuel and the absence of skilled mechanics. In order to test the willingness of the poor to work he offered a small sum of money— designedly very trivial—to have the large cistern on the

estate filled, and was delighted to watch the alacrity
with which a crowd turned out to work the wheel
while they sang in chorus Psalm cxxviii., in which
occurs the verse : " Thou shalt eat the labour of
thine hands; happy shalt thou be and it shall be
well with thee." He also had elaborate statistical
accounts of the Jaffa community prepared, and
received deputations who convinced him that the
charges which had been brought against the Jews
were without foundation.

On the way to Jerusalem he observed many signs of
improvement since his last visit, and was particularly
pleased to note that several of the fields were cultivated
by Jews. His diary gives a dramatic account of a
moonlight ride from Bab-el-Wad :—

" We waited for the rising of the moon, and at
twenty minutes past eleven o'clock started for Jerusalem. Those were exciting moments which presented
themselves to my mind now and then, as we ascended
and descended the hills and dales on the road ; the
moon throwing her long and dark shadow when behind
a rock. They recalled to memory how much exposed the traveller was in former years to the attacks
of a Bedouin, or some feudal lord. Now, thank God,
thanks to the protection of the Turkish Government,
we do not hear of such outrages on peaceable pilgrims.
Just as I concluded these meditations two Bedouins in
full speed dashed along from behind some hidden rock,
and directed their course right up to our carriage.

' Good heaven,' I thought, ' we ought not to be too
hasty here in bestowing praises on the protection of
the police.   What in the world will they do with us ? '
But Dr. Loewe, who was with me in the carriage,
suddenly called out as loud as he possibly could,
' Shálom Aleykhem, Rabbi B. S., Shálom Aleykham,
Rabbi L. S.,' and turning round to me, he said, ' These
are not Bedouins, though they are dressed exactly
like them, and gallop along the hills like the sons of
the desert, but they are simply our own brethren from
Jerusalem, who, I have no doubt, come to ascertain
the exact time of your intended entry into Jerusalem,
to give timely notice to the people to come out to
meet you.'   And so it was.   A minute afterwards they
pulled up the reins of their fiery chargers, and stood
before us.   'A happy and blessed week to you, Dr.
Loewe,' they shouted ; ' where is Sir Moses ? how is
he ? when will he enter Jerusalem ? '   As I bent my
head forward they reverentially saluted me, and stated
to me the object of their coming ; but as it was my intention purposely to avoid giving any unnecessary inconvenience to my Jerusalem friends, I declined letting
them know the exact hour.   They again saluted,
galloped off, and soon disappeared.   I was told that
they had left Jerusalem after Hábdáláh, and now intended being again in the Holy City early in the morning.   If there be many such horsemen in the Holy
Land like these two supposed Bedouins, they certainly
ought not in justice to be regarded as descendants
from sickly parents, as some persons supposed."

Notwithstanding that he had given no intimation of
the time of his intended entry into Jerusalem, he was
received with great rejoicings. Venerable Rabbis
saluted him at the gates ; crowds assembled in the
streets and enthusiastically shouted their welcome,
and even the roofs of the houses were thronged with
gaily attired women and children, who showered upon
him copies of poems especially composed in his honour.
The British Consul waited upon him, and the
Governor of the city sent his brother to express his
regret that no official reception had been arranged in
consequence of the suddenness of his arrival.

During the forty days he spent in the Holy City Sir
Moses made the most elaborate inquiries into the condition of the Jewish population, and thoroughly satisfied
himself that they were as worthy of his confidence and
support as ever. He visited the synagogues, cross-
questioned the managers of the various charities,
and had all the schools examined in secular and religious subjects by Dr. Loewe. The results were very
satisfactory. Among the congregations he visited was
a new one composed of Georgian Jews, who had settled
in the Holy Land by special permission of the Russian
Government. " Some of them," he writes, " had decorations on their breast. One of the name of Eliahu
ben Israel, had three ; he received one from the late
Emperor Nicholas, and two from the present Emperor
Alexander. When I inquired of their chief, Haham
Eliahu ben Jacob, how they came by these special
marks of distinction, he told me that, during the war of

the Russians with the Circassians, the Jewish soldiers fought most bravely ; and that when all the people in the town of Kutais deserted the place, they, the Jews, remained, and with their blood defended the treasury of the Russian Government. The soldier with the three decorations said that he received on each occasion when those decorations had been given to him an embrace from the Emperor."

Receiving distressing accounts of the spread of cholera, Sir Moses made an attempt to permanently improve the sanitary condition of Jerusalem. He ordered several houses to be whitewashed, a number of streets to be cleansed, and the refuse to be removed outside the city. He also made representations to the authorities on the subject of clearing the Pool of Bethesda, into which the sewage of the town was conducted, recommending that it should be filled with pure water, and that special pools should be dug for the reception of the refuse of the town.

Before his departure he was visited by the Sheik of the Mosque of Omar, who presented him with Arabic and Cufic inscriptions ; a deputation of Armenian priests, who expressed the friendly sentiments of the Patriarch ; a sheik of the Haram, who offered him a souvenir in the shape of some curious native flasks for oil lamps, and a Jewish emissary from Arabia Felix, who was on his way to petition the Turkish Government to free his brethren from disabilities. On the 8th August his stay terminated, and he again

bade farewell to Jerusalem. Thirty-two days later he
was offering up his grateful prayers in his Synagogue
at Ramsgate.

The opinions and propositions suggested by this
pilgrimage, Sir Moses thus sets forth at the end of
his journal :—

" The great regard which I always entertained
towards our brethren in the Holy Land has now
become, if possible, doubly increased, so that if you
were to ask me, ' Are they worthy and deserving of
assistance ? ' I would reply, ' Most decidedly.' ' Are
they willing and capable of work ? ' ' Undoubtedly.'
' Are their mental powers of a satisfactory nature ? '
' Certainly.' ' Ought we, as Israelites, in particular,
to render them support ? ' ' Learn,' I would say, ' if
your own sacred Scriptures do not satisfy you, from
non-Israelites, what degree of support those are
entitled to who consecrate their lives to the worship
of God. Go and cast a glance upon the numerous
munificent endowments; upon the magnificent institutions ; upon the annual contributions, not only in
Jerusalem, but in every part of the world ; not only by
individuals, but by almost every mighty ruler on earth.
Notice the war which had broken out within our recollection respecting a privilege of repairing a house of
devotion, all for the sole object to support religion, and
are we Israelites to stand back and say : ' We are all practical men ; let everybody in Jerusalem go and work. We
do not want a set of indolent people who, by poring over
books, teaching the Word of God, think they are per-

forming their duties in life, and wait for our support.
The Jews in Jerusalem, in every part of the Holy
Land, I tell you, do work ; are more industrious even
than many men in Europe, otherwise none of them
would remain alive ; but, when the work does not
sufficiently pay; when there is no market for the
produce of the land; when famine, cholera, and
other misfortunes befall the inhabitants, we Israelites,
unto whom God revealed Himself on Sinai, more than
any other nation, must step forward and render them
help—raise them from their state of distress.'   If you
put the question to me, saying thus :—' Now we are
willing to contribute towards a fund intended to render
them such assistance as they may require ; we are
ready to make even sacrifices of our own means if
necessary ; what scheme do you propose as best
adapted to carry out the object in view ? '   I would
reply—' Carry out simply what they themselves have
suggested ; but begin, in the first instance, with the
building of houses in Jerusalem.   Select land outside
the city; raise, in the form of a large square or
crescent, a number of suitable houses, with European
improvements ; have in the centre of the square or
crescent a synagogue, a college, and a public bath.
Let each house have in front a plot of ground large
enough to cultivate olive trees, the vine, and necessary
vegetables, so as to give the occupiers of the houses a
taste for agriculture.   The houses ought to pay a
moderate rental, by the amount of which, after securing
the sum required for the payment of a clerk and over-

seer, and the repair of the houses, there should be
established a Loan Society on safe principles, for the
benefit of the poor working class, the trader, the
agriculturist, or any poor deserving man. Two per
cent should be charged on each loan, so as to cover
thereby the expenses necessary for a special clerk, and
the rent of an appropriate house. If the amount of
your funds be sufficient, build houses in Safed,
Tiberias, and Hebron, on the same plan ; establish,
by the rental also, Loan Societies on similar principles
of security. And should you further prosper, and have
£30,000 or £50,000 to dispose of, you will, without
difficulty, be able to purchase as much land as you
would like in the vicinity of Safed, Pekeein, Tiberias,
Hebron, Jerusalem, Jaffa, and Khaifa, and you will
find in all those places a number of persons who would
be most willing to follow agricultural pursuits. There
are, according to the applications which have been
printed, more than 170 persons ready in Safed and
Tiberias alone ; Pekeein and Khaifa also offer a good
number : but there are, no doubt, persons, even in
Jerusalem, who are willing to cultivate land. And if
now you address me, saying, ' Which would be the
proper time to commence the work, supposing we
were ready to be guided by your counsel ? ' My
reply then would be, ' Commence at once ; begin the
work this day, if you can. Our brethren throughout
Europe, Persia, and Turkey, have been roused by
your promises, which have been made known to them
in the most hopeful terms, by Hebrew, German,

French, Italian, and English. periodicals. You led them to cherish the hope that you would surely make no delay in proceeding to ameliorate the condition of the Sons of Zion. They now cry out, ' Here we are, give us land, give us work ; you promised to do so. We are willing, for the sake of our love to Jerusalem, to undertake the execution of the most laborious tasks ; ' but the Representatives of the Community have no answer to give : they simply, with a cast-down countenance, say, in the words of King Solomon, ' Clouds and wind without rain.' You are then, I repeat, in sacred duty bound not to disappoint them any longer. Begin the hallowed task at once, and He who takes delight in Zion, will establish the work upon you."

These suggestions have of late years been energetically acted upon by the Montefiore Testimonial Committee. Agricultural colonies have been assisted, and, by means of loans to building societies, the beginnings of a new and beautiful city outside the Jaffa gate of Jerusalem have been made. The result to-day of Sir Moses Montefiore's persistent efforts to erect improved dwellings for the Jews of Palestine is, that the Holy City now possesses a western suburb of six hundred houses, inhabited by nearly 4,000 Israelites, many of whom own the freeholds of their dwellings.

This was Sir Moses Montefiore's last foreign journey. There is a peculiar fitness in the circumstance that he should have terminated his public

career in the very city where nearly half-a-century
before he had gathered the great inspiration of his
life. The supporters on his coat-of-arms hold aloft
banners on which the word "Jerusalem" is inscribed
in Hebrew characters, and "Jerusalem" has been the
watchword of his life—not merely in the restricted sense
of the actual city and its inhabitants, but in the wider
significance of the word as the countersign of Hebrew
tradition and the rallying cry of the Humanitarian
Ideal of Judaism. Jerusalem is more than a monument of the ancient glory of the Kingdom of God; it
is the sanctuary of the sublime aspiration which every
Israelite utters daily, "that the world may be established under the rule of the Almighty, all the children
of flesh invoke His name, and all the wicked of the
earth turn towards Him." The inner workings of
Sir Moses Montefiore's life are laid bare when we
find that this is the key-note to which it has been
attuned.

CHAPTER XVIII.

CONCLUSION.

An age that melts with unperceived decay,
And glides in modest innocence away ;
Whose peaceful Day benevolence endears,
Whose Night congratulating conscience cheers ;
The general favorite as the general friend :
Such age there is and who shall wish it end ?
DR. JOHNSON, *Vanity of Human Wishes.*

SINCE his return from Jerusalem in 1875 Sir Moses
Montefiore has lived in semi-retirement at his charming country seat near Ramsgate. Notwithstanding his
great age his heart and mind remain as actively
devoted to works of benevolence as in the prime of his
manhood. He still takes a lively interest in public
affairs, and, with the help of an English amanuensis
and a foreign secretary, carries on a voluminous correspondence in Hebrew and modern languages for the
furtherance of the philanthropic schemes to which he
has devoted his life.

On more than one occasion during the last few
years he has actively concerned himself in public
questions. In the Russo-Turkish war, six years ago—
involving, as it did, the fate of a large Jewish population—he evinced the deepest interest, and he took no
pains to hide on which side his sympathies were

engaged. As soon as the Turkish Relief Fund was
started he joined the Committee, and at the same time
addressed a sympathetic letter to Musurus Pasha, the
Turkish Ambassador in England. The following is
the text of this characteristic epistle* :—

"EAST CLIFF LODGE, RAMSGATE, *Jan.* 1, 1877.

"YOUR EXCELLENCY,

"You will, I trust, give credit to my words
when I assure you that I hail the opportunity now
presented to me to evince my gratitude to the Turkish
Government for the kind and effective protection they
have at all times extended to my co-religionists ; and
I shall never forget the glorious Hatti-Sherif given
to the Jews in the year 1840 by his late Imperial
Majesty, Abdul Medjid, assuring to the Jews the same
rights and privileges as those enjoyed by all the other
subjects of the Turkish Empire. I earnestly hope
that peace will soon be restored throughout the whole
extent of the Sultan's dominions, and that the Government of his Imperial Majesty will have every opportunity to show the world that nothing could afford His
Majesty greater satisfaction and delight than to see all
his subjects, without any distinction of creed, in the
words of Holy Writ, ' sitting under his vine and his fig-
tree,' in full enjoyment of the blessings our Heavenly
Father bestows on them.

"May I beg your Excellency to favour me by add-
ing the enclosed two cheques to the fund now being

<hr>

* *Jewish World*, Jan. 12, 1877.

raised for the relief of the wounded Turkish soldiers, one cheque for £50 in my own name, and the other for a similar amount of £50 in memory of my lamented wife, Judith, Lady Montefiore.

"With the most sincere assurance of my high esteem, respect and regard, I remain,

"Your Excellency's very obedient humble servant,

"Moses Montefiore."

Sir Moses also seconded with much energy the efforts of the Baroness Burdett Coutts in connection with the Turkish Compassionate Fund, and even offered to proceed to the East in the interests of the Fund. The circumstance was characteristic of the warm-hearted philanthropist. The Baroness having received an intimation that a large number of Jews were among the sufferers from the war, immediately communicated the fact to Sir Moses, who promptly answered by telegram as follows :—

"Greatly obliged for telegram. Deeply sympathise with sufferers. Have already forwarded my mite to Roumania, Turkey, and Holland, but will have much pleasure in sending you by to-day's post £100 for the Committee in Constantinople, over which Mr. Layard presides, to alleviate the sufferings of the people without distinction of creed. Should my presence in Constantinople or Adrianople be deemed in any way beneficial to the sufferers, I shall be ready to proceed there without delay."

In communicating this telegram to the papers the

T

Baroness wrote : "I cannot deny myself the pleasure
of enclosing you my revered and chivalrous friend's
reply, alike as characteristic of his unwearying energy
of mind and warmth of heart."

When the war was over and the Plenipotentiaries of
the Powers met at Berlin to decide upon terms of
peace, no one watched the newspaper records of their
labours more anxiously than the venerable champion
of Israel.   He corresponded with his co-religionist,
Baron von Bleichröder, on the subject of bringing the
claims of the Jews of Eastern Europe before the
Congress, and made many private representations in
other eminent quarters.   The Congress accepted the
principle of religious equality for the Danubian Princi-
palities, and Sir Moses Montefiore, on being apprised
of the fact, telegraphed his congratulations to Baron
von Bleichröder.   "Most gratified," he wrote, "with the
happy intelligence contained in your telegram, for
which I heartily thank you.   I beg to congratulate
you on the success of your unceasing efforts.   Praise
to the God of Israel for his mercy and goodness to his
people."   To Lord Beaconsfield and Lord Salisbury
he returned his personal thanks immediately on their
arrival in London.   He made a special journey to the
metropolis for the purpose, and when the Plenipotentiaries arrived at Charing Cross railway station he
was the first to greet them.

Nor are these the only instances of his public
activity during his tenth decade.   In 1880 he raised a
Relief Fund for the Jews of Persia, who had suffered

severely from famine, and in the following year promoted a similar fund for the starving population of Armenia and Kurdistan. On the occasion of the coronation of the Czar Alexander III., he addressed a letter of congratulation to the new monarch, in which he did not forget to plead implicitly for his brethren; and during the recent trial at Nyereghyaza he circulated papers refuting the Blood Accusation, among the members of the Hungarian Parliament, and also sent assistance to the accused.

The most striking feature in the character of Sir Moses Montefiore is his profound religiousness—a religiousness born and nourished of Hebrew tradition, sustaining itself by a scrupulous observance of the minute ceremonial of Rabbinism, and expressing itself in a conscientious practice of its humanitarian precepts. It is related that a Christian gentleman once asked him : " If the commandments of Judaism and Christianity are the same, wherein lies the difference ? " "We obey the commandments," was his felicitous answer. This description of Judaism may not accord with the character of every Jew, but there can be no doubt of its applicability to that of Moses Montefiore. Contemporary orthodox Judaism claims him as its brightest ornament, and with justice ; for he, more than any other man, has illustrated by his life-conduct the noblest possibilities of its teachings.

Until four years ago he was regular in his attendance at the Synagogue, and even now he reads daily every word of the prescribed prayers. He fasts on the anniversary of the capture of Jerusalem by the Romans, and on the Day of Atonement. The dietary laws he obeys to the letter, and throughout his life he has rigorously abstained from tasting the flesh of animals that divide not the hoof nor chew the cud. With these traditional observances he unites a literal adherence to the hopes of a national restoration of Israel as expressed by the Prophets and Rabbis. When questioned on the subject some years ago, he answered with a satisfied smile : " I am quite certain of it; it has been my constant dream, and I hope will be realised some day when I shall be no more." To the objection that it would be impossible to gather in the Israelites scattered in all the corners of the globe, he replied : " I do not expect that all Israelites will quit their abodes in those territories in which they feel happy, even as there are Englishmen in Hungary, Germany, America, and Japan; but Palestine must belong to the Jews, and Jerusalem is destined to become the seat of a Jewish Empire."

It is notable that critics of Judaism who find a dangerous narrowness in this creed—they call it " tribalism "—have never attempted to explain the phenomenon of its development in, the person of Moses Montefiore, of the most unrestricted humanitarianism. The noble spirit with which it has inspired him is illustrated by his entire career ; but, happily, in many of his letters he has given it a definite expression upon which those who come after him may do well to ponder. The following letter,* for example, which he addressed

* *Jewish World*, Jan. 2, 1880.

five years ago to the editor of a Jewish journal published at Philadelphia, breathes a spirit with which his co-religionists cannot be made too extensively acquainted :—

               " EAST CLIFF LODGE, RAMSGATE,
                 " *Rosh Hodesh Kislev*, 5640.

" DEAR SIR,—My attention has recently been drawn to a notice you have given in the *Jewish Record* of the 95th anniversary of my birthday, accompanied by a prayer referring to some important events in the history of Israel which occurred in our own time.

" It is not with the purpose of conveying my special thanks to you for the flattering expressions you thought proper of introducing on that occasion, that I trouble you with these lines, knowing such to have been dictated to you by the good opinion you entertain of my humble efforts to serve in a good cause, overrating the little merit I may, to a certain degree, have thereby earned ; but I am prompted to address you by a desire of manifesting to you my appreciation of the important service you render to all Hebrew communities, when recalling to their memory, from time to time, the comforting assurance that 'the Guardian of Israel neither slumbereth nor sleepeth ; ' that He shows mercy to the innocent sufferer at times when all hope had been abandoned by him ; and that the Omnipotent will never withdraw His protecting grace from all who strictly abide by the law He revealed on Sinai. Our brethren, I am happy to say, still evince that ardent

love towards one another, as in times of old ; they constitute, as it were, all over the world, one body, and
the sufferings of those who live in the remotest parts
of the globe, as soon as they become known to them,
touch their hearts, and find sympathy in every Jewish
family.   The Hebrew communities in America are pre-
eminently distinguished by that characteristic trait of
Israel.   On all occasions, when the cry of anguish
reaches their ear, promptly and most generously they
offer their noble contributions to assuage the sufferings
of the brother.   And I ascribe the cause of it to their
innate feeling of benevolence, intensely aroused by the
eloquent addresses they hear from men of great learning and piety, re-echoed from house to house by the
powerful appeals from learned and conscientious
editors of journals, raising high the banner of Israel
for the vindication of our holy religion.

" You, my dear sir, are one of those zealous brothers
who stand in the breach to defend the sacred cause ;
great is your merit, and greater still the reward you
earn by the consciousness of cordially associating yourself with all the earnest labourers in the vineyard of
God—your heart surely must be full with joy.

" Permit me, dear sir, to entertain the hope that
you will continue to avail yourself of every opportunity
to preserve, and, where necessary, to re-kindle, that
spirit of devotion, that holy zeal which constitutes the
life of Israel.   Continue to retain in the heart of our
brethren that indomitable courage which made our
forefathers plead the cause of our religion in the

presence of kings, and never felt ashamed of perform-
ing those Heavenly Commandments which are binding
upon them as Israelites.

" You will have no difficulty among our American
brethren to execute so pleasing a task. I know many
instances of their devotion to all that is good and holy,
and have every reason to believe that they will gladly
avail themselves of the opportunity to follow any of
your suggestions, by which the children may be enabled
to follow the footsteps of their fathers and forefathers
in the fear of God.

" As for myself, as long as God will bless me with
health and strength, as long as my hand is able to
move, my feet to walk, and my eyes to see, I will
not cease to remember all the mercies God has
shown to Israel, and the promises he vouchsafed
unto us.

" Zealously and cheerfully I will, conjointly with our
faithful brethren, hold high the banner of Jerusalem,
always praying that we may live to see the great day
when the name of God, as One God, will be adored
among all the nations of the earth.

" With best regards, I am, dear sir,
        " Yours very truly,
                " MOSES MONTEFIORE."

In connection with the question of the so-called
" tribalism " of Judaism, the inquiry has of late years
been raised whether orthodox Jews can be patriots;
and even in this country a prominent writer has been

found to maintain the negative of this proposition; and yet it is indubitable that the Queen of this happy realm has no subject more loyal than the orthodox Jew, Moses Montefiore. To be faithful to the land of one's adoption is a teaching to which the Jewish Rabbis have given great prominence; and on more than one occasion Sir Moses Montefiore has urged it upon his brethren, even when they have been suffering the direst persecution. One instance may here be quoted—a letter he addressed to the Jews of Morocco shortly after his return from his memorable mission to that unenlightened country. The letter was as follows :—

"EAST CLIFF LODGE, RAMSGATE,
"6th *Elul*—7th *September*, 5624—1864.

"MY DEAR BRETHREN AND FRIENDS,

"Throughout the world, a chief characteristic of the Jews is, that of being loyal, obedient, and peaceful subjects of their Sovereign. From what I have seen and know of my brethren in Morocco, I feel assured they are not exceptions to this universally-admitted truth. The precepts inculcating this conduct are enforced on us by the Sacred Scriptures, and by the wise exhortations of our Sages. Unless due respect be paid to the just exercise of legally consti-tuted authority, there can be neither order nor safety. Happily, the Imperial Edict of your August Sovereign is intended to sustain the cause of justice and humanity throughout the Moorish Empire; and though it may be that, in some places, the subordinate authorities abuse the powers with which they are entrusted, let it not be said that their severity or wrong-doing is attributable to any manifestation or disrespect on your part. You must never for a moment forget the loyalty, the affection and respect due to your Sovereign, on whom you must rely, and to whom, in case of need, you must appeal for protection against oppression, and redress for injury. Let neither actions nor words from you induce your fellow-countrymen of the Mahomedan Faith to suppose that you are in any way unmindful or regardless of your duties as subjects of His Imperial Majesty; but, on the contrary, that it is your ardent desire, and most anxious wish, to testify your love and obedience towards him, and also to cultivate the esteem and good-will of your fellow-countrymen. It is by conduct such as this, we may hope that, under the Almighty's blessing, the hearts of those who would molest or injure you will be softened ; or, that, should injustice be done, it will be speedily and surely punished. Most ardently and most anxiously do I desire your welfare. To promote this I have laboured with intense anxiety. I know full well, that these my words are conveyed to willing listeners—to those who fully recognise their truth; and I feel sure that you will, to the utmost of your ability, seek to give effect to my wishes. Over the poor and less educated classes of our brethren in Morocco, let your watchful care be exercised so far as in you lies, so that they pay due obedience and respect to the constituted authorities; let them be patient under small annoyances, but firm and reliant on their august Sovereign, who will not fail to punish those who abuse his commands, disregard his Edict, or venture to inflict serious wrong upon his Jewish subjects. I trust and believe that in such cases, the ear of your august Sovereign will ever be open to your cry.

"May it be the will of God to remove from you all further suffering, and to inspire your rulers with the spirit of humanity and justice, and to grant to your august Sovereign a long and happy reign.

" This is the heartfelt prayer of

" Yours faithfully,

" MOSES MONTEFIORE."

Not less practical than his religion has been his charity. The common form of charity—that of staying at home in one's easy chair, and signing cheques upon one's bankers whenever appealed to—has not been the charity of Moses Montefiore. In addition to his money, he has taken his personal earnestness and exertions wherever good work was to be done. It has been well observed, that "you cannot draw cheques for this sort of charity; bankers don't lock the article up in their strong-room; and dividends are not paid upon it till this world's quarter-days are over." It comes out of the endless wealth of a good heart, loving its fellows, and ready to give more than its superfluity for their sake; and where it goes, it effects what

money alone is weak to do. Sir Moses Montefiore
is as ready as he is practical. About forty years ago,
he was proposed as a candidate for a presentation
Governorship of Christ's Hospital, but was strongly
opposed by a Christian clergyman. On this his friends
related the cause of his desiring the honour. Some
weeks previously he had been travelling by water to
his country-seat at Ramsgate, when he was accosted
on board the steamer by a man, who asked him for
pecuniary assistance. He enquired into the cause of
the man's distress, and having given him a sum of
money, appointed a day for him to call at East Cliff
Lodge to be further relieved. The next morning Sir
Moses received a letter from the same individual,
stating, that being irretrievably ruined he had determined to commit suicide, and asking the philanthropist,
on whom he confessed he had no claim, to care for his
wife and son. In the course of the day the writer was
found dead at the foot of the cliff. Sir Moses
generously pensioned the widow, and determined to
make an effort to get the boy into Christ's Hospital.
This was the reason that he wished to obtain a presentation Governorship, and he was ready, in accordance with the rules of the institution, to subscribe
£500 to its funds. Needless to add, he was elected.

Of Sir Moses' courtesy and geniality many anec-
dotes are related. Coming up to town in his reserved
saloon in the Ramsgate train, he would frequently offer
a seat to strangers whom he saw incommoded by the
pressure of tourists, and sometimes in London send

them home in his own carriage, walking or taking a
cab himself.   A barrister having sent his clerk to him
with a letter after office hours, the baronet asked the
boy to read to him, and being pleased with his elocu-
tion, kept him to dinner, and gave him a copy of
" Shakespeare."   Of young folks he has always been
fond : and he possesses the rare faculty of engaging
their confidence, and making them at home.   Not
many months ago he appeared at a charity bazaar,
and bought continuously a great quantity of toys and
trinkets, which he as continuously gave away to the
hungry-eyed youngsters who crowded round him.   At
Festival seasons he delighted while Lady Montefiore
was living to ask home to his hospitable house visitors
who attended his Synagogue.   An instance of his
thoughtfulness is related by the late Mr. Sidney Samuel,
in his " Jewish Life in the East."   Describing his
visit to Jaffa, Mr. Samuel says :—

" I heard from my estimable and hospitable host
of one of those acts of politeness and kindly courtesy
on the part of Sir Moses Montefiore which contribute
so much to endear the name of one who so worthily
upholds the dignity of Judaism to all who have the
good fortune to know him.   Residing for thirteen days
in the house of my host, on the occasion of his recent
visit to the Holy Land, he noticed that the daughter
of the house, who had presented him with a beautifully
embroidered *Tephillin** bag, was a musician.   Not con-

* Phylacteries.

tent with sending the father a valuable gift, he gave
the young lady a handsome piano, and a box of musical
publications, which derive additional value from the
fact of their having belonged to the late Lady Montefiore; and he has since on the festive occasions of
Purim kept her supplied with the latest music."

Although his brethren, from their unprotected state,
have always had the first claim on his benevolence,
Sir Moses' charity has not been confined to them.
His is almost always the first response to every appeal,
irrespective of religious differences. Not a Mansion
House list is published but it includes his name; and
his private charity knows no sectarian limits. Last
year he sent to the Sheriff's fund for the relief of
prisoners discharged from Newgate a pound for every
year of his long life. The year before, Lord Shaftes-
bury, happening to meet the Delegate Chief Rabbi,
exclaimed, "Your great Judas Maccabeus has just
sent me £98 for my Ragged Schools!" Countless
charities are benefited in the same way. During the
anxieties of the Russo-Jewish persecution he found
time to send £500 towards the building fund of the
City of London College, accompanying his cheque
with a graceful and sympathetic letter.

His catholicity is equally exemplary. In 1865 the
cholera broke out in Smyrna, and the Jews suffering
severely, Mr. Hyde Clarke telegraphed for help to Sir
Moses Montefiore and Sir Francis Goldsmid. From
both he received telegrams empowering him to spend

a sum of money, and when their letters arrived they were found to be couched in almost identical terms. This is the version given by Mr. Clarke : " We have sent you money, as you have asked, for the Jews, but our practice in life has been to give alms without consideration of race or creed. If, therefore, you find there are others in greater distress than the Jews, we beg you to help them rather than the Jews." Another instance is related by Mr. Edwin Arnold. Some years ago Mr. Arnold desired to establish a hospital at Nazareth, on a piece of ground which was the very spot where the Synagogue was built, in which Jesus stood up to read the Scriptures. He applied to Sir Moses for assistance. " Certainly," was the brief, but cordial, reply. " What will you have ? Only name the sum." He gives subscriptions to churches and chapels, as well as Synagogues ; and he has obtained benefices for deserving clergymen. The late Archbishop Tait often visited East Cliff ; and Sir Moses generously assisted in Mrs. Tait's charitable labours. The busts of the Archbishop and his wife, in the latter's Orphanage at Thanet, were presented by Sir Moses. He was a subscriber to the Dean Stanley Memorial Fund. When he was High Sheriff of Kent, his chaplain was the Rev. Mr. Sicklemore, the Vicar of St. Lawrence ; and since he has resided in the county, the clergy of the various denominations have always acted as his almoners.

In Ramsgate he enjoys unbounded popularity. During his sixty-five years' residence in the neighbourhood he has been foremost in every work of

benevolence. Not a society has been started to which
he has not subscribed, and he has even assisted in
building the local churches. The schools have been
an especial object of his benevolent interest, and on
more than one occasion he has obtained holidays for
the pupils, and has entertained them by the thousand.
The inmates of the workhouses revere him. Until a
year or two ago it was his practice to pay them
periodical visits, and he always came loaded with
articles of comfort which he personally distributed
among them. One of the visiting magistrates relates
that on the first occasion of his inspecting the Union,
an old lady came forward, and on behalf of the other
inmates said: "When you see Sir Moses Montefiore,
sir, will you convey our very grateful and heartfelt
thanks to him for his benevolence to us all." On the
occasion of his ninety-ninth birthday an address
written by one of the inmates was presented "To the
Right Honourable Sir Moses Montefiore, Bart.," and,
in acknowledgment of his "unvarying kindness to the
poor," the working-men of St. Luke's Parish presented
him four years ago with a handsome Bible in Hebrew
and English. The widows and orphans of Ramsgate
fishermen are also objects of his solicitude. His own
experiences of the high seas enable him to sympathise
with those who have to brave the dangers of the deep
for a living. On his last birthday he said earnestly to
a deputation of Life-boat men, who presented him
with a congratulatory address: "You are brave
fellows. When I hear the wind blow I know you are out

in your life-boat, and I pray to God for your safety."
In 1868 the townsmen of Ramsgate subscribed for a
portrait of the benevolent Baronet, which they placed
in their Town Hall. It was painted by Mr. S. A.
Hart, R.A., and represents Sir Moses attired in the
costume of of a Deputy-Lieutenant, standing on a hill
overlooking Jerusalem, with the walls of the Holy City
and the Dome of the Mosque of St. Omar in the back-
ground. Another portrait, which hangs in the Board-
room of the Alliance Insurance Company, is by Mr.
A. B. Richmond, R.A.

On the eve of completing the hundredth year of his
life Sir Moses Montefiore is still in the enjoyment of
health, genial as ever, a cordial host, and a delightful
conversationalist. Six feet three inches in height and
stooping but slightly, he presents a striking figure to
the visitor who sees him for the first time. His attire,
with its huge white neckcloth, ample frill and high-
collared coat, is of a period that has passed into
history, but it is still arranged with the old-world
neatness and elegance of the punctilious days of the
Fourth George. But if his dress is old-fashioned, his
expression and manner are of all time. The cordial
grasp of his hand, his benign mien, the kindness and
good-humoured wisdom of his conversation, are beyond
the aging touch of fashion. His interest in public
affairs is still intelligent and keen, and he is a wide
reader of newspapers and periodicals. All his letters
have his personal attention, and he directs every detail
of the work of his secretaries. He has his favourite

books, and takes especial delight in Sturm's *Reflections* and Cicero *De Senectute.*

The order of his life is necessarily somewhat methodical. He rises at eleven, and retires to rest at nine. During the day he sits chiefly in the bay-window of his bedroom, which overlooks the sea; but occasionally he ventures into the adjoining apartment, a cheerful room, decked with portraits of Lady Montefiore, Sir Anthony de Rothschild, and Captain Keppel, and containing a bust, by Weekes, of Lord Hammond. In fine weather he drives out and visits the grave of his wife. Were he asked to reveal the secret of his longevity he would probably repeat the quaint recipe of an eminent French physiologist: " Fuir l'excès en tout; respecter les vieilles habitudes; respirer un air pur; approprier les aliments à son tempérament; fuir les médecines et les médecins; avoir le cœur tranquille, le cœur gai, l'esprit satisfait."

Such, in brief outline, is the man who now, amid a chorus of congratulations, is approaching the completion of the hundredth year of his life, a life which has been pronounced from the Throne itself to have been "useful and honourable."* Future generations will doubtless enlarge upon this Royal estimate of Sir Moses Montefiore's career; but it would not conduce to historic accuracy were the writer of these pages, in the presence of an actuality which dwarfs so much else, to attempt an anticipation of their verdict.

* Congratulatory telegram of the Queen on Sir Moses' 99th birthday.

That the history of philanthropy will write an approving word after his name none can doubt ; that Jewish history will devote a large share of its fifty-seventh century chapter to his achievements, and to the spirit by which he has been actuated, this faint record will show. But these are questions with which at present we have happily nothing to do.   Our duty now is only to congratulate the venerable philanthropist upon the happy anniversary which is to be celebrated on the 26th October.   Upon such an occasion we cannot do better than relate to the generation which has grown up since Moses Montefiore's most active work was performed the story of the life which has earned so much of the goodwill of men.   If these pages help in the performance of that duty they will have fulfilled their purpose.

THE END.

BRADBURY, AGNEW, & CO., PRINTERS, WHITEFRIARS.

For EU product safety concerns, contact us at Calle de José Abascal, 56–1°,
28003 Madrid, Spain or eugpsr@cambridge.org.